NO JACKET REQUIRED

Another Great Collection
of Recipes from InCircle

Neiman Marcus

Published by Neiman Marcus InCircle®

Dallas, Texas

Published by Neiman Marcus InCircle,
a division of The Neiman Marcus Group, Inc.

Copyright © 1995
by The Neiman Marcus Group, Inc.

Printed by Quebecor Printing.

Distributed in the United States and internationally by
Harcourt Brace & Company, New York, San Diego
and London.

Photography © 1995 John Parrish Photography.

Manufactured in the United States of America.

First Edition

10 9 8 7 6 5 4 3 2 1

ISBN 0-15-100189-8

Library of Congress Catalog Card Number: 95-068011

ACKNOWLEDGMENTS

Neiman Marcus InCircle would like to thank those whose interest, contributions, and support made this cookbook possible:

Our InCircle customers for continuing to provide us with unique recipes that are guaranteed to impress everyone.

Our stellar panel of internationally renowned chefs for their participation and recipe contributions: Joyce Goldstein (Square One, San Francisco); Matthew Kenney (Matthew's, New York); Mark Militello (Mark's Place, Miami); Stephan Pyles (Star Canyon, Dallas); and Charlie Trotter (Charlie Trotter's, Chicago).

Piero Selvaggio and Stacy Dalgleish Selvaggio for their wine selections with the recipes.

Charlotte Price for selecting the chefs and wine sommeliers who participated.

Kevin Garvin for his selection of recipes and coordination of our panel of chefs.

Burt Tansky for supporting our project and proudly signing on to write the Foreword.

Clare Adams Kittle whose design talents and management took this project from start to finish.

Laura Rivers for writing the biographies, chapter introductions, and other segments.

Susan Friedman for her precise recipe editing.

Photographer John Parrish and stylists Irene Bertolucci, Brooke Leonard, and Patricia Fly who portrayed casual elegance through the photographs in this book.

Michael Crampton for his illustrations, which are so essential to the theme.

Maunina Kaseberg and Heidi Rabel who had the difficult task of reviewing the initial recipes.

Luisa Brame, Grace Gill, and Michael Mooney for testing the recipes.

Heather Muhlick for her invaluable assistance.

The Neiman Marcus public relations team for ensuring a successful launch of *No Jacket Required* through their outstanding publicity skills.

Harcourt Brace & Company for helping to promote the book.

Michael Chartock of The Neiman Marcus Group, Inc., for his advice throughout the project.

The InCircle staff for their creative input and endless energy, which made production of this book possible.

No Jacket Required *is dedicated to the thousands of InCirclers*
who give so much of their time and energy for the good of their communities.
Without their help and enthusiasm, this third recipe book
would not have been possible.

FOREWORD

~~~~~~~~~~~~~~~~~~~~~~~~~~~~~~~~~

by Burt Tansky, *Chairman, Neiman Marcus*

When moving from New York to Dallas to join
Neiman Marcus, I looked forward to the many culinary
adventures Texas would offer: discovering barbecue, savoring
Tex-Mex, getting reacquainted with beef, and sampling the
many excellent restaurants in the region.

I was also glad to find that a strong association has existed
between Neiman Marcus and good food for a long time,
going back some 40 years to the heyday of Helen Corbitt.

It now gives me great pleasure to introduce this latest in a
series of popular cookbooks from Neiman Marcus. With
more than 200 recipes contributed by our valued InCircle
customers, *No Jacket Required* reflects the casual elegance
that defines cooking and entertaining today.

More and more of us are choosing to dine at home, whether
with family or to host an informal supper for close friends.
What easier way to plan your menu than to peruse the pages
of a cookbook filled with the favorite recipes of people who
share common interests and tastes!

In true NM style, we have engaged five of America's most celebrated chefs to share some of their specialties and to select the recipes featured here from more than 1,500 submissions by our InCircle members. As an added bonus, two well-known wine authorities (who happen to be InCirclers) have offered creative and thoughtful recommendations for many of the recipes.

A portion of the proceeds from the sale of the book will again go to charity, just as we did with *Pure & Simple* and *Pigtails and Froglegs*. I think it is highly fitting that this book will benefit the cause of literacy in America.

The Neiman Marcus cookbooks are an extension of the special relationship we have with our customers. I know you'll be proud of the delectable dishes you discover in *No Jacket Required*. Share it with a neighbor, give it as a gift, and above all, take pleasure in what you create. Enjoy!

TABLE OF CONTENTS

Our Cause

~~~~~~~~~~~~~~~~~~~~

Billy J. Payton, *Vice President, Marketing and Customer Programs*

Welcome to the third and most ambitious recipe book compiled by Neiman Marcus InCircle members. This book is all about cooking for the sheer joy of the process and presenting it with style, whether it is for a weeknight dinner or a special occasion with friends. Our recipes come from all corners of the United States, so we turned to five of America's most prestigious chefs whose regional styles are internationally recognized. Then we sought two highly regarded wine authorities to select two wines for each dish: a well-recognized label for major occasions and a more adventurous vintage for minor celebrations.

Our first recipe book, *Pure & Simple*, reflected Americans' growing interest in cooking. Our second, *Pigtails and Froglegs*, centered on the family. We are pleased that, between the two books, we have raised over $600,000 for charity. When it came to *No Jacket Required*, we settled on a single beneficiary, Literacy Volunteers of America, Inc. Two factors influenced our choice. First, literacy itself is almost universally regarded as the key to our country's future. Secondly, this organization works to train and involve volunteers at local, state, and national levels–a very effective way to achieve its goals. With a contribution from every copy of *No Jacket Required* sold worldwide, we expect to set a new record for our beneficiary.

The Chefs

Kevin Garvin, *Vice President, Food Services*

In the fall of 1994, I returned to Dallas from a stint at the Rockefeller resorts in Woodstock, Vermont, to accept the challenge of V.P. of Food Services for Neiman Marcus. I had worked at the Adolphus Hotel prior to moving to Vermont, so the move was a little like coming home.

In my new position, I found myself not only in charge of 32 restaurants in 27 stores across the country, but also an active participant in the planning and execution of this book. Let me say, it has been a challenge and a pleasure.

My first task was to chair a committee of our country's most famous chefs to review the 1,500 recipes originally submitted and reduce them to the number you see in this book. The committee consisted of these five: Joyce Goldstein of Square One, Matthew Kenney of Matthew's, Mark Militello of Mark's Place, Stephan Pyles of Star Canyon, and Charlie Trotter of Charlie Trotter's. Together, they represent the current major trends in American cuisine: California, Southwestern, multicultural, and experimental. Once the recipes were selected and tested, Piero Selvaggio and Stacy Dalgleish Selvaggio of Valentino, Primi, and Posto in Los Angeles were asked to select the wines. (The Valentino cellar is the envy of restaurant owners and the recipient of many awards.)

I hope you will gain as much satisfaction in trying these recipes for yourself as I have had helping to produce this book.

Joyce Goldstein

Long before she joined Chez Panisse as chef, and long before she opened her own restaurant in 1984, Joyce Goldstein cooked and taught cooking. And to this day, she continues to write cookbooks and teach other professionals in addition to running her own business. Those who know food say that eating Joyce Goldstein's cooking is like eating Mom's cooking–if Mom could cook as well as Joyce does. But unless you find yourself invited to join the Goldstein family for dinner every other Sunday, proceed to Square One.

Square One in San Francisco:

The menu at Square One is ever-changing, except in one regard: every morsel—even the mustard, pickles, and ice cream—is made right on the premises. The mural in the bar proclaims Il Paese della Cuccagna *(The Land of Milk and Honey.) It's no exaggeration.*

Matthew Kenney

If you ask Matthew Kenney about his culinary style, he'll skillfully dodge the question because he just won't be put into a box or a saucepan. In actuality, he cooks a little Asian, a little Moroccan, a little Italian, a little... well, you get the picture. What pleases him most is coming up with an original dish such as Ahi Tuna Tartare and having it instantly accepted by those who know food and are not easily impressed. *Food & Wine* was impressed; it named him one of the top 10 young chefs of 1994.

Matthew's in New York:

The Zagat Survey calls Matthew's "creative and breezy." It looks much like Rick's Cafe and has a creative American menu with Mediterranean influences. It's a refreshing addition to the New York scene.

Mark Militello

Although some have described Mark Militello's cooking style as "fusion," "Floribbean," or "New World," that's not how Mark sees himself. Despite a certain modesty, he is quick to say that he is "product-oriented," caring more for freshness and originality than being confined to any one cooking style. As Florida's most celebrated chef, he has turned on the food tastes for residents and visitors alike. How does he do it? By maximizing the best of local fresh offerings of the land and sea. A simple philosophy that brings superb results.

Mark's Place in Miami:

Mark Militello's restaurant is where modern American cooking meets the Caribbean and the Mediterranean. Its balmy location puts it in the best possible position for freshness in all ingredients. (Amazingly, 90 percent of all ingredients are locally produced.)

STEPHAN PYLES

"New Texas Cuisine" is what Star Canyon is all about, according to owner/chef Stephan Pyles, whose reputation was made in his first two success stories: Routh Street Cafe and Baby Routh. A fifth-generation native Texan, he helped pioneer Southwestern cuisine after returning from cooking schools in France in 1975. His first kitchen job? That of carrot peeler in a Dallas restaurant "best left unnamed." Even with today's fabulous success of Star Canyon, Stephan still continues to pursue new projects.

Star Canyon in Dallas:

Star Canyon's architecture can be described as sophisticated, contemporary western with a little cowboy whimsy thrown in. The menu features new Texas cuisine adapted from the different cultures and historical eras of the Lone Star State.

CHARLIE TROTTER

Once you've tasted the dishes served in his superb restaurant, you will know why his peers consistently acknowledge Charlie Trotter as America's most dedicated chef. (Perfection would be a good middle name for Charlie.) Not too long ago, he was studying for his degree in political science and cooking for his pals. Charlie's trophy shelf is full of awards from every source, the James Beard Foundation to Gault-Millot. He's convinced that serious vegetable cuisine is the trend of the future and is rapidly converting meat-and-potatoes Midwesterners to his sophisticated tastes.

Charlie Trotter's in Chicago:

The menu of this one-of-a-kind restaurant is presented in the French style of degustation, i.e., tastings, rather than the usual format. The idea is to have a taste of as many unusual dishes as possible without leaving the table hungry or over-satiated. It works.

Pairing Wine and Food

Editor's note: *When we needed a wine expert for* No Jacket Required, *we asked those who know, and in one voice, the answer was, "There are two–Piero and Stacy." Over the past 20 years, Piero Selvaggio and his wife, Stacy Dalgleish Selvaggio, owners of Valentino (Los Angeles), have established a wine cellar that is the envy of the restaurant world–a* Wine Spectator *Grand Award winner since the awards were first given in 1981. Watch for their wine notes throughout the book. The legend at the right defines their wine selections.*

 A classic label for major occasions.

 A wine that is adventurous for minor celebrations.

Piero Selvaggio and Stacy Dalgleish Selvaggio, *Valentino*

The matching of food with the appropriate wine is not too complicated; it is actually fun. First of all, in making such choices, there are no absolutes. Therefore, some food goes with certain wines because they complement each other, and others work because of their stark contrast. The nature of the recipes in this book reflects the American "international" style of eating. In the old days, the traditional maxim paired red wine with meat, white wine with fish, sweet wine with dessert, and Champagne with everything.

Those rules still apply. However, individual tastes and a much wider selection of new wine varietals currently govern selection. Suggesting a broad category such as Santa Ynez Valley Sauvignon Blanc with California-farmed fish is not always effective. There are too many styles of the same varietal wine and too many ways to prepare the fish. A more acceptable rule is that delicate foods need delicate wines, and heartier foods need heftier wines.

The following wine suggestions are intended to help you make informed decisions. In addition, we have made specific recommendations for many of the dishes included in this cookbook.

Appetizers: Dry, light, crispy-flavored white wines are ideal to start. The palate is awakened by their refreshing, acid edge, and they counterbalance the various flavors of cheese, smokiness, or light dressings. Champagnes and sparkling wines are also appropriate, and Rosé Champagne is more full-bodied than others for many lighter dishes.

Fish and Light Pasta: Light, dry white wine is best, as it does not mask the delicacy of flavors.

Poultry, Pork, Veal and Robust Pasta: White or red? The choice largely depends on the method of preparation, the sauce, and the spices that are being used. The simpler the preparation, the easier the pairing. Chardonnay, dry Sémillon, and light reds all partner well with these foods.

Red Meat and Game: These call for a red wine, medium or full-bodied, with a toasty, smoky aroma and enough astringency to cut through the meat's fattiness.

Asian Dishes: The use of spices such as ginger or hot peppers in these dishes calls for light wines such as Chenin Blanc, Riesling, and Gewürztraminer wrapped by a hint of sweetness, flowers, or spices. Extremely spicy dishes can be overpowering, so choose a well-chilled, off-dry white as a palate cooler.

Desserts: A delicious sweet wine and an equally great dessert pair well. Dessert wines are usually drunk in moderation at the end of the meal because of what the sugar does to the palate. (It's best to drink a sweet wine after a dry one.) Highly suggested choices are the fortified wines such as Madeira, Marsala, Sherry, and Port.

For a dinner, within a flow of several courses, there is a progression of flavors and wines. Food and wine should develop together and progress from lighter to heavier, with fruit and nutty flavors offering interesting contrasts. Remember, the subtle nuances of each dish can help us discover and exalt the quality of matching wines. Conversely, the qualities of wine complete the pleasures of the food, bringing the enjoyment of it to new heights.

NOTES

BREAKFASTS

GREAT TASTE IN THE MORNING

It's obvious InCirclers really enjoy the first meal of the day. We received enough morning recipes to fill several more recipe books. Granted, some need to be saved for more leisurely weekend brunches. But, there were still lots that are quick to make on a typical weekday morning when breakfast goes self-serve in many households. We tried the Gingerbread Waffles and deemed them heavenly. But, Terrier Toasties? The name alone warranted inclusion. And they were good, too.

APPLE-CINNAMON FRENCH TOAST

Diane Kessler
Newport Beach, CA

We had out-of-town houseguests and planned to be gone all day. With no time for cooking, I chose this unusual version of French toast which is started the day before. It was an instant hit!

2 large baking apples
5 tablespoons butter
1 cup firmly packed dark
   brown sugar
2 tablespoons dark corn syrup
1 teaspoon cinnamon
8 (1-inch-thick) slices baguette
3 large eggs
1 cup milk
1 teaspoon vanilla extract

The day before serving: Peel, core, and slice apples. Grease a 13x9-inch baking pan. In a large, heavy skillet, melt butter over medium heat. Add apples and cook, stirring occasionally, until tender. Add brown sugar, corn syrup, and cinnamon. Cook, stirring, until sugar dissolves. Pour the mixture into the baking pan and spread to an even layer, arranging apple slices in concentric circles.

Arrange bread slices in a layer on top. In a medium bowl, beat eggs, milk, and vanilla with a fork until combined; pour over bread. Cover and chill overnight.

Before serving: Preheat oven to 375°. Remove the cover from the baking pan, and bake for 30 to 35 minutes until the mixture is firm and the bread is golden. Let cool for 5 minutes. Invert a serving tray over the baking pan and carefully flip both so that the apple layer is on top. Spoon any apple slices or syrup that remain in the pan over the top.

(PHOTO, PAGE 154)

SERVES 6 TO 8

Germany: Von Kesselstatt, '93 Spätlese Riesling, Piesport

France: Hugel et Fils, '93 Sylvaner, Alsace

—

—

—

—

—

—

—

—

—

—

—

—

—

—

—

—

—

—

—

—

—

—

—

BANANA YOGURT PANCAKES

Diane A. Ward
Los Angeles, CA

Breakfast has always been my favorite meal, probably because I am a morning person and begin my day swimming laps in my pool. This recipe was inspired by Bradley Ogden's cookbook and the menus at Lark Creek Inn and One Market Place. I lightened it by using very ripe bananas and extra egg whites. This is definitely a dish to be enjoyed in your Sunday morning lounging clothes.

Peel bananas, cut into chunks, and purée with lemon juice in a food processor. Add lemon zest, vanilla, sugar, cinnamon, and melted butter; process until combined. Add yogurt and pulse six times. Add whole egg and pulse three times. Add flour and pulse gently until barely mixed. Transfer mixture to a clean mixing bowl. Gently fold egg whites into batter.

Heat skillet or griddle until a drop of water sizzles. Lightly coat with oil. Drop batter by spoonfuls onto skillet. When bubbles appear, turn pancakes. Cook on second side until just brown.

Serve immediately with sautéed bananas and maple syrup.

Note: The following substitutions can be made:
   For self-rising flour: 1/2 cup all-purpose flour,
   1 teaspoon baking powder, and
   1/4 teaspoon baking soda.
   For yogurt: 1/4 cup milk and 1/4 cup sour cream.

SERVES 2

- 2 medium bananas, very ripe
- 2 teaspoons lemon juice
  Grated zest of 1 lemon (optional)
- 1 teaspoon vanilla extract
- 2 teaspoons sugar
  Dash cinnamon
- 2 tablespoons unsalted butter, melted
- 1/2 cup yogurt
- 1 egg, beaten
- 1/2 cup self-rising flour
- 2 egg whites, beaten until stiff
  Canola or avocado oil for frying

FRENCH TOAST

Mrs. Edgar C. Sayles Sr.
Huntington Beach, CA

This has been a Sayles family favorite for over 40 years and incorporates suggestions from every family member. We've served it to guests in every city we've lived in. Part of the fun is selecting the bread to use, sometimes determined by the season.

4 large eggs
1 cup heavy whipping cream
4 tablespoons sugar
1 teaspoon salt
1 tablespoon plus 1 teaspoon vanilla extract
1 to 2 teaspoons nutmeg (optional)
8 (³/4-inch-thick) slices bread, dried
½ cup (1 stick) butter for browning

Grease a 10-inch skillet or griddle. In a shallow bowl beat eggs. Add and lightly mix cream, sugar, salt, vanilla, and nutmeg. Heat skillet over medium-high heat. Dip two bread slices, one slice at a time, in the mixture, coating each side but allowing excess to drip off before placing in skillet. Fry until browned as desired. Serve immediately. Dip and fry remaining bread in batches as space allows, removing any dark butter and bits of bread from skillet between batches and adding butter as needed.

Serve with butter, warm syrup, and confectioners' sugar. Flavored butter or flavored syrup enhance the toast. Garnish with strawberries, orange slices, fresh pineapple, or other fruit. Accompany with crisp bacon, ham, or sausage.

Note: If diners have differing preferences regarding nutmeg, it may be sprinkled on individual slices in the skillet. Some breads dry out if set out overnight; however, bread also can be dried in the oven.

MAKES 4 SERVINGS

Terrier Toasties

Scott Schwimer
Beverly Hills, CA

During college, I spent a year in France. I went to cooking school, but I never learned to make what we Americans call "French toast" until I returned home and experimented for myself. The name? That came from the day I set a plateful down on my patio table, left to call the guests to come out, and what did we find? My Scottish terrier munching away on what I now call "Terrier Toasties."

Cut bread into 2-inch cubes, discarding the crust. In a separate bowl, beat together eggs, milk, vanilla, and syrup. Pour oil 2½ inches deep into a deep pot. Slowly warm oil until it reaches a near boil. Quickly dip the bread cubes into the batter and submerge them in oil, using tongs. Fry until golden brown. Drain on a paper towel, and place on a serving tray. Smother with whipped butter and top with confectioners' sugar, cinnamon, and chocolate.

Serve this Richard Simmons nightmare with plenty of maple syrup for that extra touch.

SERVES 4 TO 6

1 loaf Kings Hawaiian Bread or challah
3 eggs
¼ cup milk
1 teaspoon vanilla extract
1 tablespoon maple syrup
2 to 3 cups cooking oil for deep frying
Whipped butter to top toast
Confectioners' sugar to top toast
Cinnamon to top toast
Sweet ground chocolate to top toast

California: Benziger of Glen Ellen, '93 Pinot Blanc

California: Robert Talbott Vineyards, '93 Chardonnay

CANADIAN BACON-POTATO BAKE

B. Rhoads Fearn
Santa Maria, CA

This hearty breakfast was created to serve as a thank-you to a group who had participated in an AIDS Walk sponsored by Open Hand. Like many Bay Area residents, I have been privileged to participate in Open Hand, which in two years expanded from serving 700 hot meals a day to over 2,000 per day.

4 large or 6 medium baking
    potatoes
2¼ teaspoons salt
    Pepper to taste
3 to 4 large cloves garlic,
    minced
1 tablespoon orange-honey
    mustard
3 cups whipping cream
1 pound Canadian bacon,
    sliced ⅛-inch thick
2 medium onions, sliced thin

Preheat oven to 325°. Peel potatoes and cut into thin slices; do not rinse. Generously grease a 2½-quart casserole dish. Whisk salt, pepper, garlic, and mustard into cream. The mixture should taste quite salty, as the potatoes will absorb it. Place half of the potatoes in the bottom of the casserole dish. Add a layer of bacon followed by a layer of onions. Pour half of the cream mixture on top. Add remaining potatoes and cream, making sure cream completely covers potatoes. Bake for 1 hour. Check casserole. If it is browning, loosely cover with parchment paper; otherwise, do not cover. Bake for 30 more minutes.

Serve with mimosas, fresh fruit cups, and sweet rolls. Leftovers are tasty the next day.

SERVES 6

 California: Maison-Deutz, Blanc de Noir
 Italy: Pio Cesare, '93 Roero Arneis DOC

SIMPLY SINFUL CASSEROLE

Fonda M. Scott
Los Angeles, CA

My mother wowed many a guest with this delicious casserole. It is very convenient to make because it can be done the day or night before. You can even make a lower fat version by using non-fat cheese, egg substitutes, less salt, and less bacon. Either way, all it needs is coffee and fresh fruit and you have a breakfast party.

DIRECTIONS FOR BASE:

Preheat oven to 350°. Cut bread into 1-inch cubes, removing crusts if desired. Lightly grease an 8x10x2-inch glass pan. Place bread cubes in the bottom of the pan. Add the remaining base ingredients.

DIRECTIONS FOR SAUCE:

Mix the sauce ingredients together and pour over the top. Cover and chill overnight.

Bake, uncovered, for 35 to 40 minutes.
Serve hot.

Note: Other seasonings such as Italian, Indian, or Mexican spices can be added to the sauce. For a health-smart version, use non-fat cheeses, egg substitutes, and a smaller amount of low-sodium bacon.

MAKES 6 SERVINGS

BASE:
- 8 (1-inch-thick) slices French bread
- 1 pound cooked bacon or sausage
- 1/2 cup shredded Monterey Jack cheese
- 1/2 cup shredded Cheddar cheese
- 1 cup sliced mushrooms
- 1 cup sliced or shredded zucchini

SAUCE:
- 1 1/2 cups milk
- 3/4 cup half-and-half
- 1 teaspoon Worcestershire sauce
- 1 teaspoon dry mustard
- 1/2 teaspoon onion powder
- 5 eggs, beaten
- Salt and pepper to taste

Gingerbread Waffles

Margaret Fletcher
Houston, TX

The recipe for this treat came from an older friend. It was given to her years ago by her Norwegian mother-in-law during a visit to Norway.

2 cups flour
1/2 teaspoon salt
1/2 teaspoon ginger
1 teaspoon cinnamon
1 cup molasses
1/2 cup (1 stick) butter
1 1/2 teaspoons baking soda
1 cup sour cream
1 egg

Preheat waffle iron on medium heat setting. Sift together flour, salt, ginger, and cinnamon; set aside. Heat molasses and butter in a saucepan until butter melts and molasses and butter can be thoroughly mixed. Remove from heat and beat in baking soda. Pour into a large, deep bowl. Stir in sour cream and egg. Add dry ingredients. Blend. Bake in waffle iron.

Serve with brown sugar and cream or fig preserves.
(PHOTO, PAGE 152)

MAKES 6 TO 8 WAFFLES

Little Brown Jug Rolls

Phyllis Katz
New Albany, OH

Years ago, when I used to entertain much more, I clipped this recipe from our local newspaper. Now I mostly entertain at brunch because I love to bake and this is a particular favorite.

1 cup chopped pecans
2 loaves frozen bread dough, thawed
1/2 cup (1 stick) butter, melted
1 (4.6-ounce) package vanilla pudding, not instant
1 tablespoon milk
1 tablespoon cinnamon
1 cup firmly packed light brown sugar

Grease a 13x9-inch pan. Sprinkle with nuts. Shape dough into walnut-sized pieces. Fill the pan with a single layer of dough balls. Combine remaining ingredients and pour over dough. Let rise in refrigerator overnight.

Preheat oven to 350°. Bake uncovered for 30 minutes. Meanwhile, line a cookie sheet with aluminum foil. When rolls are cooked, immediately invert onto prepared cookie sheet.

SERVES 6 TO 8

MUSHROOM CRUST QUICHE

Ruth M. Branham
Dallas, TX

At a beautiful inn on the California coast, this quiche was brought to our room in a basket each morning. At home, we like to serve it with assorted breads and Champagne.

Preheat oven to 350°. Grease a 9-inch pie pan. In a frying pan over medium heat, melt 3 tablespoons butter. Add mushrooms and cook until tender. Stir in crackers. Turn the mixture into the pie pan. Press evenly over the bottom and sides of the pan. In the same frying pan, melt remaining butter. Add onions and cook until tender. Spread onions over the mushroom crust. Sprinkle with shredded cheese.

In a blender, blend cottage cheese, eggs, and cayenne until smooth. Pour into the crust. Sprinkle with paprika. Bake for 30 minutes, or until a knife inserted in the center comes out clean. Let stand for 15 minutes before cutting.

Note: To serve after freezing, thaw; then heat in a 325° oven for 15 minutes.

SERVES 6

5	tablespoons butter, divided into 3 tablespoons and 2 tablespoons
8	ounces mushrooms, chopped
1/2	cup crushed saltine crackers
3/4	cup chopped green onions
2	cups shredded Swiss cheese
1	cup cottage cheese
3	eggs
1/4	teaspoon cayenne
1/4	teaspoon paprika

California: Domaine Chandon, Blanc de Noir
Washington: Hogue Cellars, '94 Sémillon

RICE PANCAKES

Karen Sheetz
Newport Beach, CA

My Norwegian grandmother used to prepare these pancakes for my father. My mother made them for me, and on birthday mornings she stuck a candle in the stack for a special surprise. What wonderful memories this recipe brings to me of the special family members who passed it on.

> 2 eggs
> 1¾ cups milk
> 1 cup flour
> 4 teaspoons baking powder
> 1 rounded tablespoon sugar
> 1 teaspoon salt
> 1 cup cooked white rice,
>   chilled overnight
> Butter for frying

Beat eggs together. Add milk, flour, baking powder, sugar, and salt. Whisk together until blended. Stir in rice. Heat a skillet and fry pancakes in butter three at a time, using a tablespoon of batter for each pancake. Batter will be thin, so scoop up a bit of rice with each pancake.

Top each pancake with a pat of butter and maple syrup.

SERVES 4

MOCHA CREAM PUNCH

Janet Wilhelmi
Joliet, IL

I first had this luscious punch at a Christmas cookie exchange years ago. Now I often serve it at brunches or with dessert at dinner parties. This recipe totally disregards calories, cholesterol, and cost!

> 1 quart cold brewed coffee
> 1 quart chocolate ice cream
> 1 quart vanilla ice cream
> ¼ teaspoon almond extract
> 1 cup whipping cream
> ½ cup sugar
> ¼ teaspoon salt
> ½ teaspoon nutmeg

Pour coffee into a punch bowl. Add ice cream, breaking up into chunks. Add almond extract. In a separate bowl, whip cream, adding sugar and salt while whipping. Fold in whipped cream.

To serve, sprinkle with nutmeg.

SERVES 8 TO 10

Poached Eggs with Cognac Hollandaise Sauce

Sylvia F. Rollins
Chicago, IL

On my 40th birthday, my boyfriend made a special breakfast for me. We decided it was entirely too early for cocktails, so we blended the cognac into the Hollandaise Sauce for the eggs.

DIRECTIONS FOR POACHED EGGS:

Preheat oven to 350°. Bake potatoes for 45 minutes. Meanwhile, prepare Hollandaise Sauce (see sauce directions) and keep warm in double boiler with lid askew and water barely simmering. When potatoes are cooked, allow them to cool; cut in half lengthwise. Gently remove potato insides and set aside. Heat oil in deep fryer and immerse potato skins until crispy. Remove from oil, drain, and set aside. Add vinegar and eggs to a pot of water and bring to a boil. Crack eggs, remove them from shells, and return them to boiling water for 3 to 4 minutes to poach. Remove eggs and let cool. Sauté spinach, seasoning with salt, pepper, and minced garlic.

DIRECTIONS FOR COGNAC HOLLANDAISE SAUCE:

Keep butter warm. In a separate saucepan, warm Tabasco®, Worcestershire, lemon juice, and cognac; keep warm on low temperature. In a double boiler, whisk together egg yolks. When they thicken, add boiling water, one tablespoon at a time, whisking continuously until mixture thickens. Beat in lemon juice mixture. Add butter, continuing to beat until smooth. Add salt, pepper, and cayenne to taste. Blend.

To serve, place spinach on individual plates, top with potato skins, and nestle a poached egg in each skin. Lavishly pour Cognac Hollandaise Sauce on top.

EGGS:
- 2 medium baking potatoes
- 2 to 3 cups olive oil for deep frying
- 2 teaspoons vinegar
- 4 eggs
- 3 ounces fresh spinach
- Salt and pepper to taste
- 1/2 teaspoon minced garlic

SAUCE:
- 1/4 cup clarified butter
- Tabasco® sauce to taste
- 1/2 teaspoon Worcestershire sauce
- 1 teaspoon lemon juice
- 1 tablespoon cognac
- 4 egg yolks
- 4 tablespoons boiling water
- Salt and pepper to taste
- Pinch cayenne

SERVES 2

California: Iron Horse Vineyards, '90 Cuvée Vrais Amis

Italy: Ca' del Bosco, Dosage Zero

GRANOLA TRADE-OFF

Karen Frommer
Bedford Corners, NY

My neighbor, a well-known soap star for over 35 years, always has a bumper crop of tomatoes, which she generously shares. To reciprocate, I keep her well supplied with this granola trade-off, which she loves. Now it's a tradition: granola for tomatoes!

5 cups rolled oats, not instant
1 cup chopped pecans
1/2 cup sliced blanched almonds
1/2 cup cashews
1/2 cup sunflower seeds
1/2 cup unsalted pumpkin seeds
1/2 cup coconut flakes (not
    shredded)
1 tablespoon orange zest
1/2 tablespoon lemon zest
1/4 teaspoon nutmeg
2 teaspoons cinnamon
3/4 cup (1 1/2 sticks) unsalted
    butter
1/2 cup honey
1/2 cup firmly packed light
    brown sugar
1/3 cup maple syrup
1/4 teaspoon vanilla extract
1 cup coarsely chopped dried
    dates, apricots, figs, or
    other fruit
1/2 cup mixture of dried
    cherries, cranberries, and
    golden raisins

Preheat oven to 325°. Lightly grease 2 (12x17-inch) baking pans. Combine oats, pecans, almonds, cashews, sunflower and pumpkin seeds, coconut, orange and lemon zests, nutmeg, and cinnamon in a large bowl. Melt butter, honey, and sugar over low heat. Add syrup and vanilla. Add the liquid mixture to the oat mixture; mix thoroughly. Scrape into baking pans, dividing evenly. Pat down the mixture to a 1/2-inch layer.

Bake for 45 to 55 minutes until golden, stirring gently once or twice to prevent burning without breaking up the granola clumps. Remove from oven. Let cool completely in pans. Transfer to a large bowl. Break large clumps. Add chopped dried fruits to taste. Store in airtight containers for about 1 month.

Serve with fresh fruit, yogurt, or milk.

Note: This dish must be made a month in advance.

MAKES 10 CUPS

SAVORY TORTE

Julie G. Oelman
Hinsdale, IL

This torte was served by the caterer at my grandparents' 50th wedding anniversary party. That caterer has long since gone out of business, but my mother has never forgotten the party or the recipe and often serves the torte to her guests.

DIRECTIONS FOR PASTRY:

Cut butter into tablespoon-sized pieces. Process in food processor twice. Add egg and process two more times. Add salt, flour, and baking powder. Process until clumps form. Gather into a ball and chill for 45 minutes. Roll out pastry. Cut a 9-inch-diameter circle and a long rectangle in the pastry to line the bottom and sides of a 9-inch springform pan. Pinch edges together and moisten seams. Freeze crust.

DIRECTIONS FOR FILLING:

Preheat oven to 325°. In a food processor, process ham until finely minced but not pureed; set aside. Process fontina; set aside. Process ricotta, cream cheese, cream, eggs, salt, pepper, and hot pepper sauce until smooth. Remove crust from freezer. Paint with mustard. Spoon filling into crust in the following order: 1 1/2 cups ricotta mix, half of the ham, and half of the fontina. Spread half of the pesto sauce on top. Repeat these layers. Bake 1 to 1 3/4 hours until golden on top.

Cool to room temperature to serve.

SERVES 12 TO 14

PASTRY:

- 1/2 cup (1 stick) unsalted butter
- 1 egg
- 1/8 teaspoon salt
- 1 1/3 cups flour
- 1 1/4 teaspoons baking powder

FILLING:

- 1/2 pound baked ham
- 1/4 pound fontina cheese, grated
- 1 1/2 pounds ricotta cheese, drained overnight in a colander lined with a cheesecloth
- 12 ounces cream cheese
- 1/4 cup whipping cream
- 4 eggs
- 1/2 teaspoon salt
- 1/4 teaspoon pepper
- Dash hot pepper sauce
- 2 tablespoons Dijon mustard
- 1 pint pesto sauce

 California: Chimney Rock, '93 Fumé Blanc

Italy: Corvo, '93 Bianco di Salaparuta

Appetizers

HELP YOURSELF TO APPETEASERS

If it's true that first impressions are the most lasting, then the hors d'oeuvres you serve had better measure up. If you plan well, you'll always have something made ahead or ready to make when the doorbell rings - such as the Pâté aux Champignons, which is always very impressive, yet can be done way ahead of time. Our appetizers have come from all corners of our country and their inspirations from all corners of the world—Italy, France, Mexico, England, and the oceans in between. Rehearse a few, then once you've established a half dozen favorites, you've got the makings of a great party.

ARTICHOKE DIP

Andrea L. Tuggle
Dallas, TX

I took this hot appetizer dip to the law office where I work as a paralegal, and everyone there seemed to enjoy it.

4 ounces Cheddar cheese, grated
4 ounces Parmesan cheese, grated
1 (14-ounce) can artichoke hearts, drained
½ cup chopped green onions
½ teaspoon garlic salt
½ cup mayonnaise
Paprika for seasoning

Preheat oven to 350°. Mix together cheeses, artichoke hearts, green onions, garlic salt, and mayonnaise. Sprinkle paprika over the top. Bake for 20 minutes, or until bubbly. Serve with tortilla chips.

MAKES ABOUT 4 CUPS

 California: Fetzer Vineyards, Barrel Select Chardonnay

 France: Tavel, Domaine Lafon des Comtes

BACON AND LETTUCE STUFFED TOMATOES

S.C. Schultz
Marietta, GA

My daughter, Erin, insisted I submit this recipe. Erin, and her brother, Brad, have always been in charge of making (and eating) them. What makes this recipe especially great is that it can easily fit into any menu from backyard barbecue to a more formal table setting just by changing the way it's presented.

20 cherry tomatoes
Salt to season tomatoes
¼ cup finely chopped Vidalia or other sweet onion
10 slices bacon, cooked crisp and crumbled
½ cup finely chopped lettuce
⅓ cup mayonnaise
Salt and pepper (optional)

Cut the top off each tomato. Using a small melon baller, carefully scoop out the pulp and seeds and discard. Lightly salt the inside of each tomato. Invert and drain on paper towels for 15 minutes. Meanwhile, in a small bowl, combine remaining ingredients. Using a pastry bag with a large tip, stuff each tomato.

Note: You can make the filling ahead of time, but don't stuff the tomatoes until an hour or so before serving.

MAKES 20 APPETIZERS

 California: Edmunds St. John, '91 Syrah, Les Côtes Sauvages

 Italy: Rocca dell' Macie, '92 Rubizzo

SIX-LAYER BOMBAY CHEESE

Caroline Bourestom
St. Cloud, MN

When I prepared and served this recipe for our choir's $100-a-plate dinner, I had many requests for the recipe. Those requests continue as friends share it with other friends.

Combine cream cheese, Cheddar, and curry; beat by hand until smooth. Shape into a 5½-inch-diameter disc about 1 inch high. Chill until firm (about 45 minutes).

To assemble platter, place cheese on a serving tray. Spread chutney on top of cheese. Sprinkle coconut, nuts, scallions, and currants over chutney.

To serve, cut apples into thin wedges and toss with lemon juice to prevent discoloration. Arrange wedges and water crackers around cheese.

Note: Cheese can be made up to 2 days in advance; cover and chill until ready to serve. The platter can be prepared up to an hour before serving if kept cool.

SERVES 6 TO 8

California: Robert Mondavi Winery,
    '93 Pinot Noir, Carneros

Italy: Luciano Sandrone, '93 Dolcetto d'Alba DOC

8 ounces cream cheese at room temperature
4 ounces sharp Cheddar cheese, grated
½ teaspoon curry powder
⅓ cup mango chutney or mixed-fruit chutney
2 tablespoons flaked coconut, unsweetened
¼ cup toasted pecans or almonds
1 tablespoon finely chopped scallions
1½ tablespoons currants
3 apples
Lemon juice to prevent apple discoloration

CRANBERRY-GLAZED BRIE

Joanna Morford
Chandler, AZ

I had been looking for a new, elegant cranberry recipe when my sister came across this one. It makes a festive presentation and has become a holiday tradition at our house.

CRANBERRY MARMALADE:
- 3 cups cranberries
- 3/4 cup firmly packed light brown sugar
- 2/3 cup dried currants
- 1/3 cup water
- 1/8 teaspoon dry mustard
- 1/8 teaspoon allspice
- 1/8 teaspoon cardamom
- 1/8 teaspoon ground cloves
- 1/8 teaspoon ginger

BRIE:
- 1 (2.2-pound) Brie cheese wheel, 8 inches in diameter
- Crackers
- Apple slices, tossed with lemon juice to prevent discoloration
- Pear slices, tossed with lemon juice to prevent discoloration

DIRECTIONS FOR CRANBERRY MARMALADE:
Combine all ingredients in a heavy non-aluminum saucepan. Cook over medium-high heat, stirring frequently, until most berries pop (about 5 minutes). Let cool to room temperature. Cover and chill for 1 to 2 hours.
Note: Marmalade can be prepared 3 days ahead.

DIRECTIONS FOR BRIE:
Preheat oven to 300°. Line a cookie sheet with aluminum foil. Using a sharp knife, carefully cut out a circle of rind from the top of the cheese wheel, leaving a 1/2-inch border around the opening; do not cut through the side rind. Place cheese in an 8-inch-diameter ceramic baking dish on prepared cookie sheet. Spread cranberry marmalade over cheese. Bake for 12 minutes, or until soft.

To serve, cool slightly and set on a large platter. Surround with crackers and fruit.

Note: The marmalade can be spread over the cut brie 6 hours ahead. Cover and chill, then set cheese out until warmed to room temperature before baking.

SERVES 10 TO 12

 California: Au Bon Climat, '92 Pinot Noir, Talley Reserve

 France: Monthélie-Douhairet, '93 Les Champs-Fulliots

CHEESE STRAWS

Mary Louise Albritton
Chattanooga, TN

After we moved from Dallas to Chattanooga, I missed spicy Texas food (and NM)! But, a ragin' Cajun friend gave me this recipe, which helps a lot. We love it with champagne or just any time we want to be "devilish."

Preheat oven to 350°. Cream butter, add cheese, and set aside. Sift together all dry ingredients and combine with butter-cheese mixture. Place in a cookie press or a pastry bag with a fairly large tip. Pipe out to form short or long straws. Bake on an ungreased cookie sheet for 10 to 15 minutes until golden brown. (PHOTO, PAGE 156)

MAKES 3 DOZEN STRAWS

1 cup (2 sticks) butter
1 pound sharp Cheddar cheese, grated
3 cups flour
1 teaspoon baking powder
1 teaspoon cayenne
1 teaspoon salt

 Oregon: Montinore Vineyards, '93 Pinot Gris, Willamette

France: Louis Roederer, Champagne, Brut Premier NV

BLEU CHEESE MEATBALLS

Judy Walke Havener
Fort Worth, TX

Whenever my late mother-in-law served these meatballs at parties, she always invoked the "FHB Rule"—Family Hold Back. If she hadn't, her children and their spouses would have scarfed down the meatballs before the guests had a chance to taste them.

Crumble cheese. Add mayonnaise, Worcestershire, mustard, salt, pepper, egg, and milk. Mix. Crumble corn flakes and add to mixture. Add ground beef and combine. Shape into 1-inch balls. Brown in oil. Serve warm.

Note: For best results, chill the mixture for a few hours before shaping the meatballs.

MAKES 2½ DOZEN MEATBALLS

¼ pound bleu cheese
¼ cup mayonnaise
2 tablespoons Worcestershire sauce
1 tablespoon dry mustard
1 teaspoon salt
¼ teaspoon pepper
1 egg, beaten
½ cup milk
2 cups corn flakes
1 pound ground beef
Vegetable oil for browning

 California: Guenoc Winery, '92 Cabernet Franc

Italy: Tenuta Caparzo, '93 Rosso di Montalcino

Pâté aux Champignons

Susan H. (Mrs. William Torry) Barbee
Weslaco, TX

After a "Murphy's Law" day, I was way behind schedule in preparing for a dinner party. This recipe was intended as a spread, but I decided to take a short cut through the food processor. In my hurry, I used the wrong blade, so I had no choice but to pass it off as pâté. It was such a hit, I have made it that way ever since!

8 ounces Neufchâtel cheese
    at room temperature
2 tablespoons butter
8 ounces mushrooms, sliced
1 medium onion, chopped
2 cloves garlic, minced
1/3 cup sherry
1/4 teaspoon salt
1 1/2 teaspoons black pepper
1 teaspoon sugar
1 1/2 teaspoons chopped fresh
    thyme, or 1/2 teaspoon
    dried
2 teaspoons Worcestershire
    sauce

Cube cheese and set aside. In a large skillet, melt butter and sauté mushrooms, onion, and garlic until tender. Pour in sherry and cook until the liquid is absorbed. Add salt, pepper, sugar, thyme, and Worcestershire and sauté for 5 minutes. Add cheese, cook until melted, and stir until combined. Purée in a food processor to desired texture. Chill until set.

MAKES 2 CUPS

California: Matanzas Creek, '93 Chardonnay
France: Taittinger, Champagne, Brut Royal,
       Pommery, or Brut La Francaise

Cognac Pâté

James D. Felter
Scottsdale, AZ

I devised this recipe with the help of a cousin who enjoys "special cooking" as much as I do. Because I am an interior designer, the presentation of each dish is very important to me. My most elegant way to serve this pâté is in a mold, on an antique English silver tray that is actually a sports trophy.

Mince onion; sauté with butter and garlic for 5 minutes. Add livers and cook over medium heat for 3 to 5 minutes, stirring often. Add cognac, salt, pepper, allspice, and nutmeg. Cook for 5 minutes, or until livers are slightly pink. Drain. Process with cream cheese in food processor for 20 seconds, or until smooth. Stir in parsley and chives; mix. Coat a mold with cooking spray; pour in liver mixture. Cover and chill for at least 8 hours.

To serve, invert mold over serving plate and surround with slices of miniature toast.

MAKES 2 1/2 TO 3 CUPS

- 1 small onion
- 1 tablespoon butter
- 1 small clove garlic, crushed
- 1 pound chicken livers
- 1/4 cup cognac
- 1/4 teaspoon salt
- 1/8 teaspoon pepper
- 1/8 teaspoon allspice
- 1/8 teaspoon nutmeg
- 8 ounces cream cheese, cubed
- 2 tablespoons chopped fresh parsley
- 1 tablespoon snipped fresh chives

Guacamole and Caviar Dip

Mrs. Robert E. Jones
Benton, AR

Before my helper came to work for me, she had scrimped and saved to earn money for a trip from California to Arkansas. However, she then lost her fare home at the races in Hot Springs. Ergo, she came to work for me and gave me this recipe. Everyone who has tasted it says it's the best. (Editor's note: No wonder, 6 ounces of Beluga caviar!)

Juice onion in blender, strain and discard pulp, reserving the juice in the blender. Peel, pit, and chop avocados. Add avocados, lemon juice, mayonnaise, and paprika. Whip until smooth. Add cream cheese and whip until smooth. Fold in caviar. Serve with potato chips or crackers.

MAKES 2 CUPS

- 1 onion
- 2 small avocados
- 2 tablespoons lemon juice
- 2 tablespoons mayonnaise
  Dash paprika
- 8 ounces cream cheese
- 6 ounces Beluga or other caviar

California: Scharffenberger Cellars, Blanc de Blanc

France: G.H. Mumm, Champagne, Extra Brut

WORLD'S BEST GUACAMOLE PICANTE

Ann Siner
Phoenix, AZ

Bon Appétit published my guacamole recipe in 1987 and twice since then. Both my parents laid claim to the recipe, but like any good gold miner, I got to the assay office first and staked my claim.

4 medium avocados
1 medium tomato
1 small onion
1 small jalapeño
2 tablespoons hot and chunky salsa
2 tablespoons Worcestershire sauce
2 tablespoons lime juice
Salt and pepper to taste

Peel, pit, and slice avocados. Chop tomato and onion. Seed and mince jalapeño. Combine all ingredients in a large bowl. Mash with a fork until slightly chunky. Adjust seasonings to taste. Serve with crudités or tortilla chips.

Note: Be careful not to overmix. The chunky texture is what makes this dip so good.

MAKES 4 CUPS

 California: Maison Deutz, Blanc de Noir
 Spain: Freixenet, Carta Nevada, Semi-Seco

CHAFING DISH OYSTERS

Carol M. Harrison
Fort Lauderdale, FL

This recipe is so good that guests often have asked to take home the leftover sauce. There are never any leftover oysters!

Cook oysters over medium heat for 2 minutes, or until edges begin to curl. Drain and set aside. Cook butter and cream cheese in a medium saucepan over low heat, stirring until melted. Add wine, and whisk until smooth. Stir in scallions, paprika, anchovy paste, cayenne, salt, and hot sauce. Bring to a boil over high heat, stirring constantly. Gently fold in oysters. Spoon oyster mixture into chafing dish, and keep warm over low flame.

To serve, fill individual pastry shells and garnish with parsley.

MAKES 20 APPETIZERS

 California: Cambria Winery & Vineyard,
'93 Chardonnay, Katherine's

 France: Louis Latour, '93 Chablis

2 (12-ounce) jars oysters,
   undrained
1/4 cup (1/2 stick) butter or
   margarine
8 ounces cream cheese,
   softened
1/2 cup plus 2 tablespoons dry
   white wine
3 tablespoons chopped
   scallions
1/2 teaspoon paprika
1/2 teaspoon anchovy paste
1/4 teaspoon cayenne
1/4 teaspoon salt
6 drops hot sauce
20 individual pastry shells
   Chopped parsley for garnish

DEVILED EGGS SUPREME

Linda G. Bishop
Dallas, TX

These eggs are very rich, but very good. I've changed it several times, and this version is, to my taste (and to that of my friends who have tasted it), the very best.

6 eggs, hard-boiled
2 tablespoons Gorgonzola cheese, crumbled
1½ teaspoons dry mustard
Pinch salt
Dash pepper
3 tablespoons mayonnaise
6 tablespoons snipped fresh chives, or frozen or freeze-dried
Paprika

Slice eggs in half lengthwise and remove yolks. Set aside whites. Mash yolks in a mixing bowl. Add cheese and mix. Add mustard, salt, pepper, and mayonnaise. Blend until smooth. Fold in chives. Fill a pastry bag with the yolk mixture and pipe into egg whites.

To serve, sprinkle paprika on top.

MAKES 12

Australia: Penfolds, '93 Sémillon-Chardonnay
France: Pol Roger, Brut Champange

POTATO SOUFFLÉS

Susan Z. Diamond
Melrose Park, IL

I was looking for a way to turn soufflés into finger food; redskins seemed the ideal solution. This recipe originally called for zucchini, but I decided to make it with potatoes. Even though I travel frequently, I still love to entertain and this is a favorite. I first served it at a New Year's Eve party.

Preheat oven to 425°. Lightly oil a cookie sheet. Bring salted water to a boil for the potatoes. Boil potatoes for 8 minutes, or until skins can be pierced easily with a fork. Using a melon baller, make a well in the top of each potato. (If you're using the larger potatoes, cut them in half and hollow out the center.) Place potatoes, hollow side up, on prepared cookie sheet. In a small saucepan, melt butter over low heat. Using a wire whisk, stir in flour. Gradually add milk, stirring with the whisk. Cook for 5 minutes, or until thickened. Remove from heat. Add mustard, salt, Worcestershire, and cheese; whisk. Add egg yolk and whisk. In a separate bowl, whip egg whites until they stand in peaks but are not dry; fold into cheese mixture. Using a pastry bag or a spoon, fill potato cups with soufflé mixture. Bake for 7 to 8 minutes until soufflés have risen and are golden brown.

Note: Potatoes will stay upright on the tray if bottoms are cut slightly. Mushroom caps may be substituted for potatoes.

MAKES 40 APPETIZERS

40 very small red-skinned potatoes, or 20 slightly larger ones
1 tablespoon butter
1 tablespoon flour
6 tablespoons milk
1/2 teaspoon Pommery mustard
Salt to taste
Dash Worcestershire sauce
2 ounces sharp Cheddar cheese, grated
1 egg, separated
1 egg white

California: Château Montelena, '92 Zinfandel

Italy: Badia a Coltibuono, '93 Chianti Cetamura

ENGLISH APPETIZER SANDWICH

Joyce Baseman
Alexandria, VA

A wonderful English friend shared her recipe with me many years ago. It's still a favorite with my guests.

1 loaf pumpernickel bread
1 cup (2 sticks) butter, softened
3 ounces cream cheese with chives
1/2 teaspoon chopped fresh marjoram, or
    1/4 teaspoon dried
1/2 teaspoon chopped fresh thyme, or
    1/4 teaspoon dried
1 tablespoon tomato paste
1/4 teaspoon pepper
1/4 teaspoon paprika
1 tablespoon grated Parmesan cheese
1 teaspoon brandy
1/8 teaspoon nutmeg

Slice bread horizontally into 4 layers and set aside. Cream butter. Divide in three parts.

To one portion of butter, add cream cheese, marjoram, and thyme; mix.

To the second portion of butter, add pepper, tomato paste, and paprika; mix.

To the remaining creamed butter, add Parmesan, brandy, and nutmeg; mix.

Spread each mixture on a slice of bread, stack the layers, and place a fourth slice on top. Place a heavy plate on top to compress sandwich slightly. Chill for at least 2 hours.

To serve, cut in slices or thin wedges.

(PHOTO, PAGE 150)

MAKES 15 TO 20 APPETIZERS

 California: Beaulieu Vineyards (BV), '93 Special Burgundy

California: Lyeth Winery, '92 Red

TOMATO PARMESAN PIE

Louise (Mrs. Robert) Jayson
Dallas, TX

I'm an avid recipe collector, and I think I picked up this one at a college alumni luncheon. One more thing, I never substitute for fat!

DIRECTIONS FOR CRUST:

Preheat oven to 350°. Sift flour and salt together. Cut in shortening quickly and lightly with a pastry blender until the mixture is coarse. Gradually stir in water until dough is the desired consistency. Roll out the crust ¼- to ⅛-inch thick. Line an 11-inch metal quiche pan with the crust. Prick several times with a fork. Bake for 10 minutes. Remove from the oven and set aside.

DIRECTIONS FOR FILLING:

Preheat oven to 400°. Sprinkle crust with 2 tablespoons Parmesan and half of onion. Cut tomatoes into ½-inch slices (you should have 6 to 7 slices). Roll in flour and place in a layer on top of cheese and onion. Sprinkle generously with salt, pepper, half of remaining cheese, remaining onion, and olives. Beat eggs with a fork; add cream. Pour egg and cream mixture over tomatoes. Sprinkle with remaining cheese. Bake for 35 to 40 minutes until set. Let cool for 15 minutes.

To serve, cut into wedges.

(PHOTO, PAGE 147)

MAKES 16 SMALL WEDGES

Italy: Ruffino, '93 Libaio
Italy: Bertani, '94 Bardolino Chiaretto

CRUST:
- 2 cups flour
- 1 teaspoon salt
- ⅔ cup shortening
- 6 to 8 tablespoons cold water as needed

FILLING:
- ¾ cup grated Parmesan cheese, divided into 2 tablespoons, 5 tablespoons, and 5 tablespoons
- ¾ cup thinly sliced green onion, with tops, divided in half
- 3 tomatoes
- Flour for dredging tomatoes
- Salt and pepper to taste
- ½ cup black olives, sliced
- 2 eggs
- 1 cup heavy cream

WHITE SANGRIA

Tomas de la Mata
Dallas, TX

Sangria is a very refreshing and inexpensive Spanish libation. This recipe was served at the Spanish Pavilion restaurant at the New York World's Fair where I first worked when I came from Spain. I am now the director of catering for Dallas' Fairmont Hotel.

1 orange
1 lemon
1 bottle dry white wine
2 tablespoons sugar
1 ounce brandy
1 ounce Cointreau
2 cups ice cubes
1 cup club soda

Cut orange in half. Cut one half into thin slices; juice the other half. Cut lemon into thin slices. Combine orange and lemon slices and orange juice with wine, sugar, brandy, and Cointreau in a decorative pitcher. Chill until ready to serve.

To serve, add ice and club soda and stir gently.

(PHOTO, PAGE 160)

MAKES ABOUT 4 SERVINGS

TERRIFIC TANTALIZING TUNA DIP

Linda K. Wind
Dallas, TX

Just for fun, I entered this recipe in a Junior League Cook-off in 1976, and it won! It tastes like crab dip (especially with lemon and Parmesan added) and can be made very low-fat.

2 (6½-ounce) cans tuna packed
    in spring water
8 ounces cream cheese, softened
1 teaspoon grated onion
    Salt and pepper to taste
½ cup mayonnaise
3 tablespoons hot sauce
2 tablespoons chopped fresh
    parsley, or 1 tablespoon dried
Dash lemon-pepper
    marinade seasoning
1 teaspoon Worcestershire sauce

Blend all ingredients. Chill overnight so that flavors mix.

Serve with lemon or lime juice and Parmesan cheese.

Note: For parties, double the recipe. For a low-fat version, use low-fat or non-fat cream cheese and mayonnaise.

MAKES 3 CUPS

 California: Trefethen Vineyards, '94 Eschol-Blanc
 California: Chalone Vineyard, '93 Pinot Blanc

VEGETABLE QUESADILLAS

Beverly Kabakoff Adilman
Chicago, IL

As a vegetarian, I am always challenged to create new, sophisticated, and exciting dishes. Vegetarian meals can be made to satisfy everyone's taste buds. In fact, this appetizer is so well liked by my guests that I am often asked to serve it as a main course.

DIRECTIONS FOR QUESADILLAS:

Preheat broiler. Heat a 12-inch-deep skillet on low heat. Add 1 tablespoon olive oil. Add green onions and sauté for 2 minutes. Add carrots with 1 tablespoon oil and sauté for 2 minutes. Add zucchini and sauté for 2 minutes. Add corn and sauté for 2 minutes. Add red pepper and sauté for 2 minutes. Add broccoli and sauté for 2 minutes. Add mushrooms and remaining oil and sauté for 2 minutes. Remove from the heat and cover. Place tortillas on the middle rack in the oven for 1 minute. Turn over and sprinkle tortilla with cheese. Broil until cheese is almost melted. Remove and immediately cover half of tortilla with vegetables, fold over, and cut in 4 equal pieces.

DIRECTIONS FOR GUACAMOLE:

Peel, pit, and dice avocados. Mash pulp with a fork until slightly chunky. Stir in lemon juice, onion, chili sauce, and Tabasco®. Cover and chill for at least 30 minutes.

Serve quesadillas hot on a large platter with guacamole, salsa, and sour cream.

Note: To keep vegetables crunchy, stir constantly while sautéing and do not overcook.

SERVES 8 TO 10

🍷 California: Bonny Doon Vineyard, Ca' del Solo

🍇 California: Calera Wine Co., Viognier

QUESADILLAS:

- 3 tablespoons olive oil, divided in thirds
- ¾ cup finely chopped green onions
- 1½ cups finely chopped carrots
- 1½ cups finely chopped zucchini
- 1 cup sweet corn kernels, cut from the cob or frozen
- 1 cup finely chopped red bell pepper
- 2 cups chopped broccoli
- 2 cups finely chopped cremini mushrooms
- 8 (6- to 8-inch-diameter) tortillas (4 white flour, 4 wheat flour)
- 12 ounces shredded, low-moisture, part-skim mozzarella cheese

GUACAMOLE:

- 4 avocados
- 2 tablespoons lemon juice
- 1 small onion, grated
- 4 tablespoons chili sauce
- 2 dashes Tabasco® sauce

Breads and Sandwiches

THE BREADS AND THE GO-BETWEENS

Up till now, nothing so identified a culture as its bread. But now, they're eating hush puppies in New York and bagels in New Orleans. A whole new world of bread making has opened up for us, whether we knead it or not, own a bread machine or not. (If you don't, just think of making bread the old-fashioned way as good, firming exercise for the upper arms and dig right in.) As for sandwiches, well, when you consider that bread usually constitutes two-thirds of a sandwich everywhere but in Copenhagen, who could question its overall importance in the scheme of things?

ANISE TOAST

Sherrie L. Reddick
Wichita Falls, TX

My husband's family is Northern Italian, and this recipe has been handed down for six generations. It is his favorite, and I fix it on special occasions or after we have disagreed!

1/4 cup (1/2 stick) butter
1 1/2 cups sugar
4 eggs
1/2 teaspoon anise oil
2 1/2 cups flour
2 teaspoons baking powder

Preheat oven to 375°. Grease a cookie sheet. Cream butter and sugar. Add eggs and beat. Add remaining ingredients and beat until a stiff dough forms. Spread the dough on the cookie sheet, making 4 loaves; each loaf should be 2 inches wide, 8 inches long, and 1/2-inch thick. Bake for 20 minutes, or until lightly brown.

To serve, slice diagonally while warm into 1/2-inch slices.

MAKES 4 LOAVES

 Italy: Castello Gancia, Brut Sparkling Wine

 France: A. Charbaut et Fils, Brut Champagne, Gold Label

BLACK-EYED PEA CORNBREAD

Mrs. John A. Manno Sr.
Shreveport, LA

I'm not a fancy cook; I just enjoy it as therapy. Although I have a bachelor's degree in home economics, I have never taught cooking. My dream is to attend the California Culinary Academy.

1 pound bulk pork sausage
1 onion, chopped
1 cup cornmeal
1/2 cup flour
1 teaspoon salt
1/2 teaspoon baking soda
2 eggs
1 cup buttermilk
1/2 cup vegetable oil
Chopped green peppers to taste
3/4 cup creamed corn
8 ounces Cheddar cheese, grated
1 (15-ounce) can or 2 cups
    black-eyed peas, cooked

Preheat oven to 350°. Grease a 9x13-inch pan. Brown sausage and onion in a hot skillet. Drain and set aside. Combine cornmeal, flour, salt, and baking soda. In a separate bowl, beat eggs, buttermilk, and oil. Combine egg mixture with dry ingredients (batter should not be smooth). Add sausage and onions and remaining ingredients. Pour in loaf pan. Bake for 50 to 55 minutes until lightly browned.

Note: If you use a cornmeal mix, you can eliminate the salt and baking soda.

(PHOTO, PAGE 163)

SERVES 8 TO 10

Corn and Chive Popovers

Mary Frances Engle Alford
Henderson, TX

This makes a great substitute for plain cornbread. I like to serve it with soup in cold weather, but it's also delicious in the summertime, when the fresh corn and herbs are at their peak.

Preheat oven to 425°. Grease and flour a 12-cup popover or muffin tin or use muffin liners. Combine flour, cornmeal, sugar, salt, and pepper. Add remaining ingredients and leave lumpy. Pour 1/4 cup batter into each muffin cup (fill approximately two-thirds full). Bake for 25 to 30 minutes until puffed and golden. While muffins are baking, whip all herb butter ingredients in food processor and chill in individual dishes.

To serve, place individual herb butter with popovers on each plate.

Note: Do not open the oven while the popovers are cooking, or they may fall.

MAKES 12 POPOVERS

POPOVERS:
- 1 cup flour
- 1 tablespoon coarse yellow cornmeal
- 1 1/2 teaspoons sugar
- 1/2 teaspoon salt
- Pepper to taste
- 1 cup 2% milk
- 3 extra-large eggs, lightly beaten
- Corn kernels from an ear of corn, or 1/2 cup frozen, thawed and lightly mashed
- 1 1/2 tablespoons snipped fresh chives, or 1/2 tablespoon dried

HERB BUTTER:
- 1/2 cup (1 stick) butter
- 1 teaspoon chopped fresh oregano, or 1/2 teaspoon dried
- 1 teaspoon chopped fresh thyme, or 1/2 teaspoon dried
- 1 teaspoon snipped fresh chives, or 1/2 teaspoon dried
- 1 teaspoon chopped fresh tarragon, or 1/2 teaspoon dried
- Salt and pepper to taste
- 2 tablespoons chopped fresh parsley, or 1 tablespoon dried, plus some fresh for garnish

Pumpernickel Rye Bread

Sylvia C. Landers
Norfolk, NE

As a small child, I used to watch my grandmother make this recipe each and every week. The aroma that filled her home was wonderful! I have kept the recipe alive ever since.

3 packages active dry yeast
1 cup warm water
1 tablespoon salt
1 to 3 tablespoons caraway
    seeds
1/2 cup molasses
1/2 cup hot water
2 tablespoons shortening
2 1/4 cups rye flour
3 1/2 to 4 cups white flour,
    divided in half
Cornmeal for sprinkling on
    cookie sheet

Grease a mixing bowl. Dissolve yeast in warm water and set aside until foamy (about 10 minutes). Meanwhile, combine salt, caraway seeds, molasses, and hot water in a large mixing bowl. Blend together, and let cool to lukewarm. Stir in dissolved yeast. Mix in shortening, rye flour, and half of white flour; beat. Add more flour until the dough is stiff and clears the side of the bowl. Knead on a board for a few minutes until smooth. Place in prepared bowl and let rise until a dent remains in the side of the dough when it is pressed lightly with a finger (1 1/2 to 2 hours).

Sprinkle a cookie sheet with cornmeal. Punch down dough, and split in half. Cover and let stand for 5 minutes. Form into 2 smooth balls. Place on opposite corners of prepared cookie sheet. Let rise for 30 to 45 minutes until size doubles, preheating oven to 375° after the first 20 minutes. Bake for 35 to 45 minutes until well-browned and bread sounds hollow when tapped.

MAKES 2 LOAVES

CHEESE BREAD

Mara Squar
Tarzana, CA

I've enjoyed baking ever since I earned my Girl Scout cooking badge. At the age of 11, my first contribution to Thanksgiving dinner was bread, and bread or dessert is still what I bring. I once baked 500 mini loaves of this Cheese Bread for the wedding of a friend's son.

Dissolve yeast in warm water, adding sugar as needed to feed it. In a ceramic or metallic bowl, combine salt, sugar, and shortening; pour in boiling water and stir. Add yeast, milk, eggs, and half the flour; beat. Add remaining flour and beat. Let rise until size doubles (about 1 hour).

Meanwhile, grease a loaf pan. When dough has risen, add cheese and beat. Place in 8x4x2½-inch loaf pan and let rise until size doubles (about 1 hour), preheating oven to 400° after the first 40 minutes. Bake for 20 to 25 minutes until golden brown.

Note: Always let dough rise in a warm place covered with a damp towel.

MAKES 1 LOAF

1 package active dry yeast
¼ cup warm water
¼ cup sugar plus 1 or 2 teaspoons for feeding yeast
1 ½ teaspoons salt
3 tablespoons shortening
½ cup boiling water
½ cup evaporated milk
2 eggs, beaten
3 ½ cups flour
1 ½ cups sharp Cheddar cheese, grated

BREADS AND SANDWICHES 51

DIPPED CHEESE BREAD

Patty (Mrs. Tignor) Thompson
Dallas, TX

One of my most treasured possessions is my mother's recipe collection. Not just because she was a terrific cook, but also because each time I read them, it brings back a flood of memories. While Mother used Cheddar cheese, I have also used other cheeses and added spices and herbs. I think she would approve.

1 (1-pound) loaf unsliced white bread
1/2 cup (1 stick) butter
1/2 pound Cheddar cheese, cubed
4 ounces cream cheese
2 whites of large eggs at room temperature

Preheat oven to 350°. Line a cookie sheet with parchment paper. Remove crust from bread, cut loaf into 5 slices, and quarter each slice. In top of double boiler, combine butter and cheeses. Cook over simmering water until melted, stirring often. Beat egg whites until stiff but not dry. Gently fold into cheese mixture. Dip bread into cheese and coat all sides. Place on prepared cookie sheet. Chill for at least 4 hours or at most overnight. Bake for 12 to 15 minutes.

Note: The following variations can be used instead of the Cheddar:

1/2 pound pepper cheese and 1/4 teaspoon cumin
1/2 pound Havarti cheese with dill
1/2 pound mozzarella cheese; 3 to 4 garlic cloves, roasted, peeled and mashed; 1/2 teaspoon crushed dried basil; and 2 tablespoons Parmesan cheese

SERVES 8 TO 10

 California: Sanford Winery, Vin Gris de Pinot Noir
 Oregon: Ponzi, '93 Pinot Noir

Dilled Potato Bread

Janet Swedburg
Axtell, NE

This bread is heavy, but wonderfully tasty. That's because it's not just potatoes, but potatoes, skins and all. I have my sister to thank for the recipe.

Chop potatoes, place in a large pot, cover with salted water, and bring to a boil. Boil until tender; remove from heat. Drain, reserving 1½ cups of the cooking water. Mash potatoes, cover to keep warm, and set aside. Cool the reserved cooking water to 110°, add yeast and sugar, and let stand 10 minutes, or until foamy. Meanwhile, grease a large mixing bowl. When yeast is dissolved and foamy, add potatoes, buttermilk, butter, salt, and dill; mix. Add flour and knead until smooth and elastic. Put dough in greased bowl and let rise until size almost doubles.

Preheat oven to 350°. Grease either 1 shallow, 12-inch-diameter pan or 2 (9x5-inch) loaf pans. Punch dough down and knead for 5 minutes. Form into large round loaf for round pan, or divide in half for loaf pans. Cover and let rise for 15 minutes. Slash top with crosses or diamonds. Lightly mist top with warm water and dust with cake flour. Bake for 1 hour for large loaf, or 35 to 50 minutes for twin loaves until lightly browned on top and bread sounds hollow when tapped.

(PHOTO, PAGE 149)

| ½ pound baking potatoes with |
| skins on |
| 1 package active dry yeast |
| 1 tablespoon sugar |
| 1 cup buttermilk |
| 2 tablespoons unsalted butter, |
| melted |
| 1 tablespoon salt |
| ¼ cup snipped fresh dill, or |
| ⅛ cup dried |
| 8 cups unbleached flour |
| ¼ cup cake flour |

MAKES 1 LARGE OR 2 SMALL LOAVES

California: Turley Cellars, '93 Zinfandel

Italy: Calatrasi, '93 Terrale

Jalapeño Cornbread Muffins

Gary Collins
Beverly Hills, CA

Looks like Mary Ann Mobley isn't the only great cook in this household.

5 jalapeño peppers, or I (4-ounce) can chopped green chilies
I cup yellow cornmeal
½ teaspoon salt
I tablespoon baking powder
⅓ cup melted bacon fat or shortening
2 large eggs, beaten
I cup cream-style canned corn
I cup sour cream, or ⅔ cup buttermilk
I medium onion, chopped
I cup shredded sharp Cheddar cheese

Preheat oven to 350°. Lightly oil a 12-cup muffin tin. Seed and chop jalapeños or drain chilies, and set aside. In a large bowl, combine cornmeal, salt, and baking powder. Stir in bacon fat. Add eggs, creamed corn, and sour cream; blend. Stir in onion. Fill each muffin cup with 2 to 3 tablespoons of the batter. Sprinkle cheese and jalapeños in each cup, and top each with a smooth layer of remaining batter. Bake for 35 to 40 minutes until a toothpick inserted in the center of a muffin comes out clean. Let cool and remove from the cups.

MAKES 12 MUFFINS

Pumpkin Bread

Barbara E. Church
San Diego, CA

My late son, Drew, conjured up this recipe while he was in college. Each time I make it now in San Diego, I recall happy times with Drew, and the autumn colors we enjoyed while living in New England.

I cup sultana raisins, or other
⅔ cup anejo rum plus small amount for soaking raisins
3½ cups flour
2 teaspoons baking soda
1½ teaspoons salt
2 teaspoons cinnamon
I teaspoon nutmeg
3 cups sugar
I cup oil
4 eggs
2 cups pumpkin, canned

Soak raisins overnight in a small amount of rum, just enough to cover them. Preheat oven to 350°. Grease 2 (9x4-inch) loaf pans. Sift together flour, baking soda, salt, cinnamon, and nutmeg; set aside. Beat sugar and oil with electric mixer. Add eggs and beat to blend. Add rum and beat to blend. Add pumpkin and beat to blend. Combine with the dry mixture. Add raisins. Pour batter in prepared loaf pans. Bake for 1 hour, or until a toothpick inserted in the center comes out clean.

Note: Dates or currants can be substituted for raisins.

SERVES 12

FRUIT BRAN MUFFINS

Brenda J. Pangborn
Bloomfield Hills, MI

I was determined to find a delicious, low-fat alternative to the common bran muffin and succeeded with this recipe, which is a composite of several others I have tried.

In a large bowl, lightly whisk eggs, oil, milk, orange juice, yogurt, and vanilla. Stir in cereal and set aside to soften (about 30 minutes). In a small bowl, combine cherries, currants, figs, and raisins.

Preheat oven to 400°. Generously grease cups of muffin pan, or use paper liners. In a medium bowl, sift flour, baking powder, cinnamon, ginger, allspice, sugar, and brown sugar. Blend in wheat germ. Pour over bran mixture, and fold lightly three or four times with a spatula to partially combine. Sprinkle fruit over batter, distributing evenly with as few strokes as possible (the batter should not be perfectly smooth). Divide mixture among muffin cups. Bake for 20 to 25 minutes until muffins are lightly browned and spring back when lightly pressed. Let muffins stand in pan for 2 minutes. Ease muffins onto a wire rack, and let cool for 20 minutes.

Note: These muffins freeze well.

(PHOTO, PAGE 164)

MAKES 40 TO 48 (2½-INCH) MUFFINS

- 4 eggs
- 1 cup safflower oil
- 1 cup skim milk
- 3 cups orange juice
- 1 cup non-fat yogurt
- 2 tablespoons vanilla extract
- 5 cups high-fiber cereal
- 2 cups dried cherries
- 1 cup currants
- 1 cup figs or dried dates
- 1 cup raisins
- 5 cups flour
- 4 tablespoons baking powder
- 1 tablespoon cinnamon
- 1 teaspoon ginger
- 2 teaspoons allspice
- 2 cups sugar
- ½ cup firmly packed light brown sugar
- ¼ cup toasted wheat germ

Whole Wheat Honey Rolls

Susan Gottlieb
Richboro, PA

It was cold, the car was not working, and I had dinner guests coming and no dinner rolls. So I improvised this recipe, and it was a big success. My husband liked them so much that I now make them in larger rolls for burgers and sandwiches. They have become my "Honey's" favorite.

1 package active dry yeast
1/2 teaspoon sugar
1 cup lukewarm water
4 cups whole wheat flour
3 cups unbleached white flour
1 1/2 teaspoons salt
1/2 cup (1 stick) butter or margarine
2 egg whites, slightly beaten
1 cup milk
1/3 to 1/2 cup honey, depending on desired sweetness

Preheat oven to 425°. Dissolve yeast and sugar in lukewarm water in a small bowl; let stand until foamy (about 10 minutes). Meanwhile, flour a board and lightly oil a large bowl. In a separate large bowl, mix together whole wheat flour, white flour, and salt. Pinch in butter by hand until the mixture resembles meal. Make a well in the flour mixture. When yeast is dissolved, pour into flour mixture. Add egg whites, milk, and honey. Mix until the dough is pliable. Knead on floured board for 10 minutes. Put dough in oiled bowl, turn once, cover, and let rise until size doubles (1 to 2 hours depending on the warmth of the room).

Grease cookie sheets. After the dough has risen, punch it down and knead lightly. Divide it into the desired number of pieces. Form the dough into balls, flatten slightly, and place 2 inches apart on cookie sheets. Cover with a cloth, and leave in a warm place until size doubles (about 20 to 30 minutes), preheating the oven to 425° after the first 10 minutes. Bake for 15 minutes for smaller rolls and 25 minutes for larger ones. Cool rolls on a wire rack.

Use large rolls for barbecues or sandwiches. Serve small rolls with dinner.

Note: If more flour is needed when kneading the dough, use white flour or the rolls may turn out too heavy.

MAKES 12 LARGE ROLLS OR 24 SMALL ROLLS

HOMEMADE ROLLS

Mrs. Jimmy J. Jones
Houston, TX

Friends like these so much that they have offered to pay me to make a batch for them.

Grease a deep bowl with oil. Dissolve yeast in 3 tablespoons warm water. In a separate bowl, mix shortening, sugar, eggs, and salt. Add dissolved yeast and remaining warm water. Beat with electric mixer. Add 3 cups flour and beat with mixer. Add 1 cup flour and beat by hand. Put dough in bowl and roll in oil. Cover with waxed paper and chill overnight. Preheat oven to 450°. Roll out dough, using as little flour as possible. Cut with a biscuit cutter, dip in melted butter, and fold over. Arrange rolls around pan. Let rise for 1 to 2 hours until size doubles. Bake for 10 minutes, or until golden brown.

MAKES 20 SMALL ROLLS

1 package active dry yeast
1 cup plus 3 tablespoons
    warm water, divided
1/2 cup shortening
1/2 cup sugar, or to taste
2 eggs
1 teaspoon salt
4 cups sifted flour, divided
    into 3 cups and 1 cup
1 teaspoon vegetable oil
3/4 to 1 cup (1 1/2 to 2 sticks)
    butter, melted, as needed

BERRY-FILLED SCONES

Patti Estabrooks
Laguna Beach, CA

I live in a lovely area of Laguna Beach called Emerald Bay. In October 1993, after several of our neighbors had lost their homes in a large fire, I hosted a tea for them and served these. They had just come out of the oven when the first guests arrived, and the smell of the scones cheered everyone.

Mix berries with jar of jam; set aside. Preheat oven to 450°. Sift flour, baking powder, salt, and sugar together. Cut in shortening. Add cream and eggs. Combine quickly into a smooth dough. Flour a surface, and roll dough to 1/4-inch thickness. Cut into rounds with a 3-inch cookie cutter. Put one spoonful of fruit filling in the center of each round. Put another round on top, and pinch together around the edges with moistened fingertips. Sprinkle the top of each scone with sugar. Bake for 10 to 15 minutes until golden brown. Serve with whipped cream.

(PHOTO, PAGE 160)

MAKES 12 SCONES

FILLING:
1 cup fresh or frozen raspberries
    or boysenberries
1 jar berry jam (same as
    berries used)
SCONES:
2 1/3 cups sifted cake flour
2 1/2 teaspoons baking powder
1/2 teaspoon salt
2 teaspoons sugar
6 tablespoons shortening
5 tablespoons light cream
2 eggs, beaten
2 tablespoons sugar

BARBECUED MEAT SANDWICHES

Jacqueline K. Pletscher
San Diego, CA

A swim class friend gave me this recipe to which I added just a little more vinegar. It's become one of our party favorites, even tempting vegetarian friends. Besides the piquant taste, I like the fact that it can be kept frozen up to three months, which means it is an easy do-ahead for larger parties.

16 ounces spaghetti sauce
3½ teaspoons dry mustard
3½ teaspoons prepared horseradish
¼ cup apple cider vinegar
¼ cup firmly packed light brown sugar
2 tablespoons Worcestershire sauce
1 pound cooked beef or pork, cut into thin slices
8 French rolls

In a medium saucepan, combine spaghetti sauce, mustard, horseradish, vinegar, brown sugar, and Worcestershire. Bring to a boil over medium-high heat. Reduce heat to medium-low, stir, and simmer for 5 minutes. Meanwhile, split rolls, and warm in a bun warmer or 100° oven. Submerge meat in the sauce, and simmer for 5 minutes, or until thoroughly heated. Transfer onto rolls.

SERVES 8

SANDWICH DE COMO

Barbara Bernstein
Los Angeles, CA

SANDWICH:
2 slices multigrain bread
1 leaf Boston or bibb lettuce
4 thin slices prosciutto
4 slices mozzarella
Fresh basil leaves to taste

DIJON-MAYONNAISE DRESSING:
1 cup mayonnaise
1 teaspoon lemon juice
1 teaspoon chopped fresh basil
2 tablespoons Dijon mustard
1 to 3 drops Tabasco® to taste
Salt and pepper to taste

Our favorite place to vacation is the Villa d'Este, near Lake Como in Italy. It was there that we were introduced to this delicious, typically Northern Italian sandwich. Whenever I make it here at home, we picture ourselves sipping wine and gazing at the beautiful lake once more.

Whisk together all dressing ingredients in a bowl. Cover, and chill for at least 1 hour.

Spread a dollop of dressing on bread. Top with lettuce, prosciutto, mozzarella, and basil.

Note: Dressing makes enough for several sandwiches and may be used as a salad dressing.

SERVES 1

CARIBBEAN CHICKEN ROTIS

Mrs. Ronald C. Prati Sr.
Irving, TX

After a day of sun, snorkeling, and sailing in the Caribbean, nearly anything served for lunch tastes great. But these sandwiches were spectacular! They were the creation of our catamaran crew, Matt and Claire, an Aussie and his British wife. Matt's love of the sea led him to work as a deckhand on a large sailing vessel. Claire, a backpacking young English woman, happened to sign on the galley crew of the same vessel in order to see the Great Barrier Reef. Their adventures entertained us nightly, and Matt's Aussie Bartending School drinks have been added to our favorite recipes.

Peel and dice potatoes. Place in a pot of water to boil. Meanwhile, heat oil in a wok or sauté pan and stir-fry chicken until cooked. When potatoes are tender, drain, and place in a large marinade container. Add chicken, onion, garlic, green onions, pepper sauce, curry, cumin, ginger, chili powder, pepper, yogurt, and salt. Stir to combine. Chill for 18 to 24 hours.

Pour enough vegetable oil in a skillet to come 1/2-inch up the sides. Over medium heat, bring oil to 350° or just smoking. Submerge each tortilla in oil for 5 seconds to soften. Drain tortillas on paper towels and cover to keep warm; do not stack. Wipe the skillet clean, and warm chicken with marinated mixture over medium-low heat. Add water, and stir to blend. Spread filling on tortillas, and fold into thirds.

Serve with Mango Sauce (Page 206), Apple Chutney (Page 202), and a selection of hot sauces.

SERVES 6

2 medium potatoes
1/4 cup olive oil
1 1/2 pounds boneless, skinless chicken breasts, cut into 1/2-inch pieces
1 medium onion, minced
3 cloves garlic, minced
2 green onions, minced
1 teaspoon yellow chili pepper sauce
3 tablespoons curry powder
1 tablespoon cumin
1/8 teaspoon ground ginger
1/8 teaspoon chili powder
1 1/2 teaspoons pepper
1/2 cup plain yogurt
Salt to taste
Vegetable oil for softening tortillas
6 (12-inch-diameter) flour tortillas (warmed in skillet)
1/3 cup water

CHICKEN ROUND-UP SANDWICHES

Kimberly Lakin
Kansas City, MO

This is a great sandwich for picnics! Chill the round-ups first, then pack them in your cooler and cut them just before eating. Kids especially like this sandwich because it doesn't look like the usual something between two slices of bread.

6 boneless, skinless chicken breasts

SPICY GRILLED
  CHICKEN MARINADE:
  2 tablespoons lime juice
  1 clove garlic, minced
  ½ teaspoon salt
  ¼ teaspoon pepper
  1 teaspoon chili powder
  2 tablespoons olive oil

CHICKEN ROUND-UP
  FILLING:
  2 (15-ounce) cans black beans
  1½ cups plus 1 tablespoon salsa, divided into 1 cup and remainder
  Salt and pepper to taste
  8 ounces cream cheese, softened
  ½ teaspoon cumin
  6 (12-inch-diameter) flour tortillas
  1 large head red leaf lettuce

Combine all marinade ingredients in a marinade container. Add chicken. Marinate for 2 hours at room temperature or chill overnight.

Prepare and light the grill. When coals are light ash in color, remove chicken from marinade, discarding the marinade, and sear chicken for 4 to 5 minutes, turning once. Cut into strips, and set aside. Rinse and drain beans; mash in a small bowl. Add 1 cup salsa, season with salt and pepper, and stir to combine. Set aside. Combine cream cheese and cumin, and spread equally over tortillas. Spread the bean-salsa mixture on top. Top with a layer of lettuce. Place a row of chicken strips in the middle of each tortilla. Spoon remaining salsa on top of chicken. Roll tortillas, wrap snugly in plastic wrap, and chill for at least 4 hours or overnight.

To serve, cut each tortilla in half. Accompany with a large, mixed-greens salad topped with pine nuts.

SERVES 10

 California: Walker Vineyard, '92 Boeger Zinfandel
Australia: Penfolds, '90 Shiraz-Cabernet

Turkish Grilled Eggplant Sandwich with Roasted Red Pepper-Walnut Spread

Joyce Goldstein
San Francisco, CA

Everyone is looking for vegetarian sandwich options. This one is particularly tasty, and all of the parts can be made ahead of time.

DIRECTIONS FOR TURKISH GRILLED EGGPLANT:

Preheat broiler or light a charcoal grill. Peel eggplant and cut into 1-inch-thick slices. Whisk together oil, garlic, cumin, and lemon juice in a shallow bowl. Dip eggplant in the mixture, sprinkle with salt and pepper, and broil or grill for 2 minutes per side, or until tender but not charred. Drain.

DIRECTIONS FOR ROASTED RED PEPPER-WALNUT SPREAD:

Roast the peppers in the broiler, over a grill or on a gas flame, turning often, until charred all over. Put in a covered plastic container to steam for about 10 to 15 minutes. Peel, seed, and dice. Put peppers, garlic, jalapeños, cumin, oil, and lemon juice in a food processor, and pulse until blended. Add walnuts and pulse to mix in, leaving the mixture chunky. Season with salt and pepper.

DIRECTIONS FOR MAYONNAISE:

Combine all mayonnaise ingredients in a small bowl.

DIRECTIONS FOR SANDWICHES:

Cut bread in half. Spread mayonnaise in bottom of pita pockets. In each pocket, add 2 mint leaves, small sprig of watercress, eggplant slice, and Red Pepper-Walnut Spread.

Note: Leftover spread can be used as a pita dip or thinned with olive oil and spooned over cooked fish. The eggplant can be cut into 1/2-inch slices and baked in a 400° oven for 10 minutes per side, or until tender.

MAKES 6 SANDWICHES

California: Simi Winery, '93 Rosé of Cabernet

Italy: Ruffino, '91 Chianti Classico Aziano

TURKISH GRILLED EGGPLANT:
- 1 large or 2 medium eggplants
- 1/3 cup olive oil
- 1 tablespoon minced garlic
- 1 tablespoon toasted ground cumin seed
- 2 tablespoons lemon juice
- Salt and pepper to taste

ROASTED RED PEPPER-WALNUT SPREAD:
- 2 large red bell peppers
- 1 tablespoon minced garlic
- 2 to 3 jalapeños, seeded and minced, to taste
- 1 tablespoon ground cumin seed
- 1/4 cup extra-virgin olive oil
- 2 tablespoons lemon juice
- 2/3 cup toasted chopped walnuts
- Salt and pepper to taste

MAYONNAISE:
- 1/2 cup mayonnaise
- 1/2 cup non-fat yogurt
- 1 teaspoon grated lemon zest
- 3 tablespoons minced fresh mint

SANDWICHES:
- 6 large pita bread rounds
- 2 bunches watercress, stems removed
- 24 mint leaves

Open-Faced Seafood Club Sandwich

———— Laura M. Taylor
Atlanta, GA

I came up with this sandwich one day as I faced leftover shellfish and vegetables, plus certain items I always keep on hand. Since then, I have served it many times for casual luncheons or brunch.

1 teaspoon butter
1 teaspoon chopped shallots
Pinch minced garlic
¼ pound crabmeat, boiled or grilled shrimp, or cooked scallops
1 to 2 tablespoons mayonnaise to taste
1 slice sour dough bread or a sandwich portion of a baguette
Sliced tomato to taste
Sliced avocado to taste
2 bacon slices, cooked
Shredded Cheddar or Swiss cheese to taste
Sliced almonds to taste

Preheat broiler. In a sauté pan over medium heat, melt butter. Add shallots, and sauté until translucent. Add garlic, and sauté a few seconds. Add crab and mayonnaise, and cook until heated through. Spoon onto bread. Top with tomato, avocado, bacon, cheese, and almonds. Broil until cheese melts and almonds are light brown.

Serve hot with a green salad and fruit.

(PHOTO, PAGE 157)

MAKES 1 SANDWICH

 Oregon: Adelsheim Vineyard, '93 Pinot Gris
 France: de Ladoucette, '92 Pouilly-Fumé

LITTLE CUBAN SANDWICHES

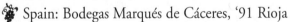

Jane Jobst
Rochester Hills, MI

Annabelle's restaurant on St. Croix in the Caribbean serves these with her delicious Dominican iced coffee and her own warm smile.

Cut bread in half lengthwise. Spread with mustard and mayonnaise. On the bottom halves, layer cheese, pickles, ham, and the top halves. In a heavy skillet, melt ½ tablespoon butter over medium heat. Cut one sandwich on an angle into 3 or 4 pieces to fit in the pan. Place in the pan, cover with aluminum foil, place a slightly smaller heavy skillet on top, and weigh down with a full teakettle or other heavy object. Cook for 3 minutes, or until bread is brown and crisp. Flip, replace foil and weight, and cook for 2 minutes, or until crisp and cheese is melted. Wrap in foil to keep warm. Melt remaining butter, and repeat the process with the remaining sandwich. Let cool for 1 minute. Cut diagonally into bite-sized pieces.

MAKES 2 SANDWICHES

2 loaves Cuban bread or narrow French bread
1 tablespoon Dijon mustard
1 tablespoon mayonnaise
¼ pound Swiss cheese, cut into thin slices
2 kosher dill pickles, sliced lengthwise into thin strips
¼ pound baked ham, cut into thin slices
1 tablespoon unsalted butter, divided in half

Spain: Bodegas Fariña, '94 Toro Zamora
Spain: Bodegas Marqués de Cáceres, '91 Rioja

Salads

Is it only a tangle of crisp greenery? Anything cold resting on a leaf of lettuce? Or, is it a main course, sometimes? It's all of those things and more. We can't think of any better opportunity for an imaginative cook to challenge her or his creativity. Certainly, the InCirclers who bombarded us with salad recipes demonstrated their creativity. Who would have thought of mixing cantaloupe and tomatoes? (It works.) In Europe, salad follows the main course. In American restaurants, it comes first. And at home, any meal without it runs the risk of being boring.

Black Bean and Rice Salad

Gail L. Coleman
Farmington Hills, MI

I've served this salad at several parties and my friends always ask for the recipe. So now I'll share it with Neiman Marcus and countless others who will enjoy the recipes in this book.

2 (14.5-ounce) cans chicken broth
1 quart plus ½ cup water, divided
1 pound long-grain rice (uncooked)
2 bay leaves
½ pound dried black turtle beans
2 red bell peppers, diced
1 green bell pepper, diced
1 medium onion, diced
1 bunch cilantro, chopped
½ cup olive oil
3 tablespoons orange juice
2 tablespoons red wine vinegar
2 teaspoons ground cumin
1 teaspoon chili powder
Salt and pepper to taste
3 sprigs cilantro

In a large, heavy saucepan over medium-high heat, bring broth and ½ cup water to a boil. Add rice and bay leaves, and bring to a boil. Reduce heat to low, cover, and cook for 20 minutes, or until liquid is absorbed. Transfer to a large bowl, and fluff with a fork; set aside. Place beans in a pot with 1 quart water. Bring to a boil over high heat, reduce heat to medium-low, and simmer for 45 to 90 minutes until beans are tender. Drain, rinse, and let cool. Add to the rice. Add peppers, onion, cilantro, oil, orange juice, vinegar, cumin, chili powder, salt, and pepper; stir to combine.

Place in a glass salad bowl. Garnish with cilantro.

Note: Beans can be cooked a day ahead. Because they are drier, older beans take longer to cook than younger beans.

MAKES 8 TO 10 SERVINGS

California: Montevina Wines,
'92 Zinfandel, Amador

France: Caves des Papas, '90 Gigondas
or Côte Rôtie, '90 Guigal

ARUGULA SALAD WITH ROASTED SWEET CORN AND PEPPERS, MARINATED TOMATOES, AND POACHED GARLIC-TOMATO VINAIGRETTE

Mark Militello
Miami, FL

This spring salad is made when Florida arugula, vine-ripened tomatoes, sweet peppers, and sweet corn are in season and at their prime. It takes 25 minutes of preparation time. The dressing tastes best if made 24 hours ahead.

Soak corn with the husks in cold water for 4 hours.

POACHED GARLIC-TOMATO VINAIGRETTE:

Cut garlic into thin slices. In a non-reactive pan, combine garlic, wine, and bay leaves. Poach garlic for 3 to 5 minutes until tender. Remove garlic and set aside, reserving wine in the pan. Boil wine until reduced to 2 tablespoons. Remove the pan from the heat, and whisk in oil and vinegars. Stir in reserved garlic and remaining vinaigrette ingredients, and set aside.

ARUGULA SALAD:

Prepare and light a hardwood or charcoal grill. When corn is done soaking, slowly grill corn over an open flame until very tender. Husk, cut the kernels off the cob, and set aside. Lightly brush peppers with 1 tablespoon olive oil, and roast over the open flame until charred. Place in a paper bag, let stand for 5 minutes, remove from the bag, and scrape off the charred skin. Core, seed, and cut into 2-inch pieces; set aside. Cut each tomato into 8 wedges, halve each wedge, and marinate in remaining oil, balsamic vinegar, and salt.

To serve, toss arugula and corn with the vinaigrette. Arrange on four salad plates. Sprinkle with cow's milk cheese or shaved aged Parmesan. Garnish with peppers and tomatoes.

(PHOTO, PAGE 153)

SERVES 4

California: Frey, '92 Petite Sirah

France: Château de la Chaize, '93 Brouilly

VINAIGRETTE:
- 1/2 cup garlic cloves, peeled
- 1 1/4 cups chardonnay
- 2 bay leaves
- 1 cup extra-virgin olive oil
- 1/4 cup white wine vinegar
- 1 teaspoon balsamic vinegar
- 1 teaspoon chopped fresh thyme
- 1 teaspoon chopped fresh basil
- 1 teaspoon chopped fresh marjoram
- 1 teaspoon sugar
- Salt and pepper to taste
- 1/3 cup peeled, seeded, diced tomatoes

SALAD:
- 2 ears corn, with husks
- 2 red bell peppers
- 2 tablespoons olive oil, divided
- 1 large red tomato
- 1 large yellow tomato
- 2 teaspoons balsamic vinegar
- Salt to taste
- 1 pound arugula

Lobster and Corn Salad with Tarragon

M. Susan Douglas
Topeka, KS

During a break from my volunteer post at a lawn and garden show several years ago, I visited a booth which was dedicated to herbs and herb farming. I purchased a tiny tarragon plant, and as they say, the rest is history. That little plant was the first step in producing what is now a glorious culinary garden. Among the garden's now diverse herbal offerings, my favorite choice remains the French tarragon. Its peppery flavor gently enhances many of my summer entrées and salads.

1 1/2 pounds boiling potatoes
1 1/2 cups corn, cut from the cob (2 to 3 ears) or frozen
1/2 cup extra-virgin olive oil, divided into 1/3 cup and remainder
3 1/2 tablespoons rice wine vinegar, divided into 1 1/2 tablespoons and remainder
2 shallots, minced, divided in half
Salt and pepper to taste
2 tablespoons heavy cream
1 pound cooked lobster meat, cut into bite-sized chunks
1/3 cup chopped fresh tarragon
Tarragon sprigs for garnish

Peel potatoes, and cut into bite-sized pieces. In a large pot, cover potatoes with water, and bring to a boil.

In a small saucepan, bring salted water to a boil for the corn. Blanch corn for 30 seconds, plunge into ice water, drain, and set aside. When potatoes and water come to a boil, boil for 15 to 20 minutes until tender. Drain, and let cool.

In a large bowl, whisk together 1/3 cup oil, 1 1/2 tablespoons vinegar, half of shallots, salt, and pepper. Add potatoes, and set aside.

In a medium bowl, whisk together remaining oil, remaining vinegar, and remaining shallots. Whisk in cream, salt, and pepper. Add lobster, and combine. Add to the potato mixture. Add corn and tarragon. Toss gently, cover, and let stand for 30 minutes.

To serve, garnish with tarragon sprigs.
(PHOTO, PAGE 146)

SERVES 4

 California: Duckhorn Vineyards, '94 Sauvignon Blanc
 Italy: Livio Felluga, '93 Pinot Grigio, Friuli

Goat Cheese and Crab Salad

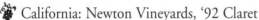

Elizabeth Romero
Los Mochis, Mexico

My grandmother's 80th birthday was coming up, and I wanted to cook something very special. This is what I prepared, and everyone enjoyed the salad as well as the whole day together.

Peel, core, and slice peaches. Pick out any shells from crabmeat. Toss peaches in a large bowl with lettuces, crabmeat, goat cheese, and walnuts. Combine all vinaigrette ingredients in a small bowl; beat vigorously until emulsified. Pour over salad, and toss to coat.

Serve with vegetable lasagna and buttered Italian bread.

SERVES 6

 California: Alban Vineyards, '93 Viognier

California: Newton Vineyards, '92 Claret

GOAT CHEESE AND CRAB SALAD:
- 3 peaches
- 3 cups cooked crabmeat, chilled
- 1 head romaine lettuce, torn into bite-sized pieces
- 2 lettuce leaves, shredded
- 1 cup crushed goat cheese
- 1/2 cup chopped walnuts

VINAIGRETTE DRESSING:
- 5 tablespoons balsamic vinegar
- 8 tablespoons extra-virgin olive oil
- 2 tablespoons Worcestershire sauce
- 1 teaspoon Dijon mustard
- 2 tablespoons peach jelly
- 3/4 teaspoon minced garlic
- 3/4 teaspoon minced jalapeño
- 1/2 teaspoon salt

Simply Sumptuous Shrimp Salad

Dr. Fay A. Riddle
La Grange, GA

A colleague of mine shared this recipe with me a few years ago when she and I were preparing to host a bridal luncheon. Don't let the shortness of the recipe fool you—this dish is sumptuous beyond belief!

1 pound small shrimp
2 cups seedless green grapes
1 cup cashew nuts
2 tablespoons minced onion
2 tablespoons chopped green
    bell pepper
1/2 cup sour cream
1/2 cup mayonnaise
1/2 teaspoon grated fresh
    gingerroot, or 1/8
    teaspoon ground ginger
1 1/2 teaspoons curry powder
    Salt to taste
1 tablespoon lemon juice

Peel and devein shrimp. Bring salted water to a boil, add shrimp, and cook for 10 minutes. Let cool. Halve grapes. Separate cashews into halves. Place shrimp, grapes, and cashews in a large bowl. Combine remaining ingredients, pour over shrimp mixture, and blend. Chill for several hours.

SERVES 4 TO 6

 California: Au Bon Climat, Chardonnay,
    Bien Nacido Reserve

 Italy: Colle Picchionie, '93 Riserva Oro, Marino

ORIENTAL CHICKEN SALAD

Liz Ghiselin Mercier
Houston, TX

My very good friend made this for a lovely surprise birthday luncheon for me years ago. Since then, it's become a frequently requested dish during Treat the Teachers Week at my stepchildren's school.

Combine all dressing ingredients in a jar and shake vigorously. In a medium bowl, combine chicken, snow peas, onions, and sprouts. Pour dressing over the salad, and toss.

To serve, arrange cabbage in a serving bowl. Top with the salad. Sprinkle with sesame seeds and walnuts.

(PHOTO, PAGE 162)

SERVES 4

 California: Louis M. Martini, '94 Gewürztraminer

 California: Richie Creek Vineyard, '94 Viognier

ORIENTAL CHICKEN SALAD:
- 2 cups chopped, cooked chicken
- 4 ounces snow peas, trimmed
- 3 green onions, sliced
- 4 ounces (1 cup) bean sprouts
- 1 medium head Chinese cabbage, shredded
- 1 tablespoon sesame seeds, lightly toasted
- 1/2 cup chopped walnuts

DRESSING:
- 1/4 cup vegetable oil
- 2 tablespoons apple cider vinegar
- 1 tablespoon soy sauce
- 2 teaspoons grated fresh gingerroot (not ground ginger)
- Pinch sugar
- 1/4 teaspoon salt

PORTOBELLO MUSHROOM SALAD

Bonnie Baker
Playa del Rey, CA

One evening at the Los Angeles Country Club's Summer Terrace dinner, I saw these funny looking things on my plate—and loved them! I like to entertain and prepare easy, but impressive dishes to serve to my guests. This salad fills the bill.

1 tablespoon sesame oil
2 tablespoons soy sauce
4 tablespoons lemon juice
2 cloves garlic, minced
4 portobello mushrooms
1½ to 2 pounds asparagus
8 leaves curly endive

In a marinade container, combine sesame oil, soy sauce, lemon juice, and garlic. Add mushrooms, and marinate for 1 hour at room temperature. Meanwhile, prepare and light grill, and preheat oven to 350°. When mushrooms are marinated and grill is ready, remove mushrooms from the marinade, reserving the marinade. Grill mushrooms for 2 minutes to brown. Transfer to a baking sheet, bake for 5 minutes, and slice. Steam asparagus slightly, making sure it remains crisp. Wrap asparagus and mushrooms in endive, using 3 to 4 spears per leaf.

To serve, place an endive wrap on each salad plate, and drizzle the reserved marinade over the top.

SERVES 8

 California: Robert Sinskey Vineyards,
'90 Cabernet Sauvignon, Aries

 Italy: Domenico Clerico, '91 Barbera Piedmont

PANZANELLA WITH BALSAMIC VINAIGRETTE

Ann-Rose Kaplan
Tarzana, CA

We like to spend our summers near Lake Como in Italy. One day, we visited the small village of San Gimignano near Sienna and lunched at a tiny hotel. They served us Tuscan bread salad, and I've been making it ever since. We especially like it with barbecued chicken.

Combine all panzanella ingredients in a salad bowl. Whisk together all vinaigrette ingredients, and toss with the salad. Cover, and chill until ready to serve.

SERVES 6

 California: Atlas Peak Vineyards,
'92 Sangiovese, Napa

Italy: Abbazia di Vallechiara,
'92 Dolcetto Barbera

PANZANELLA:
6 to 8 slices of day-old Tuscan
bread, cubed
6 medium tomatoes, diced
1/4 to 1/2 medium red onion,
diced
2 stalks celery, sliced
1/2 cup chopped black olives
6 basil leaves, chopped
2 tablespoons capers
1 1/2 to 2 hothouse (English)
cucumbers, quartered and
sliced

BALSAMIC VINAIGRETTE:
1 tablespoon Dijon mustard
1 small clove garlic,
minced (optional)
2 tablespoons balsamic vinegar
2 tablespoons lemon juice
Anchovy paste to taste
1/2 cup extra-virgin olive oil
Salt and pepper to taste

Hearts of Palm Salad

Ann S. Degenhart
Lake Worth, FL

My husband says he feels like he is in a forest when he eats this—trees and wood.

1 pound asparagus
2 (14-ounce) cans
    hearts of palm
1 pint cherry tomatoes
2 tablespoons lemon juice
2 tablespoons red wine vinegar
1 tablespoon chopped
    fresh parsley
2 tablespoons Italian seasoning
1 teaspoon salt
1/2 teaspoon sugar
1/4 teaspoon pepper
3/4 cup olive oil

Cut asparagus into bite-sized pieces. Steam until tender. Rinse hearts of palm, and cut into bite-sized pieces. Cut cherry tomatoes in half. Combine asparagus, hearts of palm, and tomatoes in a salad bowl, and toss.

In a food processor, blend lemon juice, vinegar, parsley, Italian seasoning, salt, sugar, and pepper. With the motor running, slowly add oil. Pour dressing over vegetables, and toss.

(PHOTO, PAGE 163)

MAKES 6

 California: Neiman Marcus, Cuvée CJTK, '90
 Italy: Falchini, '93 Vernaccia di San Gimignano

Copper Pennies Salad

Mrs. Guy Edward Moman
Tuscaloosa, AL

This recipe comes from my cousin, who taught second grade in Troy, Alabama, for 40 years. She made it for family, students, and their parents. She still lives in Troy, and enjoys visits from three generations of former students whom she taught to read.

Combine carrots, bell pepper, and onion in a marinade container. Whisk together remaining ingredients, pour over the vegetables, cover, and chill overnight.

Serve on a bed of lettuce.

Note: This dish can also be served hot as a vegetable side-dish. It will keep for 2 weeks in the refrigerator.

SERVES 8

California: Clos Robert, '93 Fume Blanc

Washington State: Chateau Ste. Michelle, '92 Cabernet Franc, Columbia

2 pounds sliced carrots, cooked
1 medium bell pepper, chopped
1 medium onion, chopped
1 (12-ounce) can V-8® vegetable juice
1/2 cup vegetable oil
1 cup sugar
3/4 cup apple cider vinegar
1 teaspoon dry mustard
1 teaspoon Worcestershire sauce
1 teaspoon salt
1/2 teaspoon pepper
Lettuce for garnish

Roasted Pepper and Mozzarella Salad

Lisa Klein
Houston, TX

My two sisters and I prepared an Italian dinner for my parents and some of their friends in honor of my parents' 40th anniversary. This special salad was the highlight of the whole meal.

2 red bell peppers
2 yellow bell peppers
8 ounces mozzarella cheese,
    cut into 1/4-inch slices
1/2 cup extra-virgin olive oil
1/2 teaspoon salt
1/4 teaspoon pepper
    Chopped fresh basil to taste

Spear bell peppers with a fork and hold over low heat, turning until skin darkens and splits. Place in a paper bag, and let stand for 10 minutes. Peel, seed, and cut into 1/4-inch strips. On a serving platter, arrange peppers and cheese in alternating rows. Drizzle oil over the top. Sprinkle with salt, pepper, and basil. Cover, and marinate several hours at room temperature.

(PHOTO, PAGE 162)

SERVES 4

 California: Inglenook, Vin-Rosé
 Italy: Santa Sofia, '94 Bardolino

SAVORY SALAD

Sandra Crawford
Mineral Wells, TX

This makes a very beautiful and colorful salad which I often serve to my bridge club. Add a casserole, and you have a complete dinner.

Peel, pit, and slice avocados. Tear lettuce and spinach into pieces. Cut onion and mushrooms into thin slices. Toss all salad ingredients in a large bowl. Whisk together all dressing ingredients, and pour over salad.

SERVES 12 TO 16

California: St. Clement Vineyards, '93 Chardonnay

Italy: Castello di Volpaia, '93 Chianti, Borgianni

SAVORY SALAD:

- 3 avocados
- 1 head lettuce
- 1 pound spinach
- 1 red onion
- 8 ounces mushrooms
- 2 (8-ounce) cans mandarin orange slices, drained
- 1/2 cup slivered almonds

VINAIGRETTE DRESSING:

- 1 cup raspberry vinegar
- 2 cups vegetable oil
- 1 clove garlic, crushed
- 2 tablespoons Dijon mustard
- Salt and pepper to taste

Tomato and Cantaloupe Salad

Margaret C. Carter
Dallas, TX

The idea for this salad was given to me by a dear friend years ago. Over the years, I have adjusted it somewhat. It never fails to be most interesting and the centerpiece of any menu, whether it be a brunch, buffet, or barbecue.

1 cantaloupe
1 red onion
4 large tomatoes
  Juice of 1 lemon
3 tablespoons apple cider
  vinegar
1/3 cup minced fresh parsley
2 tablespoons chopped fresh
  basil, or 2 teaspoons
  dried
1 teaspoon salt
1/2 teaspoon pepper
3/4 teaspoon dry mustard
2 teaspoons fresh minced mint
8 to 10 tablespoons oil
  as needed

Cut cantaloupe, scoop out the seeds, cut away the rind, and cut into thin slices. Dice onion, and slice tomatoes. Layer cantaloupe, onion, and tomato in a glass bowl, using onion more sparingly than cantaloupe and tomato.

In a food processor, process lemon juice, vinegar, parsley, basil, salt, pepper, mustard, and mint. With motor running, slowly add oil until mixed. Pour over the salad. Cover, and chill for up to 1 hour.

(PHOTO, PAGE 151)

SERVES 8

 California: Fetzer Vineyards, White Zinfandel
 Italy: Mario Schiopetto, '93 Müller-Thurgau

FISH

〜〜〜〜〜〜〜〜〜〜〜〜〜〜〜〜〜〜

FISHING FOR COMPLIMENTS

Aren't we all? And nothing says, "I am a confident cook," better than dinner centered around an entrée from the waters of ocean, lake or stream. First and foremost, be sure to select the freshest fish, and cook and serve it the day of purchase. If you can't serve it the same day, feel free to stash it in the freezer. In the best of all worlds, you catch it yourself or buy it right on the dock, but that's a little tricky if you live in Tucson. That said, our delectable Pickled Salmon comes from Georgia and the Seafood Gumbo from Arizona. It just goes to show there are good fish cooks everywhere!

CLAM BAKE

Janet Mothershed
Clemmons, NC

We always spend our summers at Wrightsville Beach. The traditional recipe for clam bake was pretty bland by my three sons' standards, so I jazzed it up, as you can see by the recipe. Watching the pot grow is great "hands-on" entertainment for guests, both young and old.

1 (32-ounce) bottle Clamato® juice
1 bottle chardonnay
1 (10-ounce) box chopped frozen okra
2 (14.5-ounce) cans chopped tomatoes, drained, or 4 fresh tomatoes, chopped
12 large red-skinned potatoes
12 medium sweet onions, peeled
12 chicken breasts, cleaned
¼ cup fresh chopped basil, or 1 tablespoon dried
¼ cup fresh chopped parsley, or 1 tablespoon dried
¼ cup fresh chopped oregano, or 1 tablespoon dried
¼ cup fresh snipped chives, or 1 tablespoon dried
¼ cup fresh chopped rosemary, or 1 tablespoon dried
1 tablespoon blackening seasoning
12 ears white corn, cleaned
1 pound smoked sausage, cut in 3-inch pieces
1 pound kielbasa sausage, cut in 3-inch pieces
3 dozen small clams
3 pounds large shrimp

Preheat electric roaster or oven to 350°.

Place in roaster or in a roasting pan in the oven Clamato® juice, chardonnay, okra, tomatoes, potatoes, onions, chicken, basil, parsley, oregano, chives, rosemary, and blackening seasoning. Roast for 1 hour. Add corn, smoked sausage, and kielbasa; roast for 30 minutes and spoon off excess fat. Add clams. Roast for 10 minutes, or until clams begin to open. Add shrimp; cook for 5 to 10 minutes until clams are open and shrimp have coral striations.

Serve with melted butter, cocktail sauce, and French bread.

Note: Cooking times may vary; plan on about 2 hours total. Water may need to be added to roaster as medley cooks. Other herbs can be substituted for those listed. Cooked lobster may be added to the completed dish.

SERVES 12

 California: Jade Mountain Winery, '93 Viognier-Marsanne

 California: Jordan Vineyard & Winery, '93 Chardonnay

BAKED CRABMEAT

Marilyn Jones Chapman
Seabrook, TX

When I arrived as a newlywed on Galveston Island, my in-laws insisted that I learn to catch, clean, and cook crabs. This is Aunt Mina's recipe, which I prepared when the Good Morning, Houston television crew paid a visit to my home in 1990. We've certainly enjoyed it many times since!

Soak crackers in water and squeeze dry in a cheesecloth. Preheat oven to 350°. Generously grease a 7-inch-diameter, 2¹/2-inch-deep casserole dish. Melt ¹/2 cup butter in a skillet over medium heat; sauté onions, celery, bell pepper, and garlic for 5 minutes, stirring frequently. Add basil, thyme, Worcestershire, cayenne, and seasoned salt. Stir to combine. Add crackers, egg, and crabmeat; mix. Melt remaining butter, and mix with bread crumbs. Cover casserole with bread crumb mixture.

Bake for 30 minutes.

To serve, sprinkle with chopped parsley. For an alternative plate presentation, bake in scrubbed crab shells instead of casserole dish.

SERVES 4

 California: Château St. Jean, '93 Chardonnay,
   Les Pierres

Italy: Mario Schiopetto, '93 Tocai,
   Friuli-Venezia Giulia

7 unsalted crackers
1 cup (2 sticks) butter or
  margarine, divided in half
5 green onions, chopped
1 stalk celery, chopped
¹/2 cup chopped red bell pepper
1 small clove garlic, minced
2 teaspoons fresh basil, or
  ¹/2 teaspoon dried
1 teaspoon fresh thyme, or
  ¹/2 teaspoon dried
2 tablespoons Worcestershire
  sauce
¹/4 teaspoon cayenne
¹/2 teaspoon seasoned salt
1 egg, beaten
1 pound crabmeat
1 cup bread crumbs
¹/4 cup chopped fresh parsley

CRAB QUESADILLAS WITH MANGO-JICAMA SALSA

Carol Sweet
Houston, TX

These are fresh and colorful. I always enjoy recreating recipes I have tasted elsewhere, and these are my personal favorites. They taste great and show off the Italian pottery I love to collect.

CRAB QUESADILLAS:
- 8 ounces crabmeat, fresh or canned
- Juice of 1/2 lemon
- 1 tablespoon grated onion
- 8 ounces cream cheese, softened
- 8 (8- to 10-inch-diameter) flour tortillas
- 10 ounces Monterey Jack cheese, grated
- 2 tablespoons butter
- 2 tablespoons oil
- Raspberries for garnish

MANGO-JICAMA SALSA:
- 2 mangoes
- 1 medium jicama
- 1/3 cup chopped fresh cilantro
- Juice of 1/2 lime
- 1/2 teaspoon chopped jalapeño pepper
- 1 onion, minced (optional)

DIRECTIONS FOR CRAB QUESADILLAS:

Drain crabmeat and pick out any shells. Mix crabmeat, lemon juice, onion, and cream cheese. Place a fourth of the mixture in each of 4 tortillas. Cover with Monterey Jack. Top each with another tortilla. Melt butter with oil, and sauté tortillas for 2 minutes on each side, turning when cheese melts and the bottom is slightly crisp and golden. Using a pizza cutter, slice each tortilla into 8 pieces.

DIRECTIONS FOR MANGO-JICAMA SALSA:

To make salsa, peel, pit, and dice mangoes; peel and dice jicama. Combine in a serving bowl with cilantro, lime juice, jalapeño, and onion.

Serve tortillas hot with Mango-Jicama Salsa and guacamole. Garnish with raspberries.

Note: Tortillas may be prepared ahead. To reheat, preheat oven to 350° and bake until hot and puffy (about 10 minutes). To peel, pit, and dice mangoes, cut lengthwise through the skin on both sides, peel the skin back, and cut the flesh off the pit in long vertical slices.

Caution: Mangoes are messy and juicy, mango juice stains, and many people are allergic to the skin, so you may want to use gloves.

MAKES 8 SERVINGS

 California: Cakebread Cellars, '93 Sauvignon Blanc

France: Morin, '93 Sancerre, Loire Valley

MAINE CRAB CAKES WITH GINGER, LEMON AND CUMIN SAUCE

Matthew Kenney
New York, NY

DIRECTIONS FOR MAINE CRAB CAKES WITH GINGER:

In a saucepan over medium heat, lightly sauté bell pepper and celery in vegetable oil for several minutes. Add gingerroot, scallion, cayenne, cumin, coriander, turmeric, ground ginger, paprika, and salt. Toss and cook over medium heat for 2 minutes. Add cream, and cook until reduced by half. Add crabmeat, parsley, chives, and 1 cup plus 2 tablespoons of bread crumbs. Mix and let cool. Preheat oven to 400°. Form mixture by hand into small cakes. Dip top and bottom lightly into remaining bread crumbs. Brown crab cakes in vegetable oil in a shallow sauté pan. Heat in oven for 2 minutes. Cut cucumbers into thin slices. Toss with lemon juice and olive oil.

DIRECTIONS FOR CUMIN SAUCE:

Mix egg, juices, and cumin seed in food processor. With machine running, slowly add oil. Add salt and pepper.

To serve, place cucumber on serving plates in circular format with slices overlapping each other. Top with crab cakes. Garnish with cumin sauce and sprig of parsley and chives.

(PHOTO, PAGE 149)

MAKES 8 TO 10 CRAB CAKES

 California: Edna Valley Vineyard, '93 Chardonnay

Italy: Pio Cesare, '93 Cortese di Gavi

MAINE CRAB CAKES WITH GINGER:
- 1 small red bell pepper, diced
- 2 stalks celery, diced
- Vegetable oil for sautéing vegetables and browning cakes
- 1 (2-inch) piece gingerroot, minced
- 1/8 cup thin slices of scallion
- Pinch cayenne
- 1/2 teaspoon cumin
- 1/2 teaspoon ground coriander
- 1/2 tablespoon turmeric
- 1/2 teaspoon ground ginger
- 1/2 teaspoon paprika
- Salt to taste
- 1 1/2 cups heavy cream
- 1 pound crabmeat, cleaned
- 1/8 cup chopped parsley
- 1/8 cup snipped fresh chives
- 1 1/2 cups Japanese bread crumbs, divided into 1 cup plus 2 tablespoons and remainder
- 3 cucumbers
- Lemon juice and olive oil for tossing cucumber slices

LEMON AND CUMIN SAUCE:
- 1 small egg
- Juice of 1 lemon
- 1/4 cup orange juice
- 1 tablespoon toasted and ground cumin seed
- 1 cup canola oil
- Salt and pepper to taste

FISH 85

Sautéed Prawns

Joyce Goldstein
San Francisco, CA

This is fast, easy, and can be as exciting to eat as the amount of cracked black pepper you use. Serve with lots of bread to sop up the sauce or with potatoes and a leafy green such as spinach.

2 pounds prawns (about 6 to 8 per person, depending upon the size)
Salt for seasoning
2 tablespoons olive oil
1 cup dry white wine
1¼ cups chicken stock
1 tablespoon garlic, minced
1½ teaspoons grated lemon zest
2 tablespoons lemon juice
1½ to 2 tablespoons cracked black pepper
¼ cup extra-virgin olive oil, or 4 tablespoons unsalted butter
3 tablespoons chopped flat-leaf Italian parsley

Shell and devein prawns. Sprinkle lightly with salt. Heat oil in a large sauté pan and sear prawns on both sides over high heat. Remove prawns from the pan and set aside. Deglaze the pan with wine, stock, garlic, lemon zest, lemon juice, and pepper, reducing liquids by half (about 1¼ cups). Return prawns to the pan, and swirl in extra-virgin olive oil to smooth out the sauce.

To serve, sprinkle with parsley.

SERVES 6

 California: Kalin Cellars, '93 Chardonnay, Cuvee LD

 France: Albert Morey, '93 Chassagne-Montrachet

Poached Halibut Steaks
with Mustard Mint or Red Pepper Sauce

Pamela Baxter
New York, NY

I served this at a bridal shower luncheon and everyone remarked how wonderful it tasted. Most of our friends are watching their "fat grams" and this dish truly is elegant and healthy. The two sauces may sound complicated, but are not. It's nice to offer guests a choice.

DIRECTIONS FOR MUSTARD MINT SAUCE:

Combine mustard, brown sugar, vinegar, and dry mustard in a food processor and process for a few seconds. With machine running, pour in oil in a steady stream and process until the sauce is thick and smooth. Pour into a small bowl and add 3 tablespoons or more mint to taste. Chill for at least 2 hours.

DIRECTIONS FOR HALIBUT:

Place fish in a skillet or fish poacher and cover with enough water and wine, in equal portions, to come halfway up the sides of the fish. Bring to a simmer, cover, and simmer for 8 to 9 minutes until a toothpick inserted in the thickest part of fish encounters some resistance in the center. Remove fish from the poaching liquid, leaving the liquid in the skillet for Red Pepper Sauce; cover fish with aluminum foil to keep warm.

DIRECTIONS FOR RED PEPPER SAUCE:

Spear red bell pepper with a fork and hold over low heat, turning until skin darkens and splits. Peel and purée. Set aside. Reduce poaching liquid from fish to 3 tablespoons. Add puréed red pepper, basil, and mint.

To serve, place chilled Mustard Mint Sauce and warm Red Pepper Sauce in decorative bowls and let diners help themselves, or place individual sauce portions on each plate with fish.

SERVES 2

MUSTARD MINT SAUCE:

- ½ cup coarse-grain mustard
- 3 tablespoons firmly packed dark brown sugar
- 2 tablespoons apple cider vinegar
- 1 teaspoon dry mustard
- ⅓ cup safflower oil
- 3 tablespoons chopped fresh mint, or more to taste

HALIBUT:

- 1 pound halibut steaks
- White wine for poaching

RED PEPPER SAUCE:

- 1 red bell pepper
- 2 teaspoons chopped fresh basil, or 1 teaspoon dried
- 2 teaspoons chopped fresh mint, or 1 teaspoon dried

California: Byron Vineyard & Winery, '94 Sauvignon Blanc Reserve

California: Ferrari-Carano Winery, '93 Chardonnay Reserve

CREOLE SPINY LOBSTER

Once on the far side of St. Martin, we stumbled upon a restaurant that was built on a cliff over the water. At one point, our 2-year-old daughter disappeared. We found her looking down a hole that plunged 30 feet to the ocean. Attached to the railing around the hole were a rope and a basket. When it came time to order, you would haul up the basket and choose your lobster. The chef would cook it however you wanted it: grilled with cognac, for example, or sauteed in a spicy Creole sauce.

This wasn't simply a dish from the Caribbean. It WAS the Caribbean: the sweetness of spiny lobster, the fragrance of the fresh thyme, the sting of the scotch bonnet chili.

6 (1½ pound) spiny lobsters

MARINADE:
½ cup extra-virgin olive oil
½ cup dry white wine
Juice of 4 limes

SAUCE:
2 tablespoons extra-virgin olive oil
2 tablespoons minced garlic
½ cup diced onion
½ cup diced red bell pepper
1 scotch bonnet chili, seeded and minced
1½ tablespoons curry powder
½ cup dry Spanish sherry
4 medium tomatoes, peeled, seeded, and diced
2 cups lobster or fish stock
½ cup fresh corn kernels (cut off the cob)
½ cup diced christophene (chayote) squash
½ cup diced calabaza
½ cup diced Jamaican yellow yam

Cut lobsters in half lengthwise and remove entrails.

DIRECTIONS FOR MARINADE:
Combine marinade ingredients in a shallow pan. Add lobsters and marinate for 30 minutes. Preheat hardwood or charcoal grill.

DIRECTIONS FOR SAUCE:
Heat oil in a large sauté pan over medium heat. Add garlic, onion, bell pepper, and chili. Cook for 3 minutes, or until onion is translucent. Stir in curry powder and cook for 2 minutes. Stir in sherry, raise heat setting to medium-high, and boil until reduced by half. Add tomatoes and stock and bring to a boil. Reduce heat to low and simmer for 15 minutes. Pass the sauce through a food mill fitted with a fine grate or through a food processor with a special attachment into a clean saucepan. Place the pan over low heat. Add corn, squash, calabaza, yam, and conch. Simmer for 15 minutes.

Grill lobsters for 8 to 10 minutes.

To serve, place 2 lobster halves on each plate. Spoon sauce over and around them. Sprinkle with thyme, parsley, salt, and pepper.

WITH FRESH CONCH SAUCE

Mark Militello
Miami, FL

SAUCE, CONTINUED:
3/4 cup ground fresh conch
2 tablespoons chopped fresh
    thyme leaves
2 tablespoons chopped flat-leaf
    Italian parsley
Salt and pepper to taste

CHEF'S NOTES:

The best way to grind conch is in a meat grinder, but a food processor also can be used. Spiny, or Florida lobster is found along the coasts of Florida and California and in the Caribbean. Frozen spiny lobster tails often are identified as rock lobster or langouste.

Christophene, also known as chayote or mireliton, is an avocado-shaped squash that tastes like boiled pear. Calabaza is a hard West Indian pumpkin. Jamaican yellow yam is a starchy tuber that tastes a little like a potato. All three vegetables are available at West Indian grocery stores.

As an alternative grilling method for the lobsters, remove the heads, split the tails, brown them in olive oil, and simmer them briefly in the sauce.

SERVES 6

California: Iron Horse Vineyards,
        '92 Sauvignon Blanc, Alexander Valley
California: Calera Wine Co., '92 Viognier

SHRIMP JAMBALAYA

Patricia A. Wilson
Channelview, TX

The art of Creole cooking is an acquired taste. Generations of my family have prepared the same dishes, yet no two versions are quite alike. Recently, we have been experimenting to find healthier versions of our favorites with less salt, fat, and carbohydrates while keeping the wonderful flavor. This particular recipe was passed to me by my father.

¼ cup vegetable oil
2 medium onions, chopped
2 large stalks celery, chopped
4 cloves garlic, minced or crushed
1 green bell pepper, chopped
1 teaspoon chopped fresh parsley, or ½ teaspoon dried
1 teaspoon chopped fresh thyme, or ½ teaspoon dried
1 (16-ounce) can stewed tomatoes
1 tablespoon crushed red peppers
2 pounds medium or large shrimp, cleaned and deveined
1 heaping tablespoon filé
2 cups cooked rice (from ⅔ cup uncooked)

In a large saucepan over medium-high heat, warm oil, and sauté onions, celery, garlic, bell pepper, parsley, and thyme until tender. Toss in tomatoes and red peppers. Cover and simmer for 30 minutes, stirring occasionally. Add shrimp. Remove from heat. Stir in filé, simmer for 15 minutes, or until shrimp are tender.

To serve, toss with rice or ladle over rice.

Note: Filé, a Native American seasoning of powdered baby sassafras leaves, lends this dish its characteristic stickiness and spiciness.

SERVES 4 TO 6

 California: CinnabarVineyards, '93 Chardonnay, Santa Cruz Mountains

 California: Peter Michael Winery, '93 Sauvignon Blanc, L' après Midi

SHRIMP WITH RADICCHIO AND ARUGULA

Margane M. Gatto
Miami Lakes, FL

I usually keep shrimp, radicchio, arugula, and endive on hand. One day after shopping with a friend, I invited her to stay for dinner. And wanting something warm, I improvised this quick stir-fry dish, which I served with Italian toast.

Cut a skin-deep X in the top of each tomato. Drop into boiling water and blanch for 15 seconds. Remove from pan and immediately plunge into ice water. Slip off skins. Dice tomatoes and place in a small bowl. Chop garlic, keeping amounts divided; add 1 chopped clove to bowl. Add 2 basil leaves, 2 teaspoons oil, vinegar, salt, and pepper. Set aside. Shred radicchio and endive; set aside. Separate arugula; set aside. In a non-stick sauté pan, sauté 3 chopped cloves garlic in 1 tablespoon oil for 2 minutes without browning. Add shrimp, and sauté until shrimp are almost tender. Add tomatoes, radicchio, endive, and arugula; stir-fry for 1 minute, taking care not to overcook. Cut bread into 8 (½-inch-thick) slices; brush with oil, scrape a piece of remaining garlic on each side, and toast.

To serve, place a portion of shrimp and lettuce trio on a serving plate. Arrange remaining basil leaves on top. Place 2 pieces toast on each plate.

Note: It's important not to overcook shrimp, as it will toughen, or to overcook lettuce trio, as it will lose its crunchy texture.

(PHOTO, PAGE 159)

SERVES 4

2	large beefsteak or plum tomatoes
6	large cloves garlic, divided into 1 clove, 3 cloves, and 2 cloves
10	fresh basil leaves, divided into 2 and 8 leaves
1	tablespoon plus 2 teaspoons extra-virgin olive oil, divided
1	teaspoon balsamic vinegar
½	teaspoon salt
1	teaspoon pepper
1	head radicchio
1	large head Belgian endive
1	bunch arugula
1½	to 2 pounds jumbo shrimp, peeled and deveined
1	loaf Italian bread
	Olive oil for brushing on toast

California: Franciscan Vineyards, '94 Estancia Chardonnay

Italy: Villa Banfi, Gavi Principessa

Shrimp-Mango Enchiladas with Tropical Black Bean

This is another good example of using enchilada fillings other than the stereotypical beef or cheese you find in most Southwestern or Mexican restaurants. I have always been fond of the combination of seafood and tropical fruit, and it's a natural pairing that occurs throughout the coastal regions of the Gulf, the Caribbean, and Central America. Papaya or even pineapple can be substituted for the mango.

SHRIMP-MANGO ENCHILADAS:

2 pounds medium shrimp
1 mango
4 poblano chilies
2 tablespoons olive oil
2 onions, diced
2 tablespoons minced garlic
3 tablespoons chopped cilantro
6 tablespoons ancho chili
    purée, divided into 4
    tablespoons and
    remainder
14 ounces grated Chihuahua or
    Monterey Jack cheese,
    divided into 3/4 cup and
    remainder
Salt and pepper to taste
Vegetable or canola oil for
    softening tortillas
18 (10-inch) corn tortillas
3 tablespoons water

DIRECTIONS FOR SHRIMP-MANGO ENCHILADAS:

Peel and devein shrimp. Cut into 1/2-inch pieces and set aside. Peel, pit, and dice mango and set aside. Roast, peel, seed, and dice poblanos and set aside. Preheat oven to 350°. Heat oil in a large skillet until lightly smoking, and sauté onions and garlic for 2 minutes, or until lightly browned. Add shrimp and cook until shrimp have coral striations. Add cilantro, 4 tablespoons ancho purée, mango, and poblanos; cook for 30 seconds. Remove from the heat and add 3/4 cup cheese. Season with salt and pepper. Mix and set aside. Pour enough vegetable oil in a skillet to come 1/2-inch up the sides. Over medium heat, bring oil to 350° or just smoking. Submerge each tortilla in oil for 5 seconds to soften. Drain tortillas on paper towels, and cover to keep warm; do not stack. In a bowl, combine remaining ancho chili purée and water. Dip each tortilla in the mixture, lightly coating both sides.

To assemble the enchiladas, divide the shrimp mixture among tortillas, spreading mixture evenly down the middle of each. Roll up tortillas and place, seam side down, on a baking sheet or in a baking dish, placing them snugly together. Sprinkle remaining cheese on top and cover with foil. Bake for 3 to 5 minutes until cheese melts.

Note: To peel, pit, and dice mango, cut lengthwise through the skin on both sides, peel skin back, and cut flesh off the pit in long vertical slices. You may want to use gloves when working with mangoes and chilies. Mangoes are messy, the juice stains, and many people are allergic to the skin. Many people are sensitive to chilies as well.

Salsa and Avocado-Tomatillo Salsa

Stephan Pyles
Dallas, TX

DIRECTIONS FOR TROPICAL BLACK BEAN SALSA:
Husk, rinse, and dice tomatillos; set aside. Drain beans and place in a saucepan with ham hock. Cover with water and bring to a boil. Reduce heat and simmer for 50 minutes. Strain to remove ham hock and beans, reserving cooking liquid. Discard ham hock and let beans cool completely. Combine beans with all ingredients in a mixing bowl, and let stand for at least 1 hour. Reduce reserved cooking liquid in half to form a glaze.

DIRECTIONS FOR AVOCADO-TOMATILLO SALSA:
Peel, pit, and dice avocados. Husk, rinse, and dice tomatillos. Combine avocados, half of tomatillos, red and green bell peppers, and scallion in a large mixing bowl. Place garlic, cilantro, serranos, lime juice, and remaining tomatillos in a blender, and purée until smooth. Slowly drizzle in oil. Pour purée into the mixing bowl, combine thoroughly, and season with salt. Let stand for 30 minutes.

Serve 3 enchiladas per plate, together with salsas.

SERVES 6

🍷 France: Luciaen Albrecht, '93 Pinot Blanc

🍇 Italy: Luigi Righetti, '88 Amarone, Veneto,
Capitel de Roari

TROPICAL BLACK BEAN SALSA:
- 2 medium tomatillos
- 8 ounces (I cup) black beans, soaked overnight
- I small ham hock
- 2 tablespoons diced mango
- 2 tablespoons diced pineapple
- I small clove garlic, minced
- 2 scallions (white parts only), sliced into thin discs
- I serrano chili, seeded and minced
- 2 teaspoons chopped fresh cilantro
- 2 teaspoons lime juice
- 2 tablespoons vinaigrette
- Salt to taste

AVOCADO-TOMATILLO SALSA:
- 2 large avocados
- 4 tomatillos
- I teaspoon diced red bell pepper
- I teaspoon diced green bell pepper
- I tablespoon diced scallion
- I clove garlic, minced
- 2 tablespoons chopped fresh cilantro leaves
- 2 serrano chilies, seeded and diced
- 2 teaspoons lime juice
- 3 tablespoons olive oil
- Salt to taste

SEAFOOD GUMBO

New Orleans is one of my very favorite places to visit--and eat! The first few times I tried to make seafood gumbo, making the roux was the hardest part. So I developed this technique, and none of the flavor is lost. I've served it many times at parties.

1 (28-ounce) can whole tomatoes
8 strips bacon, cut into 1½-inch pieces
1 large onion, chopped into large pieces
3 cloves garlic, minced
1 green bell pepper, chopped into bite-sized pieces
1 (14-ounce) can stewed tomatoes
1 (8-ounce) bottle clam juice
1 cup dry white wine
1 tablespoon lemon juice
1 tablespoon chopped fresh basil, or 1 teaspoon dried
¼ teaspoon cayenne
2 bay leaves
¼ cup chopped fresh parsley, or 1 tablespoon dried
1 tablespoon Worcestershire sauce
Few drops Tabasco® (optional)
1 teaspoon salt
Pepper to taste
½ pound cut fresh or frozen okra
1 pint oysters, rinsed, shelled, drained, and cut in half if large

Thaw any frozen ingredients. Using a spoon, break up tomatoes in a large bowl; do not drain.

In a large stockpot, cook bacon until crisp. Remove from the pot, and set aside. Pour off and discard all but 2 tablespoons bacon fat. Sauté onion and garlic in bacon fat over medium heat until golden. Add green pepper, broken up and stewed tomatoes, clam juice, wine, lemon juice, basil, cayenne, bay leaves, parsley, Worcestershire, Tabasco®, salt, and pepper. Bring to a boil. Reduce heat, cover, and simmer for 20 minutes. Add reserved bacon, okra, oysters, scallops, shrimp, crabmeat, and clams. Cover and simmer for 15 minutes. Remove from heat, and stir in filé. Cover, and let stand for 10 minutes. Remove bay leaves.

Serve hot with French bread or over rice.

Selma Young
Scottsdale, AZ

Note: If bacon is omitted, sauté onions and garlic in olive oil or vegetable oil. Filé, a Native American seasoning of powdered baby sassafras leaves, lends this dish its characteristic Creole flavor.

SERVES 10 TO 12

 California: Matanzas Creek Winery,
'94 Sauvignon Blanc, Sonoma

California: Louis M. Martini, '94 Sémillon

CONTINUED:

- ¾ pound whole bay scallops, or halved sea scallops
- ¾ pound medium shrimp, shelled and deveined
- ½ pound fresh or frozen crabmeat
- 1 (10-ounce) can whole baby clams
- 1 tablespoon filé

GREEK-STYLE FISH

Jackie Kanner
St. Petersburg, FL

We are fortunate to live in a coastal city where I can buy great fresh fish. I go, not to the supermarket, but to the fish wholesaler's facility, where the local restaurant chefs buy. A woman there told me how to cook fish with feta cheese. It is so good, that when my teenage son caught a large grouper, he wanted to cook it himself using this recipe.

Preheat oven to 450°. Oil a baking dish. Sprinkle fish with lemon juice, and lay in the baking dish. Add onion, green pepper, and tomato. Crumble feta on vegetables. Sprinkle olive oil, oregano, and basil on top. Pour wine around fillets. Bake for 15 to 20 minutes until fish is flaky. Raise oven temperature to highest setting and broil for several minutes until cheese browns. (PHOTO, PAGE 145)

SERVES 4

California: Beringer Vineyards, '94 Chenin Blanc

France: F.E. Trimbach, '93 Pinot Blanc

- 2 pounds fillets grouper, snapper, or other lean fish
- 2 tablespoons lemon juice
- 1 red onion, cut into thin slices
- 1 green bell pepper, cut into thin slices
- 1 tomato, chopped
- 4 ounces feta cheese
- 2 tablespoons olive oil
- 1 teaspoon oregano
- 1 teaspoon basil
- ½ cup white wine

SEAFOOD RISOTTO

Elizabeth Morris Minahan
Dallas, TX

While vacationing in the Mediterranean, I tasted many different risottos and numerous mussel dishes and loved them all. When I returned home, I couldn't find the exact combination of tastes and seasonings that I was seeking in any cookbook. This risotto is my best effort at recreating those delicious dishes that linger in my mind along with my vacation memories.

1 pound mussels, debearded and scrubbed clean
4 cups water
1 small white onion, chopped
3 cloves garlic, minced
2 tablespoons olive oil
3 cleaned squid, sliced into thin rounds
1 (14.5-ounce) can diced tomatoes, drained
1 tablespoon paprika
2 cups arborio rice
1 cup dry white wine
Salt and pepper to taste
1/2 pound large shrimp or crayfish, cleaned
8 ounces (1 cup) shredded Parmesan cheese, divided into 3/4 cup and remainder

In a stockpot, cover mussels with water and simmer until the shells open. Remove, reserving stock, and cover to keep warm. In a deep-sided pan, sauté onion and garlic in oil until onion is translucent. Add squid and stir lightly. Add tomatoes, paprika, and rice. Cook, stirring constantly, for 3 minutes, or until rice is opaque. Add reserved stock and wine and bring to a boil. Boil gently, uncovered, stirring frequently, for 20 minutes, or until tender. Reduce heat and stir until creamy. Add salt and pepper. Stir in shrimp and cook until shrimp have coral striations. Stir in 3/4 cup cheese.

To serve, spoon onto a warm platter or individual plates. Place mussels on top or around the sides and sprinkle remaining cheese over the top. Serve with a salad of mixed greens and crusty bread.

Note: Any type of fish or shellfish may be used. Fresh clams in the shell make a nice addition.

SERVES 3

 California: Beringer Vineyards, '94 Pinot Blanc
 Italy: Antinori Marchesi L & P,
'93 Cervaro della Sala

AHI TUNA TARTARE

Matthew Kenney
New York, NY

DIRECTIONS FOR AHI TUNA TARTARE:

Using a very sharp knife, dice tuna into ⅛-inch cubes, rubbing the knife on a lightly oiled towel periodically to keep it clean. With a spoon, mix tuna with lemon peel, oil, soy sauce, and chives. Add Tabasco® and season with salt and pepper. Chill until ready to serve.

DIRECTIONS FOR GREEN OLIVE TAPENADE:

Purée olives, anchovy, and capers. Add lemon juice. With blender or food processor running, add oil and sufficient water to thin the mixture until blended but still coarse; purée until smooth. Season with salt and pepper. Force through a strainer.

DIRECTIONS FOR FENNEL:

Wash fennel, pull apart the bulb, and dice the pieces. Combine lemon juice, vinegar, coriander, shallots, and walnut oil. Season with salt and pepper. Dress fennel with mixture.

DIRECTIONS FOR CARAWAY TOAST:

Mix butter with caraway seeds and salt. Spread on brioche and grill. Sprinkle anise seed on top. Quarter each slice.

To serve, place a serving of fennel in the middle of each individual plate. Top with seasoned tuna. Spoon a serving of tapenade on each plate and on the tuna. (Tuna can be prepared up to 1 hour in advance and chilled.)

SERVES 4

GARNISH WITH:

Sliced picholine olives
Cracked pepper
Snipped chives
Minced fennel sprigs

 California: Long Vineyards, '94 Pinot Grigio
 California: Kistler Vineyards, '94 Chardonnay, Estate

AHI TUNA TARTARE:

8 ounces very fresh sushi-grade tuna
1 tablespoon grated lemon peel
1 tablespoon olive oil
1 teaspoon light soy sauce
3 tablespoons snipped fresh chives
Dash Tabasco®
Salt and pepper to taste

GREEN OLIVE TAPENADE:

2 ounces picholine olives, pitted
1 anchovy
1 teaspoon small capers
1 teaspoon lemon juice
4 tablespoons olive oil
Coarse salt and pepper to taste

FENNEL:

1 bulb fennel with sprigs
2 tablespoons lemon juice
1 tablespoon sherry vinegar
½ teaspoon ground coriander seeds
1 tablespoon minced shallots
⅓ to ½ cup walnut oil as needed
Salt and pepper to taste

CARAWAY TOAST:

1 teaspoon butter
1 teaspoon ground toasted caraway seeds
Pinch salt
4 slices brioche
¼ teaspoon toasted anise seed

SALMON WITH TOMATOES AND CAPERS

Emma Afra
Miami, FL

My husband challenged me to come up with a fish dish that was neither bland, nor dry. This moist, wonderful salmon recipe was my answer to the challenge.

4 tomatoes
6 (4- to 6-ounce) salmon
    fillets
  Juice of 1 lemon
1 tablespoon extra-virgin olive
    oil
1 tablespoon salt
1 tablespoon seafood seasoning
2 tablespoons butter
1½ tablespoons capers
1 small bunch (a handful)
    fresh basil, stems removed
1 small bunch (a handful) flat-
    leaf Italian parsley, stems
    removed
  Salt and pepper to taste

Cut a skin-deep X in the top of each tomato. Drop into boiling water and blanch for 15 seconds. Remove from pan and immediately plunge into ice water. Slip off skins. Seed, cut into strips, and set aside.

Sprinkle salmon with lemon juice. Brush both sides with olive oil. Sprinkle lightly with salt and seafood seasoning. Broil on a baking sheet for 10 to 15 minutes, taking care not to overcook.

Melt butter in a skillet over medium-high heat. Add tomatoes and stir to coat. Stir in capers, basil, and parsley. Cook for 2 minutes. Add salt and pepper.

To serve, arrange salmon on a serving platter or individual dishes and spoon tomato-caper mixture on top.

SERVES 6

 California: Grgich Hills Cellar, '94 Fumé Blanc
 Italy: Teruzzi & Puthold, Terre di Tufi

Roast Salmon on Fennel Gratin

Joyce Goldstein
San Francisco, CA

This dish can be assembled ahead of time and then baked when you need it. If you have refrigerated the assembled dishes, add about 10 minutes to the baking time.

Core and slice fennel bulbs into ¼-inch thick-slices (you should have about 6 cups). Preheat oven to 450°.

Melt butter in a large sauté pan and sauté sliced fennel over moderate heat, stirring often, until golden. Add stock and fennel seed and cook until fennel is tender and glazed and stock is syrupy. Season with nutmeg, salt, and pepper. Transfer fennel to six gratin dishes or one large baking dish.

Place fish fillets over fennel. Sprinkle with salt and pepper. Drizzle with white wine. Top with toasted bread crumbs and Parmesan. Bake for 8 to 10 minutes until fish is cooked through.

To serve, sprinkle with chopped fennel fronds.

Note: It is important not to overcook fish, as it will become hard and dry. There are several methods of testing whether fish is cooked: when it flakes easily with a fork, after 10 minutes of cooking time for each inch of thickness, or when the flesh is opaque and doesn't cling to the bones at its thickest part. Fish will continue to cook from retained heat after it is removed from the oven.

SERVES 6

3 to 4 large fennel bulbs
3 tablespoons unsalted butter
½ cup fish or chicken stock
1 teaspoon ground fennel seed
¼ teaspoon nutmeg
Salt and pepper to taste
6 (6-ounce) fillets salmon, halibut, or sea bass
½ cup white wine
½ cup toasted bread crumbs
2 ounces Parmesan cheese, grated (optional)
Chopped fennel fronds for garnish

California: Fetzer Vineyards, '94 Bonterra Chardonnay

California: Carmenet Vineyard, Cabernet Franc

PICKLED SALMON

Saundra Reiter Shapiro
Marietta, GA

When we lived in Montreal, my parents would take us out to this very fancy restaurant. I always ordered the Pickled Salmon. Now we live in Atlanta and I still yearn for that Pickled Salmon. My mother, being the "greatest cook on this earth" that she is, devised her own recipe for this. Personally, I think it's the best!

3/4 cup vinegar
2 tablespoons pickling spices
1/2 cup sugar
1/8 to 1/4 cup ketchup to taste
1 or 2 plum tomatoes, sliced
1 1/4 cups water
1 1/2 to 2 pounds salmon fillets
1 onion, sliced

Place vinegar, pickling spices, sugar, ketchup, and tomatoes in water in a stockpot and bring to a boil. Remove any skin and bones from salmon, cut into 2-inch cubes, and add to the pot. Cover and simmer for 7 minutes.

To serve, place salmon on each plate with some of the juice and some of the cooked tomato pieces. Garnish with sliced onion and serve with hot French bread.

SERVES 4 TO 6

 California: Domaine Chandon, Blanc de Noir

 Oregon: Evesham Wood, '93 Pinot Gris, Willamette

Salmon in a Jacket

Dottie Lyons
Santa Maria, CA

I often donate complete dinners for auction to worthy community organizations, such as the Literacy Council of Santa Maria Valley. So far, my top selling price has been $2,150. While experimenting to come up with a spectacular beginning of an important dinner, I developed Salmon in a Jacket. Since then, it has been requested as an appetizer or entrée almost every time one of my dinners is listed in a catalog of auction items.

Thaw the sheet of puff pastry in the refrigerator overnight. Preheat oven to 425°. Poach salmon in wine; let cool. Melt butter in a skillet over medium heat and sauté mushrooms in butter and pepper until tender. Let cool. Roll out pastry sheet and cut into 4 (8-inch) squares. Place 4 ounces of salmon in the center of each. Top with mushrooms and Brie. Brush the outer edges of the pastry with egg white; gather and twist to seal. Brush the outside of the pastry jacket with egg white. Bake for 20 minutes, or until golden brown.

To serve, place on a serving dish and garnish with a sprig of parsley.

(PHOTO, PAGE 153)

1 pound puff pastry, frozen
1 pound salmon fillets
1 cup chardonnay
1 tablespoon unsalted butter
8 ounces mushrooms, sliced
Dash white pepper
1/2 pound Brie cheese
One egg white, beaten
Parsley for garnish

SERVES 4

California: Murphy-Goode, '93 Sauvignon Blanc
California: Joseph Phelps Vineyard, '93 Viognier

MEATS

~~~~~~

A MEATING OF THE MINDS

Beef, pork, or lamb... it's what's most often on dinner tables.
Could be as comfortable as Roast Pork Boulanger or as grand as
Filets Mignon with Porcini and Shiitake Mushrooms. We can talk
vegetables till we're blue in the face, but it's meat that matters to
most of us. And there's an art to cooking it. You start by carefully
selecting the lean and tasty cuts, then trimming away some of the
fat, marinating for flavor and tenderness, cooking fast or slow as
the cut demands, and finally, slicing for a beautiful presentation.
Now, light the fire and get the grill just right.

BURRLADAS

Barbara (Mrs. Gary) Kent
Las Vegas, NV

One afternoon, my two little girls were disagreeing about what they wanted for dinner that night. One wanted burritos and the other insisted upon enchiladas. I told them they would each get their wish and created a new Mexican dish I named Burrladas. Today, both daughters are married and Burrladas are a favorite in their families.

1½ pounds ground beef
1 onion, diced
1 clove garlic, minced
1 (30-ounce) can refried beans
1 (14-ounce) can stewed
   tomatoes
1 green bell pepper, diced
1 teaspoon chili powder
1 teaspoon jalapeños, seeded
   and diced
½ teaspoon oregano
1 (28-ounce) can enchilada
   sauce, divided into 1 cup
   and remainder
12 (8- to 10-inch) flour tortillas
1 pound Monterey Jack cheese,
   divided in half
1 pound Cheddar cheese,
   divided in half
½ head lettuce, shredded
2 tomatoes, diced
1 avocado, peeled, pitted, and
   diced
1 pint sour cream, or to taste
12 cherry tomatoes

Preheat oven to 350°. Brown ground beef and onion in a large skillet over medium heat. Add garlic, beans, stewed tomatoes, bell pepper, chili powder, jalapeños, oregano, and 1 cup enchilada sauce. Simmer for 15 minutes. Spread on tortillas; top with both cheeses, reserving half of each cheese. Roll up tortillas. Place in an oblong 2½-quart casserole. Pour any remaining mixture over tortillas. Cover with remaining cheese and remaining enchilada sauce. Bake, uncovered, for 1 hour.

To serve, top each tortilla with lettuce, tomatoes, avocado, and a mound of sour cream. Place a cherry tomato on sour cream, sundae-fashion.

SERVES 8 TO 10

 California: Marietta Cellars, '90 Petite Sirah
 Spain: Bodegas Fariña, '90 Colegiata, Toro

TENDERLOIN WITH MUSHROOM-ROQUEFORT SAUCE

Karol Wilson
Dallas, TX

My fellow board members of the American Heart Association sneak over to my house for this. They proclaim it worth the "danger."

DIRECTIONS FOR TENDERLOIN:

Wash tenderloin and pat dry. Rub with garlic and press pepper onto sides. In a large baking dish, combine Worcestershire and soy, and marinate beef for 2 to 3 hours at room temperature.

Preheat oven to 500°. Drain tenderloin, discarding marinade. Pour bouillon over beef. Put into oven and immediately reduce heat to 350°. Cook for 18 minutes per pound for rare; 20 minutes per pound for medium; or until internal temperature reaches 135° to 140°.

DIRECTIONS FOR MUSHROOM-ROQUEFORT SAUCE:

In a medium saucepan over low heat, combine cheese, butter, garlic, Worcestershire, and caraway. Stir until melted. Add green onions and mushrooms. Cook for 3 minutes.

SERVES 8

🍷 Chile: Château Lafite-Rothschild & Los Vascos, '88 Cabernet Sauvignon

🍇 Italy: Castello di Ama, '88 Chianti Classico

TENDERLOIN:
- 1 (4-pound) beef tenderloin
- 2 to 4 cloves garlic to taste, minced
- 4 to 6 tablespoons coarsely ground black pepper to taste
- 3/4 cup Worcestershire sauce
- 1 1/2 cups soy sauce
- 1 1/3 cups beef bouillon

SAUCE:
- 4 ounces Roquefort cheese
- 1/2 cup (1 stick) butter
- 2 to 4 cloves garlic to taste, minced
- 1 tablespoon Worcestershire sauce
- 1/4 teaspoon caraway seeds
- 1/2 cup chopped green onions, with tops
- 8 ounces mushrooms, sliced

TENDERLOIN TO TASTE

We raise registered Hereford cattle, so I have prepared every cut of beef in countless ways. But for special occasions, I like to serve this, hot or cold, sauced or not. For a spicy Southwestern flavor, I serve it with Poblano-Tomatillos Sauce. For a more traditional taste, I use Green Peppercorn Sauce.

TENDERLOIN:

- 1 (4- to 5-pound) beef tenderloin
- 3 cloves garlic, minced
- Coarsely ground black pepper for seasoning
- 1 bunch rosemary
- 1 bunch thyme
- Salt to taste

POBLANO-TOMATILLOS SAUCE:

- ½ of a large red bell pepper
- 1 poblano chili
- 2 cups tomatillos
- 2 cloves garlic
- 1 cup beef stock, divided into ¼ cup and remainder
- ½ cup red wine
- Salt and pepper to taste
- 2 tablespoons chopped fresh cilantro, or 1 tablespoon dried

DIRECTIONS FOR TENDERLOIN:

Preheat oven to 425°. Trim and tie tenderloin. Sprinkle garlic and pepper over tenderloin and pat into the meat. Place in a shallow roasting pan and cover with rosemary and thyme. Roast for 10 minutes. Reduce oven temperature to 350° and roast for 25 to 35 minutes until internal temperature is 140° to 145° for medium. Remove from oven; sprinkle with salt; and let stand for 10 minutes before slicing.

DIRECTIONS FOR POBLANO-TOMATILLOS SAUCE:

Spear red bell pepper with a fork and hold over low heat, turning until skin darkens and splits. Peel, seed, and dice; set aside. Spear and roast poblano; peel, seed, and dice; set aside. Husk, rinse, and quarter tomatillos. Place in food processor with garlic and ¼ cup of beef stock; purée. Transfer to a saucepan saucepan with remaining stock and wine. Simmer over medium-low heat for 15 minutes, or until sauce thickens. Add poblanos, red pepper, salt, and pepper. Simmer until heated through; do not boil. Stir in cilantro.

Ginger (Mrs. John E.) Dudley
Comanche, TX

DIRECTIONS FOR GREEN PEPPERCORN SAUCE:

In a saucepan over medium-high heat, sauté shallots in 2 tablespoons butter for 2 to 3 minutes until tender. Add Burgundy and cook until the liquid is reduced by half. Add cream, mustard, salt, and pepper. Reduce the heat to its lowest setting to keep the sauce warm. In a separate skillet, sauté peppercorns in remaining butter.

To serve, top each tenderloin slice with a spoonful of Poblano-Tomatillos Sauce or Green Peppercorn Sauce and serve remainder on side. If serving Green Peppercorn Sauce, top with sautéed peppercorns.

SERVES 6 TO 8

California: Della Valle, '91 Cabernet Sauvignon, Estate

France: Louis Jadot, '90 Ruchottes-Chambertin

GREEN PEPPERCORN SAUCE:
- 3 tablespoons minced shallots
- 3 tablespoons butter, divided into 2 tablespoons and remainder
- ½ cup Burgundy
- ½ cup cream
- 1 teaspoon Dijon mustard
- Salt and pepper to taste
- 2 tablespoons green peppercorns, drained

Ragout of Beef Provencale

Cheryl Q. Behan
St. Louis, MO

This is a classic recipe to which I added my own favorite touches such as bacon, mushrooms, and green peppercorns. It's a good upgrade from a plain winter stew. My advice is to make a lot and invite friends.

6 strips bacon
2 pounds lean boneless beef
¼ cup flour
1 large onion, cut in chunks
8 ounces mushroom caps
1¼ cups beef broth
1 cup Burgundy
4 carrots, cut in 1-inch pieces
1 tablespoon green
    peppercorns, drained
1 teaspoon herbes de Provence
1 teaspoon tomato paste
Watercress leaves for garnish

Fry bacon until crisp. Remove bacon from the pan and set aside, reserving the drippings. Cut beef into 1-inch cubes, dredge in flour, and brown in the drippings. Add onion and mushrooms; sauté for several minutes. Add beef broth, wine, carrots, peppercorns, herbs, and tomato paste. Cover and simmer over low heat for 1 hour. Cut bacon into 1-inch pieces.

To serve, place ragout in serving dish, garnish with watercress and bacon, and serve over rice.

MAKES 8 SERVINGS

 California: Seghesio Winery, '91 Sangiovese

California: Château Montelena,
        '92 Cabernet Sauvignon

FILETS MIGNON WITH PORCINI AND SHIITAKE MUSHROOMS

Louise Kazanjian
Pompano Beach, FL

Most of my cooking is done during the holidays, when I like to make appetizers and bake desserts. But in summer, we often barbecue for 25 or 30 friends at a time, and these filets on the grill please them all.

Soak porcinis in hot water in a bowl for 15 to 20 minutes until softened. Drain, reserving ½ cup of the liquid. Remove and discard stems; slice mushrooms, and set aside. In a small bowl, combine arrowroot and cream; set aside. In a saucepan, bring stock, wine, shallots, tomato paste, thyme, peppercorns, and reserved soaking liquid to a boil over high heat; boil until reduced to 1 cup. Stir in the arrowroot mixture; cook for 1 minute, or until thick.

Pat filets dry and sprinkle with salt and pepper. In a hot skillet, melt 1 tablespoon butter with oil, and cook filets over medium-high heat for 3 to 4 minutes on each side for medium-rare. Transfer filets to a plate and keep warm in a 100° oven.

Discard fat from the skillet and cook porcinis and shiitakes in remaining butter over medium-high heat, stirring constantly, for 3 minutes, or until the mushroom liquid evaporates. Strain the wine sauce into the skillet and season with salt and pepper. Simmer for 1 minute, and add any juices that have accumulated on the plate.

To serve, nap the filets mignon with the sauce. Garnish with parsley.

SERVES 2

California: Chappellet Vineyards, '91 Merlot
Italy: Cosimo Taurino, '89 Salice Salentino, Puglia

½ ounce dried porcini, or cèpe, mushrooms
1 cup hot water
2 teaspoons arrowroot
2 tablespoons heavy cream
1 cup brown stock or beef broth
½ cup Burgundy or other dry red wine
¼ cup minced shallots
1 teaspoon tomato paste
¼ teaspoon dried thyme, crumbled
¼ teaspoon peppercorns, crushed
2 (1-inch-thick) filets mignon, each weighing 6 to 7 ounces
Salt and pepper to taste
2 tablespoons unsalted butter, divided in half
1 tablespoon vegetable oil
2 ounces shiitake mushrooms, sliced
Minced fresh parsley leaves for garnish

Salt and Pepper Crusted Steak

Patricia J. Dutt
Chicago, IL

We enjoy this mostly in the summer, especially around the 4th of July when we have many friends over for a barbecue. In the winter, particularly around the holidays, I often use a prime rib instead of steak. Either way, it's superb.

1 (4- to 5-pound) boneless
   sirloin steak,
   3 inches thick
1/3 cup corn oil
1/3 cup Dijon mustard
1 cup Kosher salt
2 tablespoons cracked
   peppercorns

Prepare and light grill. Trim excess fat from steak. Slash the fatty edge of steak to prevent curling. Mix oil and mustard, and spread generously over both sides of steak. Mix salt and pepper; coat steak, pressing mixture firmly onto steak. Place steak on waxed paper and let stand for 30 minutes at room temperature.

Grill 6 inches above gray coals for 20 minutes on each side for rare, 25 minutes for medium, turning with tongs to keep from piercing the meat. Break the crust from the steak. Cut meat into thin slices across the grain.

Serve on thickly sliced toasted French bread. Accompany with corn, relish, baked potatoes with chive butter, and beefsteak tomatoes.

MAKES 6 TO 8 SERVINGS

California: Laurel Glen Vineyards,
   '93 Cabernet Sauvignon, Sonoma Mountain
California: Pahlmeyer, '93 Red

SANTA FE STEAK

Evilon (Mrs. Eric) Littlejohn
Dallas, TX

My husband and I love going to Santa Fe and eating Southwestern cuisine made with red chili peppers. He loves to grill in our back yard, using only the wood from our own trees: black walnut, mesquite, and chinaberry. No charcoal! This is his recipe.

MARINADE:

Combine all marinade ingredients, squeezing the juice from lime and adding lime and juice to marinade container. Add steaks, turning to cover with marinade. Let stand at room temperature for 2 hours, turning once. Cook immediately (see directions below) or chill overnight, turning occasionally.

SAUCE:

Combine all sauce ingredients in a cast-iron skillet, squeezing the juice from lime and adding lime and juice to the pan. Cook over medium-low heat until peppers soften.

Meanwhile, start a wood fire on one side of a lidded grill. When the fire is ablaze, close the lid to build up smoke. Put steaks over the fire, and put the cast-iron skillet with sauce on the non-fire side. Close the lid and smoke/grill for about 2 minutes. Raise the lid, dip steaks in sauce, return to the grill, close the lid, and grill for 2 minutes. Repeat this procedure every 2 minutes until steaks are cooked to desired doneness (8 to 10 minutes total for medium-rare).

Serve with sauce for dipping.

SERVES 4

4 steaks

MARINADE:

3 tablespoons water
3/4 cup teriyaki sauce
1/3 cup red wine
3 cloves garlic, crushed
1 lime

SAUCE:

3 dried red chili peppers, seeded
1 (18-ounce) bottle KC-style barbecue sauce
2 ounces bourbon
1/2 ounce honey
1 lime
2 ounces beer

 California: Markham Vineyards, '92 Merlot, Napa Valley

Spain: Marqués de Riscal, '91 Rioja, Reserva

Flank Steak with Jack Daniel's® Sauce

Bess Worden
Wauwatosa, WI

This recipe always is a great opportunity for my husband to show off his carving skills. He sharpens the carving knife and slices the steak in very thin strips on an angle, across the grain of the meat. Only then, after his ritual, can we eat.

1 (1-pound) beef flank steak

MARINADE:
- ¼ cup soy sauce
- 3 cloves garlic, minced
- 2 teaspoons red wine vinegar
- 2 teaspoons Worcestershire sauce
- ⅛ teaspoon Tabasco® sauce

JACK DANIEL'S SAUCE:
- 2 tablespoons olive oil
- ¼ cup minced onion
- 2 cloves garlic, minced
- ½ cup Jack Daniel's® whiskey
- 2 teaspoons Dijon mustard
- 2 teaspoons cornstarch
- 1 cup beef broth
- 2 teaspoons chopped fresh parsley
- Salt and pepper to taste

MARINADE:

Combine all marinade ingredients. Place flank steak in marinade and turn several times to coat. Cover and chill for at least 30 minutes or overnight.

JACK DANIEL'S® SAUCE:

In a small saucepan over medium heat, heat oil. Add onion and garlic, and sauté for 2 minutes. Add whiskey and mustard, and stir to combine. Cook, stirring occasionally, for 2 to 3 minutes until the mixture is reduced by half and a thin glaze forms. In a separate pan, sprinkle cornstarch over broth, and stir to dissolve. Add whiskey mixture, parsley, salt, and pepper; stir to combine.

Reduce heat to low, and simmer, stirring occasionally, for 4 to 5 minutes until thick. Maintain at low setting to keep warm. Preheat broiler to highest temperature. Transfer steak to a broiling pan, discarding marinade. Broil, turning once, for 4 minutes on each side, or until steak is rare.

To serve, slice steak across the grain with your sharpest knife. Top with sauce and serve with Japanese-style rice.

SERVES 4

 California: Kendall-Jackson Winery, '91 Cardinale, The Proprietor's Red

 Washington State: Leonetti, '91 Merlot

KOREAN-STYLE SHORT RIBS

Rona L. Freedland
Bloomfield Hills, MI

When my daughter became engaged, her fiancé, now our son-in-law, insisted on a pre-nuptial agreement that I would give him this recipe. We all like to marinate it overnight and cook it outside on the grill in the summer.

In a mixing bowl, stir together soy sauce, water, onions, sesame seeds, sugar, garlic, and pepper. Pour over ribs and marinate, chilled, overnight. Grill or broil for 15 to 20 minutes until cooked to desired doneness.

SERVES 6 TO 8

🍷 California: Hop Kiln, '92 Zinfandel, Sonoma

🍇 France: Pourra, '91 Gigondas

- 1/4 cup soy sauce
- 1/2 cup water
- 1/4 cup sliced green onions
- 2 tablespoons toasted sesame seeds
- 2 tablespoons sugar
- 2 cloves garlic, crushed
- 1/2 teaspoon pepper
- 4 pounds short ribs, cut between the bones

MADEIRA WINE ROAST

Annlyn C. Stufflebeam
Plano, TX

Our son was home for a week after serving a four-month military tour in the Mediterranean. He was ravenously hungry for our family's favorite roast, and this is the recipe for it.

ROAST:
- ½ cup flour
- 1 teaspoon salt
- ¼ teaspoon pepper
- 1 (4- to 5-pound) rump or sirloin roast
- 1 tablespoon olive oil

MADEIRA WINE SAUCE:
- ¾ cup Madeira wine
- ¼ cup Worcestershire sauce
- ¼ cup soy sauce
- 1 tablespoon hot sauce
- 1 tablespoon minced garlic
- ¼ cup chopped onion
- 1 tablespoon capers
- 1 tablespoon crushed green peppercorns
- ¼ cup sliced carrots
- 1 bay leaf
- 1 tablespoon cornstarch
- ¼ cup water

Preheat oven to 375°. Season flour with salt and pepper. Dredge roast in flour. Brown in a Dutch oven with olive oil. Remove from the pan and set aside, reserving oil and drippings in the Dutch oven. Add wine, Worcestershire, soy sauce, hot sauce, garlic, onion, capers, peppercorns, and carrots. Cook over medium heat, scraping reserved oil and drippings from the bottom to blend with ingredients, for 1 to 2 minutes until blended. Add roast and bay leaf. Roast for 15 minutes per pound. Transfer roast to a serving platter, reserving sauce in the roasting pan.

In a measuring cup, mix cornstarch and water. Add to sauce and cook over medium-high heat, stirring constantly, for 2 minutes, or until thickened.

To serve, ladle sauce into a gravy boat to accompany roast.

(PHOTO, PAGE 161)

SERVES 6 TO 8

 California: Ravenswood Winery, '92 Zinfandel

 Spain: Marqués de Murrieta, '91 Rioja, Reserva

Sweet and Sour Pot Roast

Melodie Finks
Salem, IL

After a long trip to visit friends in Florida, I found this wonderful dish awaiting my arrival. Since then, I have decided that it is wonderful any time, especially on a cold winter day. It's my Dad's favorite, so I make it for him every Father's Day.

Heat shortening in a heavy skillet with a tight-fitting lid. Add roast and onions. Brown, turning frequently. Add remaining ingredients, cover, and simmer over low heat for 3 to 3½ hours until meat is very tender, turning every 45 minutes and uncovering for the last 15 minutes to reduce the juices.

SERVES 6 TO 8

California: E. & J. Gallo Winery, '93 Zinfandel

France: E. and M. Guigal, '92 Côte Rôtie or
Côte du Rhône

1 tablespoon shortening
4 pounds arm or chuck roast
2 onions, sliced
¼ teaspoon pepper
¼ teaspoon ground cloves
¼ cup honey
¼ cup sugar
Juice of 2 lemons
Salt to taste

SPINACH-STUFFED LAMB SHOULDER

Edna B. Benna
Reno, NV

I have served this lamb dish to guests from Russia, China, India, and Lebanon on many different occasions, and they all enjoyed it. In my own family, it's the requested entrée for birthday dinners.

SPINACH STUFFING:

- 1/4 cup (1/2 stick) butter or margarine
- 2 cups sliced fresh mushrooms, or 1 (6-ounce) can sliced mushrooms
- 1/4 cup chopped green onions
- 1 clove garlic, crushed
- 1 (10-ounce) package spinach (thawed and drained if frozen)
- 1/2 teaspoon salt
- 1/4 teaspoon pepper
- 1/4 teaspoon mace

LAMB:

- 1 (4-pound) lamb shoulder, boneless
- 1 clove garlic, crushed
- 1 teaspoon dried thyme leaves
- 1 teaspoon salt
- 1/2 teaspoon pepper
- 1 tablespoon olive oil
- 1 carrot, peeled and sliced
- 1 onion, sliced
- 1 (10 1/2-ounce) can condensed beef broth or consommé
- 1/2 cup dry white wine or dry vermouth
- 2 tablespoons flour
- 2 tablespoons water

In a skillet over medium-high heat, melt butter for stuffing and sauté mushrooms until slightly browned. Add onions and garlic; sauté for 2 minutes. Add spinach, salt, pepper, and mace. Cook, stirring, for 1 minute, or until spinach is slightly wilted. Remove from the heat and set aside. Preheat oven to 450°. Trim excess fat from lamb. Mix garlic, thyme, salt, and pepper; rub over both sides of lamb. Spread out lamb, smooth side down. Place stuffing over half of lamb, about 1 inch from the edges. Fold the other lamb half over. Fasten the edges with skewers. Tie in 2 or 3 places with string. Brush with olive oil. Roast in a roasting pan in the oven for 20 minutes to brown. Add carrot and onion. Pour beef broth and wine over the top; cover. Reduce heat to 350°. Braise, basting occasionally with the pan juices, for 2 1/2 hours, or until meat is tender when pierced with a fork. Transfer lamb to a platter, reserving pan juices in the roasting pan. Remove the trussing from lamb, cover with aluminum foil, reduce oven temperature to 100°, and return lamb to oven to stay warm. In a measuring cup, stir flour into water until smooth. Stir into pan juices. Cook on medium-high heat, stirring constantly, until mixture thickens and boils. Boil for 2 minutes. Strain.

To serve, ladle gravy into a gravy boat. Cut lamb into 1/2-inch-thick slices, against the grain. Accompany with a western grain or rice pilaf.

SERVES 6

 California: Silver Oak Wine Cellars, '91 Cabernet Sauvignon

 Italy: Biondi-Santi, '91 Sassoalloro

Rack of Lamb Persille

Nancy K. Galdi
Tucson, AZ

Our Easter visitors expected traditional spring lamb (which my husband does not care for.) I was in a difficult spot, so I decided to try a very different way of preparing lamb. This is the result and it is now an Easter tradition at our house.

Preheat oven to 450°. French lamb (see note below). Rub the fat side of each rack with mustard.

In a sauté pan, melt butter over medium-low heat and cook shallot for 2 minutes, stirring constantly. Remove from the heat. Add thyme, bread crumbs, salt, and pepper. Stir to combine, and let cool. Add parsley. Season lamb with salt and pepper, pat the crumb mixture evenly over mustard, and arrange, crumb side up, in a roasting pan. Roast for 30 minutes, or until a meat thermometer registers 130° to 140° for medium-rare. Carefully remove from the oven and let stand for 10 minutes.

To serve, interlock the ribs, transfer to a serving platter, and cut the chops.

Note: To French the lamb, trim the tips of the ribs to the bone and form the rack into a crown. For an elegant touch, adorn the tips of the ribs with paper frills.

SERVES 4

- 2 (7-rib) racks lamb (about 1 1/4 pounds each)
- 3 tablespoons Dijon mustard
- 1/4 cup (1/2 stick) unsalted butter
- 1/3 cup minced shallot
- 1/4 teaspoon dried thyme, crumbled
- 1 1/2 cups Italian-style bread crumbs
- Salt and pepper to taste
- 1/3 cup minced Italian flat-leaf parsley

California: Eisele Vineyard, '91 Cabernet Sauvignon, Araujo Estate

France: Ch. de Beaucastel, '92 Châteauneuf-du-Pape, Red

CURRIED LAMB KEBOBS

Carol (Mrs. Luis) Flores
Houston, TX

I first tasted this dish at Trader Vic's. It doesn't taste like any other lamb you've eaten. It's very tender, and I've often found guests surprised to discover that it was lamb.

2 pounds boneless lamb

MARINADE:

- 1/3 cup olive oil
- 1/3 cup Dijon or hot mustard
- 1/4 cup grated onion
- 1/4 cup white wine vinegar
- 1 tablespoon Worcestershire sauce
- 1 tablespoon curry powder, or to taste
- 2 cloves garlic, crushed
  Few drops sesame oil
- 1 1/2 teaspoons marjoram
- 1 teaspoon salt
- 1/2 teaspoon pepper

CURRIED LAMB KEBOBS:

- 8 ounces mushrooms
- 1 large red or green bell pepper
- 1 medium onion
- 4 cherry tomatoes

DIRECTIONS FOR MARINADE:

In a 1 1/2-quart glass or stainless steel bowl, whisk olive oil, mustard, onion, vinegar, Worcestershire, curry powder, garlic, and sesame oil. Mix in marjoram, salt, and pepper. Trim lamb, cut into 1 1/2-inch pieces, and place in marinade mixture, turning to coat. Cover and chill for 3 to 4 hours.

DIRECTIONS FOR CURRIED LAMB KEBOBS:

Clean mushrooms; remove and discard stems. Seed bell pepper and cut into 12 pieces. Peel onion and cut into eighths. Remove lamb from marinade, reserving marinade. Preheat broiler. Place on each of four 12-inch skewers a piece of lamb, a mushroom cap, a piece of pepper, and a piece of onion. Repeat twice, and finish with lamb. Place the kebobs on a broiler pan 3 inches from the heat source for 20 minutes, turning occasionally and basting with marinade. Add a cherry tomato to the ends of the kebobs after 10 minutes.

Accompany with chutneys, watermelon pickles, and rice.
(PHOTO, PAGE 151)

SERVES 4

 California: Babcock Vineyards,
'93 Pinot Noir, Estate
 California: Zaca Mesa Winery, '91 Syrah

Roast Pork Boulanger

Cheryl Bennett
Forest Park, IL

One of our favorite pastimes is cooking for our friends. This is one dish that always gets accolades and allows us to showcase my husband's collection of wines.

Preheat oven to 425°. Rub pork with garlic. Cut slits in crevices between bones and insert garlic. Combine salt, thyme, bay leaf, and pepper, and rub over meat to coat. In a shallow roasting pan, place 1/2 cup onion, carrot, and parsley, reserving 1 tablespoon of parsley for potatoes. Place meat, fat side up, on vegetables. Roast for 20 minutes. Reduce the temperature to 400°, and roast for 40 minutes. Remove pork from the pan. Pour off and discard all but 1 tablespoon of fat from the pan, leaving the vegetables in the pan. Stir flour into drippings. Brown over low heat. Gradually stir in 1 cup chicken broth until combined. Stir in water. Raise heat setting to medium-high, and bring to a boil. Reduce heat to medium-low, and simmer until gravy is brown and thick. Strain through a sieve into a saucepan, discarding the solids and set gravy aside. Toss potatoes with remaining onion, remaining parsley, salt, and pepper. Return roast to pan. Arrange potatoes around roast. Heat remaining chicken broth to boiling. Pour over potatoes. Brush potatoes with butter. Roast for 1 hour, or until potatoes are crispy brown and tender. Reheat gravy.

To serve, garnish with additional chopped parsley.

SERVES 6 TO 8

California: Havens Wine Cellars, '93 Merlot

France: Ducru-Beaucaillou, '93

- 1 (5-pound) pork rib roast, center cut
- 2 cloves garlic, slivered
- 1 1/2 teaspoons salt
- 1 tablespoon chopped fresh thyme, or 1 teaspoon dried
- 1 bay leaf, crumbled
- 1/4 teaspoon pepper
- 1 1/2 cups chopped onion (1 1/2 medium onions), divided into 1/2 cup and remainder
- 1/2 cup chopped carrot (about 1 carrot)
- 2 parsley sprigs, chopped, plus more for garnish
- 2 tablespoons flour
- 1 (10 3/4-ounce) can condensed chicken broth, divided into 1 cup and remainder
- 3/4 cup water
- 3 pounds potatoes, peeled and sliced thin
- Salt and pepper
- 1/4 cup (1/2 stick) butter, melted

SAUTÉED PORK TENDERLOIN WITH VERMOUTH

Barbara Frederich
San Jose, CA

I love to entertain, and I do so often. This recipe is one of my favorites and always gets rave reviews. Some say it tastes like it was prepared in a four-star restaurant, but it's really very easy. I like to serve it with wild rice for a delicious fall dinner.

1 tablespoon butter
1 tablespoon oil
2 pork tenderloins (about ¾ pound each)
½ teaspoon dried rosemary leaves, crumbled
½ teaspoon dried thyme
½ teaspoon salt
¼ teaspoon pepper
1 cup dry vermouth
½ cup half-and-half

Preheat oven to 100°. In a skillet over high heat, heat butter and oil until hot. Add tenderloins and sear until brown on all sides. Add rosemary, thyme, salt, pepper, and vermouth. Cover, reduce heat to medium-low, and simmer for 10 minutes, or until pork is 160°. Remove tenderloins, and keep warm in oven, reserving sauce in skillet. Over high heat, boil sauce rapidly until reduced by half. Reduce heat to medium-low, stir in half-and-half, and heat through; do not boil. Remove pork from oven and cut into ½-inch slices.

To serve, arrange pork on a platter and pour sauce over top. Accompany with wild rice.

SERVES 4

 California: Laurel Glen Vineyards,
'93 Terra Rosa, Sonoma

California: Ridge Vineyards,
'91 Cabernet Sauvignon, Monte Bello

PORK ROAST

Karen Benning
Dallas, TX

When my sister made this for a family gathering, we all refused to leave until she parted with the recipe. Needless to say, she came through.

Preheat oven to 325°. Cut a lengthwise slit into tenderloin to make a long pocket, or untie string and unfold; set aside. In a hot skillet, melt butter and sauté green pepper, onion, celery, and garlic. Stir in black pepper, salt, white pepper, cayenne, paprika, thyme, and mustard. Fill the pocket of tenderloin, or place the filling in center, roll up, and re-tie. Roast for 2 to 3 hours until internal temperature is 170°.

SERVES 6 TO 8

California: Silverado Vineyards, '91 Merlot

Italy: Elio Altare, '92 Dolcetto d'Alba, Piedmont

1 (4-pound) pork tenderloin
1/2 cup (1 stick) butter
1 green bell pepper, chopped
1 medium onion, chopped
2 celery stalks, chopped
2 cloves garlic, minced
2 teaspoons black pepper
2 teaspoons salt
1 teaspoon white pepper
1 teaspoon cayenne
1 teaspoon paprika
1 tablespoon chopped
   fresh thyme, or
    1 teaspoon dried
1/2 teaspoon dry mustard

Marinated Pork Tenderloin

Elaine D. Montgomery
Garland, TX

I come from a large Italian family and this dish was our special Christmas tradition. I particularly love marinated meats and this uses fresh basil, mint, and parsley, which I grow in my garden. One of the best things about this tenderloin is that it can be grilled ahead of time and served cold or reheated.

1 (2-pound) pork tenderloin
½ teaspoon ground ginger
½ medium onion, minced
3 large cloves garlic, minced
5 leaves fresh basil
4 sprigs fresh parsley
3 tablespoons soy sauce
2 tablespoons vegetable oil

Prepare and light the grill, then slice tenderloin into ¾-inch medallions. Combine remaining ingredients and process in food processor. Pour over meat, and marinate for at least 3 hours or overnight. Grill for 3 to 5 minutes on each side until pork is no longer pink in the middle.

MAKES 4 TO 6 SERVINGS

 California: Ridge Vineyards, '92 Cabernet Sauvignon, York Creek

 Italy: Aldo Conterno, '92 Barbera d' Alba

VEAL SCALLOP

Carol Grimm
Coral Springs, FL

My husband has always liked me to cook recipes that go well with wine. About two years ago, we were introduced to the California Wine Club through the InCircle newsletter. Each month, we receive two bottles of wine from small, select vineyards and a newsletter that makes wine collecting fun. Thank you, NM, for an excellent introduction.

Flatten veal with a wooden mallet or the side of a cleaver. Season with salt and pepper. Sprinkle lightly with flour.

Melt 3 tablespoons butter in a hot skillet and sauté veal on low heat for 5 to 6 minutes on each side until golden brown. Transfer to a warm serving dish, reserving butter in the skillet. Clean and slice mushrooms; add to skillet and sauté over medium heat until tender. Add shallots and cook until soft. Pour in wine and cook until the liquid is reduced by half. Add tomatoes and cook until the liquid is again reduced by half. Swirl in remaining butter until it melts. Add parsley and tarragon and pour over veal.

SERVES 4

California: Shafer Vineyards, '91 Merlot

Italy: Polizano, '90 Vino Nobile di Montepulciano

2 pounds veal, cut from the leg in slices less than ½-inch thick
Salt and pepper for seasoning
Flour for browning
4 tablespoons butter, divided into 3 tablespoons and remainder
8 mushrooms
2 shallots, minced
½ cup dry white wine
1 (14.5-ounce) can stewed tomatoes
½ teaspoon chopped fresh parsley, or ¼ teaspoon dried
1 teaspoon chopped fresh tarragon, or ½ teaspoon dried

CURRIED VEAL CHOPS

Esther W. Goldman
New Rochelle, NY

When I first saw this recipe, it called for pork. But, I keep kosher, so I substituted veal. Of course, you could also use chicken.

1 Bartlett pear
1 tablespoon lemon juice
1/4 cup chopped dried apricots
3 tablespoons raisins
1 (5 1/2-ounce) can pear or
   apricot nectar
3/4 cup chicken broth
1 tablespoon oil
4 (1/2-inch- to 1-inch-thick)
   veal chops
   Salt and pepper to taste
1 onion, chopped
1 clove garlic
1 tablespoon curry powder
2 teaspoons flour

Preheat oven to 375°. Peel, core, and dice pear. Combine with lemon juice, apricots, raisins, nectar, and broth in a small bowl. Set aside.

Heat oil in a skillet and cook chops over medium heat for 3 minutes per side, or until golden on each side. Sprinkle with salt and pepper. Transfer veal to a glass baking dish and set aside, reserving oil and drippings in skillet. Sauté onion and garlic in skillet over medium-high heat for 2 minutes. Combine curry and flour, and sprinkle over onion mixture. Cook, stirring constantly, for 2 minutes. Stir in fruit mixture. Bring to a boil, scraping browned bits from the bottom to blend with ingredients. Reduce heat and simmer, stirring constantly, for 2 minutes. Spoon over chops. Cover with aluminum foil. Bake for 20 minutes. Uncover and bake for 15 minutes.

Serve over rice.

SERVES 4

 California: Dry Creek Vineyard, Zinfandel
 Italy: Bertani, '83 Recioto della Valpolicella Amarone

INTERNATIONAL VEAL SHANKS

Mr. and Mrs. V.W. Sanders
Beverly Hills, CA

When my great-grandmother brought this recipe from Germany, it was called "Kalbshop." It's undergone several subtle changes since then. An Italian neighbor introduced tomato paste, and a conversation with a Russian woman influenced us to substitute brandy for white wine. So, here is our recipe for a very international dish.

Dredge veal shanks in flour, salt, and pepper. Heat oil and butter together in a large skillet and brown meat on all sides, handling carefully to avoid losing marrow from the bones. Transfer veal to an enameled cast-iron Dutch oven, standing each piece on edge so the marrow will not fall out as it cooks.

Deglaze skillet with brandy. Strain the liquid into the Dutch oven. Add tomato paste and chicken broth. Bring to a boil over medium-high heat. Add onion, leeks, garlic, carrots, celery, lemon peel, and rosemary. Cover, reduce heat to medium-low, and simmer for 2 hours. Transfer veal shanks to a serving platter, and strain liquid and vegetables into a sauce boat.

To serve, surround veal with spaetzle. Garnish with fresh parsley. Serve sauce on the side. If desired, use a heated serving platter.

SERVES 6

California: Ridge Vineyards, '91 Zinfandel, Lytton Springs

Italy: Altesino, '90 Palazzo Altesi

9 (1½-inch-thick) pieces veal shank
⅓ cup flour
2 teaspoons salt
½ teaspoon pepper
3 tablespoons vegetable oil
3 tablespoons butter
½ cup Courvosier or other brandy
2 tablespoons tomato paste
1¼ cups chicken broth
1 medium onion, minced
2 leeks, white part only, minced
2 cloves garlic, minced
2 small carrots, diced
1 stalk celery, diced
1 tablespoon grated lemon peel
1 tablespoon chopped fresh rosemary, or 1 teaspoon dried
1½ tablespoons chopped fresh parsley for garnish

PASTA

~~~~~~

WHEN IT COMES TO PASTA, EVERYBODY'S ITALIAN

And our InCirclers' recipes are the proof of that. Some of the best versions, both traditional and innovative, came from the Prices, the Sublewskis, and the Jhins. And not one recipe for spaghetti and meatballs in the whole lot! Pasta is so versatile that it can be a quick-serve meal if you use the packaged kind, or a labor of love if you choose to make your own from scratch on the pasta machine you had to have. Beyond that, it's all up to the sauces and the cook's imagination. For example, have you ever had Salmon Lasagna Wheels or Rose-Lime Pasta? We bet you will have both soon!

CALIFORNIA PASTA

Gayle Price
Pacific Grove, CA

I'm always looking for low-calorie pasta dishes and consequently try to keep sun-dried tomatoes, mushrooms, and other things that work well with pasta on hand. This one is easy and makes a good do-ahead dinner.

1 cup chicken stock
1 cup sun-dried tomatoes
2 tablespoons olive oil, or more as needed
2 boneless, skinless chicken breasts
1 pound eggless rigatoni
3 shallots, chopped
4 cloves garlic, minced
1/4 cup chopped fresh parsley
10 mushrooms, sliced
8 ounces (1 cup) tomato purée
1 cup red wine
1 tablespoon cornstarch
Salt and pepper to taste

In a small saucepan, heat stock until boiling. Add sun-dried tomatoes; boil 15 minutes. Bring salted water to a boil for the pasta. Heat 1 tablespoon oil in a sauté pan over medium-high heat. Sauté chicken for 8 to 10 minutes until brown. Remove chicken, and set aside. When water is boiling, cook pasta according to the package directions, drain, toss with 1 tablespoon olive oil, and set aside. Add more oil to the sauté pan if necessary, and add shallots, garlic, and parsley. Sauté for 2 minutes. Add mushrooms, and cook for 8 minutes, or until mushrooms are tender. Add stock with tomatoes, tomato purée, and wine, reserving 2 tablespoons wine. Dissolve cornstarch in reserved wine; add to sauce. Cook for 1 minute, or until thick and translucent. Add salt and pepper. Shred chicken into bite-sized pieces, and add to sauce. Toss sauce over cooked pasta.

To serve, sprinkle with grated Parmesan cheese. Accompany with a salad and French bread.

SERVES 4

 California: Louis M. Martini, '92 Fresco Rosso
 France: Louis Jadot, '93 Beaujolais Fleurie

FUSILLI WITH SHRIMP AND GRILLED ZUCCHINI

Dawn Adels Fine
Miami, FL

My best friend and I dream of publishing an Italian cookbook. She is Italian and has taught me much about cooking. With luck, our cookbook will be out in a year.

Preheat broiler to 450°. Line a cookie sheet with aluminum foil; brush with oil. Slice zucchini into ¼-inch rounds and place on foil. Brush zucchini on both sides with 3 tablespoons oil. Sprinkle both sides with rosemary, salt, and pepper. Broil until brown, turn, and brown other side. Remove from oven, squeeze lemon juice over zucchini, and set aside. Sauté onion in remaining oil until translucent. Add garlic, and cook over low heat for 3 minutes. Add shrimp, wine, salt, and pepper; cook over medium heat until tender and wine evaporates slightly. Add zucchini, and reduce heat to low to keep warm. Boil salted water for fusilli. Cook fusilli until al dente, toss with zucchini mixture, and sprinkle with parsley.

(PHOTO, PAGE 159)

SERVES 4

- 6 tablespoons extra-virgin olive oil, divided in half, plus more to brush on foil
- 1 to 1½ pounds zucchini
- 2 tablespoons ground rosemary
- Salt and pepper to taste
- Juice of 1 lemon
- 1 Vidalia onion, chopped
- 4 cloves garlic, crushed
- 1 pound large shrimp, peeled and deveined
- ½ cup white wine
- 1 pound fusilli
- 1 handful Italian flat-leaf parsley, chopped

California: Kenwood Vineyards, '94 Sauvignon Blanc
Italy: Maculan, '93 Chardonnay

Linguini with Chicken a la Béchamel

Mona Ghazal
Houston, TX

Years ago, as a young woman, my grandmother visited Sicily, where she first tasted this pasta dish. Typically, she cooked by taste, rather than specifically measuring ingredients. I was able to work out the measurements in order to share the recipe with my friends.

LINGUINI:

- 2 pounds boneless, skinless chicken breasts
- 1/4 teaspoon nutmeg
- Salt to taste
- Juice of 1/2 lemon
- 1 small onion, divided in half
- 1 teaspoon olive oil
- 8 ounces linguini
- 1 cup Gruyère or Swiss cheese
- 1/2 cup grated Parmesan cheese

BÉCHAMEL SAUCE:

- 4 cups milk
- 6 tablespoons butter
- 3/4 cup flour
- 1/2 teaspoon salt
- 1/4 teaspoon pepper
- 1/4 teaspoon cinnamon
- 1/4 teaspoon nutmeg
- 8 ounces frozen peas, cooked and drained
- 8 ounces mushrooms, chopped

DIRECTIONS FOR LINGUINI:

Preheat oven to 375°. Bring salted water to a boil for the pasta. Clean chicken and season with nutmeg and salt. Place in a saucepan. Add lemon juice, half of onion, and enough water to cover chicken. Simmer until chicken is cooked. Strain, discarding onion. Cut chicken into bite-sized pieces, and set aside. When water is boiling, add oil and cook linguini for 10 minutes, or until al dente. In a 9x11-inch baking pan, arrange a third of the pasta. Top with a third of Gruyère, half of chicken, and a third of the sauce. Sprinkle with Parmesan. Repeat the process, eliminating chicken on the third layer. Cover with aluminum foil. Bake for 45 minutes. Uncover, raise heat to the highest temperature, and broil for 5 minutes, or until golden.

DIRECTIONS FOR BÉCHAMEL SAUCE:

In a saucepan, heat milk until just under boiling (160°). Meanwhile, melt butter in a saucepan over medium heat. Add flour and stir until golden. Reduce heat to medium-low. Add milk, 1/4 cup at a time, stirring constantly. Raise heat to medium, and cook, stirring constantly, until the mixture boils. Add remaining ingredients, and cook for 5 minutes, stirring constantly.

Serve with salad and an oregano vinaigrette.

SERVES 6 TO 8

 California: Atlas Peak, '93 Sangiovese

Italy: Lungarotti, '93 Rubesco

Baked Manicotti with Cheese Filling

Liz Sublewski
Chicago, IL

Highwood, Illinois has many northern Italian families who came to the U.S. after World War II, bringing with them many delicious recipes. This is Mama Santi's recipe using homemade manicotti and red sauce. No other manicotti will ever taste as good once you've tried this version.

Heat oil for the sauce in a 5-quart Dutch oven. Sauté onions and garlic for 5 minutes. Mix in remaining sauce ingredients, mashing tomatoes with a fork. Bring to a boil. Reduce heat, cover, and simmer, stirring occasionally, for 1 hour. Meanwhile, to prepare manicotti, combine all manicotti ingredients in a medium bowl. Beat with an electric mixer until smooth. Let stand for at least 30 minutes.

Heat an 8-inch skillet over medium heat. Pour in 3 tablespoons of the batter, rotating the skillet quickly to spread the batter evenly over the skillet. Cook until the top is dry without allowing the bottom to brown. Let cool on a wire rack. Repeat the process with the remaining batter, stacking manicotti between waxed paper on the rack.

Preheat oven to 350°. In a large bowl, combine ricotta, mozzarella, 1/3 cup Parmesan, eggs, salt, pepper, and parsley; beat with a wooden spoon to blend. Spread 1/4 cup of the filling in the center of each manicotti, and roll up. Spoon 1 1/2 cups sauce into each of 2 (12x8x2-inch) baking dishes. Place 8 rolled manicotti, seam side down, in a single layer; top with 5 more. Cover with 1 cup sauce; sprinkle with remaining Parmesan. Bake, uncovered, for 30 minutes, or until bubbly.

MAKES 6 SERVINGS

 California: Forest Glen, '93 Merlot

Italy: Fontodi, '92 Chianti Classico

SAUCE:
- 1/3 cup olive or vegetable oil
- 3 medium onions, minced
- 1 clove garlic, crushed
- 1 (6-ounce) can tomato paste
- 2 tablespoons chopped parsley
- 1 tablespoon sugar
- 1 tablespoon chopped basil, or 1 teaspoon dried
- 1 1/2 cups water
- 2 (14.5-ounce) cans plus 1 (6-ounce) can whole Italian tomatoes, drained
- 1 tablespoon salt
- 1/4 teaspoon pepper
- 1 tablespoon chopped oregano, or 1 teaspoon dried

MANICOTTI:
- 6 eggs at room temperature
- 1/2 teaspoon salt
- 1 1/2 cups flour
- 1 1/2 cups water

FILLING:
- 2 pounds ricotta cheese
- 8 ounces mozzarella cheese, diced
- 1/3 cup grated Parmesan cheese, plus 1/4 cup for assembly
- 2 eggs
- 1 teaspoon salt
- 1/4 teaspoon pepper
- 1 tablespoon chopped parsley

ORIENTAL MUSSELS AND NOODLES

Angela Jhin
Tiburon, CA

In Paris, the fast-food restaurants serve a dish similar to this—even with sandwiches! If you love mussels marinière as much as I do, you'll find this even heartier and tastier.

1 pound mussels, washed and debearded
1 pound egg noodles
2 tablespoons corn or olive oil
1 teaspoon black bean-garlic sauce
1 large onion, chopped
8 stalks celery, chopped
¼ cup white wine
2 cups chicken broth

Soak mussels in water for at least 1 hour, changing water at least once. Bring salted water to a boil for noodles. Drain, wash, and scrub mussels, discarding any remaining beard. When water is boiling, cook noodles until al dente; rinse with cold water, and drain. Divide noodles into 4 deep soup bowls; set aside. Heat oil in a sauté pan over medium heat. Add sauce, onion, and celery; sauté for 5 minutes. Add mussels, and sauté for 30 seconds. Pour wine into the center of the sauté pan. Add broth, cover, reduce heat to low, and steam for 5 minutes, or until mussels open.

To serve, pour mussel mixture over noodles.

Note: Black bean-garlic sauce is available in Oriental markets. To debeard mussels, pull out threads of tissue protruding from the shell.

SERVES 4

 California: Thomas Fogarty Winery,
'94 Gewürztraminer
 Italy: Villa Simone, '94 Frascati

Pepper Pasta

Rosalind Hertzog
Scarsdale, NY

This is an easy, versatile dish, perfect for working women. I have served it as a luncheon dish or dinner entrée with the addition of some chicken. Cold leftovers disappear at our house.

Bring salted water to a boil for the pasta. Cut bell peppers and onion into ½-inch strips. When water is boiling, cook pasta until al dente; drain, and set aside. Heat oil in a 12-inch skillet over medium heat. Add peppers, onion, and salt. Cook for 10 minutes, or until vegetables are tender. Stir in sugar, vinegar, basil, and pepper. Cook until heated through.

To serve, toss pepper mixture with pasta.

(PHOTO, PAGE 150)

SERVES 4

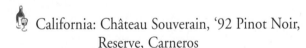 California: Château Souverain, '92 Pinot Noir, Reserve, Carneros

Italy: Frescobaldi, '93 Chianti Rufina, Remole

1 large red bell pepper
1 large green bell pepper
1 large yellow bell pepper
1 large onion
1 pound penne or mostaccioli
3 tablespoons olive or vegetable oil
½ teaspoon salt
1 tablespoon sugar
3 tablespoons balsamic or red wine vinegar
¾ teaspoon dried basil
½ teaspoon pepper

Pasta Lovers' Sauce

— Carole Warburton
Sherman Oaks, CA

We eat pasta quite often. One night, I just decided to toss in a bunch of our favorite ingredients. And, voila!

> 2 tablespoons butter
> 1/2 cup olive oil
> 10 cloves garlic, minced
> 1 cup chicken broth
> Chopped fresh basil to taste
> Chopped fresh parsley leaves to taste
> Pepper to taste
> 1/2 cup heavy cream
> 2 ounces sun-dried tomatoes, chopped
> Pasta

Melt butter with oil in a saucepan over medium heat. Sauté garlic until lightly browned. Add remaining ingredients, reduce heat to low, and simmer for 7 to 10 minutes until flavors blend.

Serve over your favorite pasta.

MAKES 1 1/2 CUPS

PASTITSIO

Eileen H. Swartz
Swampscott, MA

About 20 years ago, a young woman from Paris came to work for me as a mother's helper. She was part French, and part Greek and cooked many unusual dishes that my family enjoyed. Now that I am teaching my daughter to cook, I wish I had saved more of her recipes. But this is certainly one of our favorites.

Preheat oven to 350°. Melt butter for meat mixture over low heat in a large skillet. Sauté onions until soft. Add beef slowly, and cook over high heat, crumbling meat with a fork, until brown. In a small bowl, blend tomato paste into 1 cup wine; add to meat. Reduce heat to low, add nutmeg, pepper, salt and cinnamon, and mix. Simmer, uncovered, for 1 hour. Meanwhile, bring a large pot of water to a boil for the pasta. Add oil to keep the pasta from sticking, and cook the pasta until al dente. Drain, and set aside. In a hot saucepan, scald milk. Remove from the heat, and set aside. Melt butter in a 4-quart pot over low heat. Slowly sift in flour, stirring constantly to prevent lumping. Cook for 5 minutes. Add a dash of nutmeg. Slowly add milk, beating vigorously with a wire whisk. Add remaining nutmeg. Cook until smooth with the consistency of heavy cream, stirring constantly with the whisk. Remove from the heat, and let cool. When beef begins to stick to the pan just before the cooking time is finished, add remaining wine. To assemble the pastitsio, stir half of bread crumbs and half of cheese into the meat mixture. Grease the sides and bottom of a 16x10x2-inch baking pan. Sprinkle with 2 tablespoons bread crumbs. Spread half of cooked pasta evenly in baking pan. Sprinkle with ½ cup cheese. Spread the meat mixture evenly over pasta and set aside. In a separate bowl, beat eggs, combine with remaining pasta, and spread over the meat. Pour sauce over all. Sprinkle with remaining Parmesan and bread crumbs. Bake for 50 minutes, or until golden brown.

SERVES 8 TO 10

Calif: Guenoc Winery, '93 Cabernet Franc

Calif: Chalone, '93 Pinot Noir

MEAT MIXTURE:
- 3 tablespoons butter
- 2 large onions, grated
- 2 pounds ground beef
- 4 tablespoons tomato paste
- 1¼ cups dry red wine, divided into 1 cup and remainder
- 1 teaspoon nutmeg
- ¼ teaspoon pepper
- 1 tablespoon salt
- ½ teaspoon cinnamon

MACARONI AND CREAM SAUCE:
- 1½ teaspoons oil
- 1 pound macaroni or ziti
- 6 cups milk
- 1 cup (2 sticks) butter
- ½ cup flour
- 2 dashes nutmeg, divided in half

PASTITSIO:
- ¼ cup plus 2 tablespoons unseasoned bread crumbs, divided into 3 tablespoons, 2 tablespoons, and 1 tablespoon
- 3 cups grated Parmesan cheese, divided into half, then ½ cup, with remainder
- 6 large eggs at room temperature

PICNIC PINWHEEL PASTA

Janet Shepherd
Atlanta, GA

I often make this for casual dinners and everyone finds the veal a unique surprise. Although my husband finds it quite "gourmet," it's really very easy. And, even my toddler likes it.

5 tablespoons olive oil, plus more for tossing with pasta and drizzling over casserole
4 cloves garlic, minced
1/2 pound ground veal, or ground turkey
1 (14.5-ounce) can Italian tomatoes, puréed
24 ounces cooked fresh peas, or uncooked frozen
1 cup yellow corn cut from the cob (about 2 ears)
1 bunch basil leaves, chopped
Salt and pepper to taste
1 pound pinwheel pasta
1 pound mozzarella cheese, diced
1/2 cup grated Romano cheese
1/2 cup toasted bread crumbs
1/4 cup grated Parmesan cheese

Preheat oven to 400°. Grease a 9x13-inch casserole dish. Heat oil in a skillet, and cook garlic and veal for 8 minutes, or until veal is cooked. Add tomatoes, peas, corn, basil, salt, and pepper. Cook over low heat until the pasta is ready.

Boil salted water for the pasta, and cook the pasta until al dente. Drain. Toss with oil in a large bowl. Pour sauce over the pasta. Add mozzarella and Romano. Transfer to prepared casserole dish. Top with bread crumbs and Parmesan cheese. Drizzle with olive oil. Bake for 20 minutes, or until golden brown. Let cool.

To serve, cut in squares.

SERVES 8

 California: Seghesio Winery, '92 Zinfandel, Sonoma
 France: Matrot, '93 Volnay-Santenots

Rose-Lime Pasta

Gem Wallis Klinar
Kingsport, TN

The first time I tasted lime-flavored pasta, I loved it. Then I remembered a college friend who received a loaf of wheat bread baked with rose petals from her grandmother. I decided to toss a few petals into the pasta for color and see what would happen. This turned out to be a happy combination.

Bring salted water to a boil for pasta. Pluck rose petals from the bulb. When water is boiling, cook pasta until al dente. Drain. Toss with butter, lime juice, and Parmesan. Top with rose petals and lime slices.
(PHOTO, PAGE 156)

9 ounces angel hair or other thin pasta
1 tablespoon butter, salted
2 to 3 tablespoons lime juice
4 ounces Parmesan cheese, grated
2 organically grown roses
Lime slices

SERVES 2

 California: Iron Horse Vineyards, Blanc de Blanc

California: Honig Cellars, '94 Sauvignon Blanc

Fusilli Roma

Paula Robinson
Houston, TX

I have been part of a couples' dinner club for 22 years. Each month, the host couple provides the main course and assigns recipes to the other four couples. This is one of our many favorite recipes.

Boil water to blanch tomatoes. Cut a skin-deep X in the top of each tomato. Drop into boiling water, and blanch for 15 seconds. Remove from the pan and immediately plunge into ice water. Peel tomatoes, and set aside. Boil salted water for pasta. Seed and dice tomatoes; place in a large bowl and season with salt, pepper, and basil. When water is boiling, cook pasta for 8 minutes, or until al dente. In a large sauté pan over medium heat, simmer cooked pasta, oil, garlic, and tomatoes for 5 minutes. To serve, sprinkle mozzarella over the top.

12 Roma tomatoes
8 cups salted water
2 teaspoons salt
1 teaspoon white pepper
1/2 cup torn fresh basil leaves
1 pound fusilli
1/2 cup extra-virgin olive oil
2 tablespoons minced garlic
8 ounces mozzarella cheese, diced

SERVES 4

Italy: Ruffino, '90 Chianti Classico

Italy: Tenuta Caparzo, '90 Ca' del Pazzo, Tuscany

SALMON LASAGNA WHEELS

Christine Horner Lewis
Plano, TX

This dish was created for my daughter's sixth birthday dinner. It had to include salmon, her very favorite. It needed to look festive, be delicate in flavor, fun to eat, and light on kitchen time. It was all of those things—and a hit!

LASAGNA:

- 1 tablespoon olive oil
- 6 lasagna noodles
- 10 ounces ricotta cheese
- 4 ounces Romano cheese, grated
- 2 eggs, beaten
- 3 tablespoons minced fresh basil, or 1 tablespoon dried
- 1 tablespoon minced fresh oregano, or 1 teaspoon dried
- 6 slices (about 4 ounces) smoked Nova salmon
- 3 green onions, blanched

SAUCE:

- 4 tablespoons butter
- 1 pound mushrooms, chopped
- 4 shallots, chopped
- 1/2 cup white wine
- 1 (4-ounce) bottle clam juice
- 1 pint whipping cream

DIRECTIONS FOR LASAGNA:

Bring salted water in a large pot to a boil for the pasta. Add oil and pasta, stir to prevent sticking, and cook until al dente. Drain, rinse under cold water until cool, and drain again. Separate noodles, lay 2 inches apart on waxed paper to keep them from sticking together, and let cool. Preheat oven to 300°. In a medium bowl, combine ricotta, Romano, eggs, basil, and oregano; set aside. Place a salmon slice between 2 sheets of waxed paper. Using a rolling pin, gently stretch the length and width of salmon. Repeat the process with remaining salmon slices. Spread a sixth of the ricotta mixture on each noodle, leaving 1/2-inch uncovered on each end. Lay a salmon slice on each. Gently roll up noodle into a pinwheel. Cut green onions lengthwise to form 6 ribbons. Tie pinwheels with onion ribbons. Coat a shallow baking pan with cooking spray. Place pinwheels, seam down, in the pan. Cover, and bake for 30 minutes.

DIRECTIONS FOR SAUCE:

Melt butter in a large heavy skillet over medium heat. Add mushrooms and shallots; sauté for 6 minutes, or until tender. Add wine and clam juice; cook for 5 minutes. Add cream; cook for 20 minutes. Strain into a bowl with a pour spout, pressing on the vegetables with the back of a spoon to release all juices. Return the liquid to medium heat, and cook until thick enough to lightly coat a spoon.

To serve, ladle sauce evenly between 6 serving plates. Place a lasagna wheel in the center of each. Top with grated Parmesan cheese. (PHOTO, PAGE 146)

MAKES 6 SERVINGS

California: Caymus Vineyards,
'93 Premium White Blend, Conundrum
Italy: Duca di Salaparuta, '94 Terre D'Agala, Sicily

SHRIMP STIR-FRY WITH PASTA

Ronnie Milsap
Nashville, TN

This stir-fry with shrimp is music to our ears!

Peel and devein shrimp; set aside. In a small bowl, whisk together broth, mayonnaise, and juice; set aside.

Spray a wok or large skillet with cooking spray. Add oil, and heat over medium-high temperature until hot. Add garlic and ginger; stir-fry for 1 minute. Add shrimp and asparagus; stir-fry for 3 to 4 minutes until shrimp have coral striations. Add mayonnaise mixture and pasta. Mix, and cook for 2 to 3 minutes until thoroughly heated. Sprinkle with pepper.

SERVES 2

 California: Chalone Vineyard, '93 Chenin Blanc

Italy: Borgo Conventi, '93 Tocai, Fruili

1/2 pound medium shrimp
1/4 cup chicken broth
1/4 cup mayonnaise
1 tablespoon lemon juice
Cooking spray to coat wok
2 teaspoons vegetable oil
2 cloves garlic, minced
1 tablespoon grated fresh gingerroot
3 to 4 spears asparagus, sliced in 1-inch pieces (about 1 cup)
2 cups hot cooked rotini pasta
1/4 teaspoon pepper

PASTA WITH SPICY SPINACH AND TOMATOES

Sandy Mallin
Las Vegas, NV

This is a great way to use your own fresh garden tomatoes. I'm delighted it was accepted—now I've had recipes in all three Neiman Marcus InCircle cookbooks!

1 (16-ounce) box angel hair pasta
¼ cup olive oil, divided into 1 tablespoon and remainder
8 plum tomatoes
1 dried chili pepper, seeded and crushed
5 anchovy fillets, rinsed and drained
2 large cloves garlic, finely chopped
10 ounces spinach, chopped
¾ cup grated Parmesan cheese
Pepper to taste

Cook pasta according to the package directions, drain, toss with 1 tablespoon olive oil, cover, and set aside. Cut a skin-deep X in the top of each tomato. Drop into boiling water and blanch for 15 seconds. Remove from the pan and immediately plunge into ice water. Peel, seed, and dice; set aside.

In a small saucepan over medium heat, cook chili pepper in remaining olive oil until brown. Strain oil into a large sauté pan, discarding pepper. Over medium heat, cook anchovies and garlic in reserved oil, stirring constantly for 1 minute, or until garlic browns. Add spinach and tomatoes, toss, and cook until spinach is wilted. Add pasta and toss until heated through.

To serve, stir in cheese and pepper, and toss.

SERVES 4

California: Vichon Winery, '93 Merlot, Napa Valley
Italy: Ruffino, '90 Cabreo Il Pareto

Shells with Chicken, Prosciutto, Sun-Dried Tomatoes, and Mushrooms

Janys Abate
Eastchester, NY

My son, who taught himself to make hamburgers at the age of 7, likes this. Now he is a senior at the Culinary Institute of America. But, he makes such a mess that I won't allow him to cook in my kitchen!

In a food processor, chop garlic, tomatoes, prosciutto, and basil. In a Dutch oven, stir together chicken broth and water. Add the prosciutto mixture and chicken. Cook over low heat for 15 minutes, or until chicken is cooked. Bring salted water to a boil for the pasta. Add creminis and portobellos to the Dutch oven and cook for 10 minutes. Season with salt and red pepper. When water boils, cook shells until al dente; drain. Add cream and wine to the sauce; cook until heated through.

To serve, toss shells with sauce and sprinkle with cheeses.

SERVES 4 TO 6

California: Husch Vineyards, '93 Pinot Noir, Anderson Valley

Italy: Altesino, '88 Brunello di Montalcino

2 cloves garlic
4 ounces sun-dried tomatoes in oil, drained
1/4 pound prosciutto
1 tablespoon chopped fresh basil
2 envelopes chicken broth mix
1 cup water
2 boneless, skinless chicken breasts, cut into pieces
4 ounces cremini mushrooms, cleaned and chopped
2 medium portobello mushrooms, cleaned and chopped
  Salt to taste
  Pinch red pepper
1 pound large shells
1 cup heavy cream
1/2 cup white wine
  Grated Romano or Asiago cheese for seasoning

THAI NOODLE MEDLEY

Paul-Michael Klein
North Miami Beach, FL

So, you think you can't duplicate those exquisite, luscious ethnic restaurant dishes at home using everyday ingredients? Well, this recipe could change your thinking. It's delicious, much easier than you may think, and low in calories and fat as well.

SAUCE:

- ½ cup peanut butter
- ½ cup soy sauce
- ¾ teaspoon finely minced garlic
- 3 tablespoons sesame oil
- 3 tablespoons honey
- ½ teaspoon chili oil
- ½ teaspoon anise oil
- ¼ teaspoon white pepper
- 1 teaspoon balsamic vinegar (optional)

NOODLE MEDLEY:

- ½ pound chicken breast
- ½ pound boneless pork tenderloin
- 8 green onions
- 1 pound dry flat Oriental noodles or fettucini
- 1 tablespoon vegetable oil
- 1 teaspoon sesame oil
- ½ teaspoon finely minced garlic
- 1 extra-large white or yellow onion, diced
- 6 ounces titi (miniature) shrimp

Blend all sauce ingredients in a blender or food processor; set aside at room temperature. Boil water for the pasta. Cut chicken and pork into pencil-thin strips; set aside. Cut the white portion of green onions into thin discs; julienne the green portion; set aside. Prepare noodles according to the package directions, drain, and mix in all but ¼ cup of the sauce. Heat vegetable oil and sesame oil in a wok or large skillet over high heat, swirl in garlic, and cook until brown. Add chicken, pork, and diced white onion. Stir-fry for up to 6 minutes until meats are cooked. Add green onion discs and shrimp; stir-fry for 2 minutes. Add green onion stalks and remaining sauce; stir until the mixture is coated with sauce.

Note: For a health-smart version of the sauce, use fresh peanut butter, cut honey to 2 tablespoons, and substitute light tamari for soy sauce, 1 teaspoon of gosamaisu for sesame oil, and ½ teaspoon of Tabasco® for chili oil. For a health-smart noodle medley, eliminate sesame oil, shrimp, and pork, and triple the amount of chicken. The sauce can be prepared in advance.

To serve, top noodles with medley. Garnish with green onion parasols. To make green onion parasols, trim and discard some of the green tops from green onions. Cut off and discard the white bulb of each onion. Make numerous lengthwise slits in each onion leaf, starting at the dark green end and stopping halfway through the leaf. The shape will resemble a feather duster. Soak onions in chilled water for a few seconds to curl.

SERVES 4 TO 6

TOMATO CREAM SAUCE PASTA

Janina Parrott Jacobs
St. Clair Shores, MI

I was a houseguest of friends in Bal Harbour when their daughter, Andrea, decided that she would cook dinner for "company." I was a little apprehensive since Andrea barely could boil water, but this recipe from her grandmother looked simple enough for her to handle. Was I surprised by the rich taste! Four stars to Grandma and an honorary chef's toque to Andrea!

Melt butter in a saucepan. Add onion, carrot, celery, tomatoes, salt, and sugar; simmer for 1 hour. Transfer to blender; purée. Return to the saucepan over low heat. Add cream until sauce is fairly thick and creamy and light orange in color; keep sauce warm over low heat, stirring occasionally.

In a large pot, boil salted water and cook ravioli for 5 to 7 minutes until al dente.

To serve, pout hot sauce over ravioli. Sprinkle with Parmesan.

SERVES 4

🍷 Italy: Casal Thaulero, '92 Montepulciano d' Abruzzo
🍇 Italy: Tenuta di Capezzana, '92 Barco Reale, Tuscany

½ cup (1 stick) butter
3 tablespoons chopped onion
3 tablespoons chopped carrot
3 tablespoons chopped celery
1 (20-ounce) can Italian-style tomatoes, undrained
2 teaspoons salt
¾ teaspoons sugar
¼ to ½ cup heavy cream as needed
1 pound cheese-filled ravioli
Parmesan cheese or Romano cheese, grated, for seasoning

PASTA WITH TOMATO AND RED BELL PEPPER SAUCE

A. Bremer
Houston, TX

With a heart surgeon as head of our family, I am continuously in search of healthy recipes that do not sacrifice taste for reduced fat. After numerous experiments, I finally found this winner that is easy to prepare and full of flavor.

1 tablespoon olive oil
1 large onion, diced
2 large red bell peppers, diced
2 cloves garlic, crushed
1 (28-ounce) can plum
      tomatoes, undrained
1 bay leaf
   Pinch dried red pepper
      flakes
   Salt and pepper to taste
1 pound linguini
⅛ cup grated Romano cheese

In a sauté pan, heat oil over medium heat. Sauté onion for 5 minutes. Add bell pepper and garlic; sauté for 5 minutes. Add tomatoes, bay leaf, and pepper flakes; simmer for 30 minutes. Bring water to a boil for the pasta. Discard bay leaf from the sauce mixture. Transfer to blender; purée. Strain into a bowl with a pour spout, pressing with a spoon to release all liquids. Discard solids, and return liquid to the sauté pan. Add salt and pepper. Simmer for 5 to 10 minutes until mixture is reduced by a fourth.

Cook linguini according to the package directions. Toss with sauce and top with Romano.

Serve with salad and French bread. For a heartier version, brown Italian sausage, slice, and toss with pasta.

SERVES 4

 California: Steele, '91 Zinfandel, Clear Lake
 Italy: Marchesi L & P Antinori, '93 Chianti,
      Santa Cristina

JOYCE GOLDSTEIN

"What is casual elegance? I'd say it's serving cassoulet on fine china... or maybe, it's lobster on paper plates."

Broccoli and Olives with Garlic
and Hot Pepper Vinaigrette,
Page 219

Greek-Style Fish,
Page 95

145

ABOVE
Salmon Lasagna Wheels,
Page 138

BELOW
Lobster and Corn Salad
with Tarragon, Page 68

ABOVE
Carrot Loaf, Page 220

BELOW
Tomato Parmesan Pie, Page 43

ABOVE
Apricot Cake, Page 246

BELOW
Golden Cointreau®
Cake, Page 252

MATTHEW KENNEY

"What is casual elegance to me? It's food that is sophisticated and creative, enjoyed in a relaxed ambiance."

Maine Crab Cakes
with Ginger, Lemon and Cumin Sauce, Page 85

Dilled Potato Bread, Page 53

ABOVE
English Appetizer Sandwich,
Page 42

BELOW
Pepper Pasta, Page 133

ABOVE
Tomato and Cantaloupe
Salad, Page 78

BELOW
East Indian Cauliflower, Page 221
Curried Lamb Kebobs, Page 118

Big Dipper Biscotti,
Page 267

Gingerbread Waffles,
Page 24

Mark Militello

"Casual elegance? That's eating well in your shorts."

Arugula Salad with Roasted Sweet Corn and Peppers, Marinated Tomatoes and Poached Garlic-Tomato Vinaigrette, Page 67

Salmon in a Jacket, Page 101

Marinated Asparagus,
Page 214

BELOW
Spicy Mayonnaise, Page 208
Apple Cinnamon French Toast,
Page 18

Grilled Quail with Fourth of July
Salsa, Page 181

White Gazpacho Soup, Page 199
Cheese Straws, Page 35

BELOW
Rose-Lime Pasta, Page 137

STEPHAN PYLES

*"I think I helped invent
casual elegance...
it's sophistication, style and
creativity in a comfortable setting."*

Chilled Yellow Pepper Soup
with Scallop Ceviche Verde, Page 193

Open-Faced
Seafood Club
Sandwich,
Page 62

157

Absolutely Divine
Devil's Food Cake, Page 253

BELOW
Duck a l'Orange, Page 183
Cranberry Wild Rice,
Page 234

ABOVE
Shrimp with Radicchio and
Arugula, Page 91

Pistachio-White Chocolate Chip
Cookies, Page 268

Berry-Filled Scones, Page 57

White Sangria, Page 44

French Fresh Fruit
Flan, Page 273

160

CHARLIE TROTTER

"Casual elegance, to me is perfect service in a perfect setting, that is warm, friendly and knowledgeable. If not done properly, it is an exercise in mediocrity."

Shallot Compote, Page 235

Madeira Wine Roast, Page 114

Oriental Chicken Salad,
Page 71

Roasted Pepper and Mozzarella
Salad, Page 76

ABOVE
Hearts of Palm
Salad, Page 74

Black-Eyed Pea
Cornbread,
Page 48

Fruit Bran Muffins,
Page 55

Fresh Lemon Ice Cream,
Page 257

POULTRY

CHICKEN FEED EXTRAORDINAIRE

Delicious and different every time. Judging by the number and variety of recipes we've perused, people must eat chicken three or four times a week. And they love it. Why else would aficionados of such exotica as alligator, rabbit, rattlesnake, etc., always proclaim, "It tastes just like chicken?" Paella had us clapping our hands like a flamenco troupe, and Chicken Breasts on a Bed of Spinach had an up-and-at-'em flavor. Truth to tell, we loved every chicken recipe we tested, and that made this one of the hardest chapters to put together. Try them all, and don't miss the quail and duck recipes you'll find nesting with the chickens.

GRILLED BALSAMIC CHICKEN

Montelle Kline
Miami, FL

Of all my recipes, I think this is my personal favorite. I especially like to serve it at summer dinner parties. It is just the right touch as an entrée.

DRESSING:
- ¼ cup vinegar
- ¾ cup olive oil
- 1 teaspoon salt
- ¼ teaspoon pepper
- 1 tablespoon balsamic vinegar
- 2 teaspoons lemon juice

CHICKEN:
- 6 portobello mushrooms
- 4 boneless, skinless chicken breasts
- 1 bunch broccoli
- 1 (16-ounce) package thin spaghetti
- Twist of lemon for garnish

THE DAY BEFORE SERVING:

Mix all dressing ingredients in a bottle. Remove mushroom stems, and lay mushrooms in a shallow baking dish. Pour half of the dressing over them. Cover and marinate for 24 hours, turning once. Chill remaining dressing for 24 hours.

WHEN READY TO GRILL:

Transfer mushrooms to a plate and set aside, reserving dressing from marinade container. Trim excess fat from chicken breasts, and marinate breasts in reserved dressing for 30 minutes. Meanwhile, to prepare grill, make holes in aluminum foil, place on grill, and heat on low setting. Bring salted water to a boil for spaghetti. Cut broccoli into florets, discard stems, and steam florets until tender when pierced with a fork; set aside. When water is boiling, cook spaghetti until al dente. Meanwhile, grill chicken on foil until the bottom is cooked; turn and cook the other side. During the last 5 to 10 minutes of grillling, add mushrooms. When pasta is done, drain, rinse, and combine with broccoli. Pour remaining dressing over pasta.

To serve, place pasta on a platter. Top with chicken breasts. Arrange mushrooms around chicken.

Garnish with twisted lemon.

Note: Can be served over wild rice or couscous.

SERVES 4

 California: Santa Barbara Winery, '92 Pinot Noir
Australia: Penfolds, Sémillon Chardonnay, Kooruinga Hill

Quick Chicken Breasts with Fontina Cheese and Mushrooms

Barbara Bush
Houston, TX

Mrs. Bush continues to crusade for literacy with this easily prepared entrée.

Season the chicken with salt and pepper; set aside. In a skillet over medium heat, sauté garlic in oil until it colors but doesn't brown.

Preheat broiler. Add chicken to garlic, raise the heat to medium-high, and brown on both sides. Add a layer of mushrooms, a layer of fontina, and a generous sprinkling of Parmesan. Reduce heat to low, cover, and cook until cheese melts. Broil until bubbly.

Accompany with steamed rice with poppy seeds.

MAKES 4 SERVINGS

4 boneless chicken breasts, halved
Kosher salt and black or white pepper to taste
Crushed garlic to taste
Olive oil for sautéing
8 ounces mushrooms, sliced
8 thick slices fontina or mozzarella cheese
Grated Parmesan cheese to taste

Italy: Altare, '91 Nebbiolo, Piedmont
Italy: Castello di Gabbiano, '93 Ania

HONOLULU CHICKEN CURRY

Jean Hankin
Honolulu, HI

In my work as a nutrition research doctor, I travel all over the Pacific Rim countries–Taiwan, Singapore, Japan, Korea, and the various Pacific Islands. I entertain in spurts, and this recipe has made my reputation as a Honolulu hostess.

6 tablespoons butter or margarine
1 small onion, grated
1 clove garlic, peeled
6 tablespoons flour
2 teaspoons chopped fresh gingerroot
1 1/2 teaspoons salt
2 tablespoons curry powder, or to taste
2 cups milk
1/2 cup coconut milk
1 cup chicken broth
3 1/2 pounds cooked chicken, diced (3 cups)

Melt butter in a large saucepan over medium heat. Add onion and garlic, and sauté for 5 minutes. Remove garlic clove. Combine flour, ginger, salt, and curry powder; add to the pan and blend. Add milk, coconut milk, and broth. Reduce heat to low, and cook, stirring constantly, until thick. Add chicken and cook until heated through.

Serve with rice and individual bowls of the following toppings: chutney, flaked coconut, chopped peanuts, raisins, crisp and crumbled bacon, and chopped green onion tops.

SERVES 8

 California: Joseph Phelps Vineyard, '94 Riesling
 California: St. Francis Vineyards, '93 Gewürztraminer

COQ AU VIN

Joan Chognard
Menlo Park, CA

My father-in-law was French and lived in Paris. He served as a naval officer and was an excellent cook. I followed him around his tiny kitchen and made copious notes. This is one of my favorite recipes from his repertoire.

In a skillet over medium heat, melt 1 tablespoon butter in oil. Sauté onions for several minutes. Add mushrooms, and sauté until onions are soft. Add bouillon, 1/4 cup wine, salt, pepper, parsley, 1/2 bay leaf, and 1/4 teaspoon thyme. Cover, and reduce heat to simmer. In a mixing bowl, blend 2 tablespoons softened butter and flour until smooth. Whisk into hot liquid or beat in by hand. Simmer for 1 to 2 minutes, stirring constantly, until the sauce is thick enough to lightly coat a spoon. Set aside. Melt remaining 2 tablespoons of butter in a 10-inch casserole dish. Sauté bacon over low heat until light brown. Remove bacon and set aside, reserving butter and drippings in the casserole dish. Add chicken, season with salt and pepper, and brown. Add bacon, cover, and cook over low heat for 10 minutes, turning chicken once. Add cognac, light with a long match, and wait until the flame subsides. Pour in remaining wine and chicken stock. Add tomato paste, garlic, remaining thyme, and remaining bay leaf. Cover, and simmer for 25 to 30 minutes until chicken is cooked. Remove chicken and set aside, reserving remaining mixture in the casserole dish. Simmer cooking liquid for 1 to 2 minutes until fat can be skimmed off. Raise heat, bring to a boil, and boil rapidly until the liquid is reduced to 2 1/4 cups. Remove bay leaf. Return chicken to the casserole dish. Add onion-mushroom sauce. Cover, and simmer, basting occasionally for 4 to 5 minutes until chicken is hot.

Serve from the casserole dish or arrange on a warm plate. Decorate with fresh parsley and accompany with potatoes and fresh green peas.

3 tablespoons butter, divided into 1 tablespoon and 2 tablespoons
1 tablespoon oil
18 pearl onions
8 ounces mushrooms, sliced
1/2 cup beef bouillon
3 1/4 cups red wine, divided into 1/4 cup and remainder
Salt and pepper to taste
1/4 cup chopped fresh parsley, or 2 tablespoons dried
1 1/2 bay leaves, divided into 1 leaf and 1/2 leaf
1/2 teaspoon dried thyme, divided in half
3 tablespoons flour
2 tablespoons butter, softened
4 ounces bacon
1 (3- to 3 1/2-pound) frying chicken, cut in pieces
1/4 cup cognac
2 cups chicken or beef stock
1 1/2 teaspoons tomato paste
2 cloves garlic, crushed
Fresh parsley for garnish

SERVES 4

 Calif: Rodney Strong Vineyards, '92 Pinot Noir, River Estate

 France: Chateau Lagrange '90 Pomerol

CHICKEN MOLINO

S. Kelly Young-Finkel
Fort Lauderdale, FL

I'm a hard-working interior designer with a new baby, so I don't have much time to cook. When I do, I like to feel my dishes are beautifully presented, usually on my silver pieces. This is my favorite party recipe, warm or cold, as an entrée or just using wings or drumsticks for a great appetizer.

1 head garlic, peeled and finely puréed
¾ cup chopped fresh oregano, or ¼ cup dried
Coarse salt and black pepper to taste
½ cup red wine vinegar
½ cup olive oil
8 ounces pitted prunes
4 ounces pitted Spanish green olives
4 ounces capers with a bit of juice
6 bay leaves
10 pounds chicken wings and drumsticks
1 cup firmly packed light brown sugar
1 cup white wine
½ cup minced fresh cilantro, or 3 tablespoons dried

In a large bowl, combine garlic, oregano, salt, pepper, vinegar, oil, prunes, olives, capers and juice, and bay leaves. Add chicken, cover, and chill overnight.

Preheat oven to 350°. Remove chicken from the marinade, reserving marinade, and arrange in a single layer in 1 or 2 shallow baking pans. Spoon marinade over, sprinkle with brown sugar, and pour wine around the sides of the pan. Bake for 50 minutes, basting frequently with pan juices.

To serve, transfer chicken, prunes, olives, and capers to a serving platter, using a slotted spoon. Moisten with a few spoonfuls of pan juices. Sprinkle with cilantro. Serve remaining juices in a sauceboat.

SERVES 10 TO 12

 California: La Crema, '93 Pinot Noir, Reserve
 Italy: Renato Ratti, '93 Nebbiolo

CHICKEN MONTEREY

Nancy Adams
Rancho Santa Fe, CA

This was a favorite dish that my mother would make for special occasions. It's a wonderful meal with its thick green sauce. Other chicken dishes pale in comparison, and my guests always beg for more.

Grease a 3-quart baking dish. Place chicken breasts between 2 pieces of waxed paper and pound until ¼ inch thick. Lightly sprinkle with salt and pepper; dust with flour. Melt ¼ cup butter in a large skillet over medium heat, and brown chicken. Transfer to prepared baking dish in a single layer, and set aside.

Preheat oven to 350°. In the skillet, melt remaining butter over medium-low heat, and sauté onion, garlic, and mushrooms until vegetables are tender. Stir in 2 tablespoons flour, celery salt, white pepper, chicken stock, and wine. Cook over low heat for 4 to 5 minutes until thick. Stir in avocado and ½ cup cheese to blend. Adjust seasonings to taste. Spoon avocado mixture on chicken breasts. Top with remaining cheese. Bake for 10 to 15 minutes until chicken is cooked and cheese is melted.

SERVES 6 TO 8

France: Château Citran, '92 Haut Medoc
Italy: Lungarotti, '88 Cabernet Sauvignon

4 large boneless, skinless chicken breasts, halved
Salt and pepper to season
2 tablespoons flour, plus more for dusting
½ cup (1 stick) butter, divided in half
½ medium onion, chopped
1 clove garlic, minced
8 large mushrooms, diced
1 teaspoon celery salt
½ teaspoon white pepper
½ cup chicken stock
½ cup white wine
1 avocado, pitted, peeled, and mashed
¾ cup grated Monterey Jack cheese, divided into ½ cup and remainder

Chicken Honey Nut Stir-Fry

Mrs. Terrell Newberry Jr.
Spring, TX

We've enjoyed this recipe for a number of years, having learned to watch our fats and to exercise. What I know about cooking I learned from my mother and my mother-in-law. As for my daughter, she is engaged, but has not learned to cook as yet.

2 to 2½ cups rice (uncooked)
¾ cup orange juice
⅓ cup honey
3 tablespoons soy sauce
1 tablespoon cornstarch
1 teaspoon minced fresh
    gingerroot, or ⅓
    teaspoon ground
2 tablespoons vegetable oil,
    divided in half
2 large carrots, cut diagonally
    into small pieces
2 stalks celery, cut diagonally
    into 2-inch pieces
1 pound boneless, skinless
    chicken breasts, cut into
    thin strips
½ cup cashews or peanuts

Prepare rice according to the package directions, and set aside in the covered pot to stay warm. Meanwhile, in a small bowl, combine orange juice, honey, soy sauce, cornstarch, and ginger; set aside. Heat 1 tablespoon oil in a large skillet over medium heat. Add carrots and celery; stir-fry for 3 minutes. Remove the vegetables; set aside.

Pour remaining oil into the skillet. Add chicken; stir-fry for 3 minutes. Return vegetables to the skillet. Add the sauce mixture and nuts. Cook over medium-high heat, stirring constantly, until the sauce thickens.

To serve, spoon stir-fry mixture over hot rice.

MAKES 4 TO 6 SERVINGS

 California: Inglenook-Napa Valley,
    '94 French Colombard
 France: Hugel et Fils, '92 Sylvaner, Alsace

CHICKEN BREASTS WITH SAUCE SUPREME ON A BED OF SPINACH

Freda D. Cronic
Griffin, GA

This is actually my daughter's recipe. I like to cook it for special occasions, such as entertaining my bridge club and my husband's employees at Christmastime.

DIRECTIONS FOR CHICKEN BREASTS:

Preheat oven to 425°. Sprinkle chicken with salt and pepper; set aside. Pick over spinach, discarding any tough stems and blemished leaves. Rinse and drain leaves; set aside. Heat half of butter in a heavy skillet over medium heat. Add chicken, skin side down, and cook for 2 minutes, or until skin browns. Turn and cook for 2 minutes. Remove chicken from the pan; set aside. Melt remaining butter in the skillet. Add mushrooms, shallots, salt, and pepper. Cook, stirring frequently, for 3 minutes, or until the mushroom liquid is almost evaporated. Add spinach and cook until wilted. Add nutmeg, and stir. Lay out 4 squares of aluminum foil large enough to enclose the chicken and spinach securely. Spoon equal portions of the spinach mixture onto the center of each square. Sprinkle each portion with 1 tablespoon cheese. Top each portion with a piece of chicken, skin side up. Fold over the foil to enclose securely, making each as airtight as possible. Place in a baking dish, and bake for 20 minutes.

DIRECTIONS FOR SAUCE SUPREME:

Melt butter in a saucepan over medium heat. Add flour, stirring with a whisk until combined. Add broth, stirring rapidly with the whisk until thick and smooth. Cook for 5 minutes. Add remaining ingredients, and cook until heated through; do not boil.

To serve, open the foil packages and place on 4 heated plates. Spoon Sauce Supreme over the top.

MAKES 4 SERVINGS

CHICKEN BREASTS:

2 boneless chicken breasts, halved (about 2 pounds total)
Salt and pepper to taste
1 pound bulk spinach, stems removed, or 1 (10-ounce) package of spinach leaves
1/4 cup (1/2 stick) butter, divided in half
8 ounces mushrooms, cut into thin slices
3 tablespoons minced shallots
1/8 teaspoon grated fresh nutmeg
4 tablespoons Parmesan cheese, grated

SAUCE:

2 tablespoons butter
2 tablespoons flour
1 1/4 cups chicken broth
1/2 cup heavy cream
Juice of 1/2 lemon
Salt and pepper to taste

California: Williams Selyem, '93 Pinot Noir, Sonoma
Italy: Rocca dell' Macie, '92 Chianti Classico

Lemon Chicken with Moroccan Olive-Pine Nut Sauce,

2 (3-pound) chickens
Chopped chives, scallions, or
cilantro leaves for garnish

MARINADE:
1/2 cup olive oil
2 lemons, preserved if available
1 tablespoon chopped fresh
cilantro
2 teaspoons minced gingerroot
Pinch crushed red pepper
flakes
1 teaspoon white pepper

MOROCCAN OLIVE-PINE
NUT SAUCE:
2 tablespoons olive oil
5 tablespoons grated white
onion
1 teaspoon minced garlic
1 tablespoon minced gingerroot
Pinch crushed red pepper
flakes
1 vial saffron threads, crushed,
or pinch powdered
1/3 cup sliced Moroccan green
olives
1/3 cup toasted pine nuts
2 tablespoons chopped
preserved lemon, or
3 tablespoons lemon juice
3 tablespoons honey

DIRECTIONS FOR MARINADE:
Remove neck and giblets from chickens. Rinse and dry chickens. Combine all marinade ingredients in a deep container. Add chickens and marinate, chill for 6 to 24 hours.

DIRECTIONS FOR LEMON CHICKEN WITH MOROCCAN OLIVE-PINE NUT SAUCE:
Preheat oven to 375°. Remove chickens from marinade, discarding marinade, season body cavities and skin with salt and pepper, and truss. Heat a roasting pan over high heat on the stovetop, add oil, and brown chickens on both sides. Place in oven and roast for 50 minutes, or until juices are pale yellow. Remove chickens from the roasting pan, brown further under the broiler if necessary, and set aside. Pour off excess fat, reserving 3 tablespoons. Add onion, garlic, and ginger, place on the stovetop over medium heat, and cook until onion begins to brown. Add red pepper, saffron, olives, and pine nuts. Deglaze the pan with lemon juice over high heat, or add preserved lemons. Add honey and stock, and cook until liquids are reduced by half. Add butter, salt, pepper, parsley, and cilantro. Reduce heat to low to keep warm.

Toasted Garlic, and Couscous

Matthew Kenney
New York, NY

DIRECTIONS FOR COUSCOUS:

In a small saucepan over medium heat, bring chicken stock to a simmer. In a large sauté pan, place carrot, bell pepper, onion, and zucchini. Cover, and sweat over medium-low heat for 3 to 4 minutes until tender. Add saffron, turmeric, and stock. Transfer to a large bowl, add couscous, and stir to combine. Cover with plastic wrap, and let stand for 15 minutes.

To serve, remove trussing from chicken and carve. Place a serving portion on each plate. Add a serving of couscous to each plate, fluffing with a fork and seasoning to taste with salt, pepper, and parsley. Accompany with garlic-flavored spinach, greens, and grilled flatbread. Drizzle sauce over chicken. Garnish chicken with chopped chives, scallions, or cilantro leaves and couscous with pignoli nuts and olives.

Note: Lemons preserved in salt are commonly used to enhance Moroccan dishes.

SERVES 4

California: Bonny Doon Vineyard, '92 Rhône Blend Old Telegram

France: Chapoutier, '92 Hermatage Rouge, La Sizeranne (Rhône Valley)

MOROCCAN OLIVE-PINE NUT SAUCE, CONTINUED:
- 1 quart chicken stock
- 2 tablespoons butter
- Salt and pepper to taste
- 1 teaspoon chopped fresh parsley
- 1 tablespoon chopped fresh cilantro

COUSCOUS:
- 2 cups chicken stock
- 1 carrot, diced into ¼-inch cubes
- 1 red bell pepper, seeded and diced
- 1 red onion, diced
- 1 zucchini, diced into ¼-inch cubes
- 2 cups medium-grain couscous (uncooked)
- 1 vial saffron, or pinch powdered
- 1 tablespoon turmeric
- 4 tablespoons fresh chopped parsley for seasoning
- Pignoli nuts and olives for garnish

Honey Mustard Marinated Chicken

Sarah Magner
Chicago, IL

The fabulous smell of this chicken cooking brings all the neighborhood children to my back door for dinner. Try it for yourself, and see!

¼ cup vegetable oil
¼ cup apple cider vinegar
2 tablespoons honey
1 tablespoon chutney (any kind)
2 teaspoons coarse-grain
    mustard
1 teaspoon Worcestershire sauce
½ small onion, minced
4 boneless, skinless chicken
    breasts

Combine oil, vinegar, honey, chutney, mustard, Worcestershire, and onion in a marinade dish. Add chicken and chill overnight.

Prepare grill. Remove chicken from marinade, and grill until cooked.

SERVES 4

 California: Au Bon Climat, '91 Pinot Noir, Santa Maria

 California: Navarro Vineyards, '92 Sauvignon Blanc, Mendocino

Low-Fat Chicken

Mrs. Harold Fishman
St. Louis, MO

We all seem to be watching our fat intake these days. Recently, I made a big batch of this chicken, enough for my daughter to take some home, and some for me to take to a friend who is on a special diet. It's very flavorful and freezes well.

10 boneless, skinless chicken
    breasts
1 cup plum jam or jelly
6 tablespoons red wine vinegar
½ cup onions or scallions
¼ cup soy sauce
1 tablespoon dry mustard
    Pinch ground cloves
    Pinch cayenne

Preheat oven to 375°. Lay chicken breasts in a large baking dish; set aside.

Combine all other ingredients in a saucepan, and cook over medium heat until heated through. Pour over chicken and bake, uncovered, for 1 hour.

SERVES 6 TO 8

 California: Chalone, '94 Chardonnay, Gavilan

 France: Georges Duboeuf, '93 Moulin-a-Vent

SESAME CHICKEN

Janet Rosenblatt
Boston, MA

I've had this recipe for years, and it's always well-received by guests. My mother-in-law gave me many silver serving pieces when she moved into an apartment, and I love to serve this chicken, garnished with lemons, tomatoes, and greens, on one of her silver platters.

Preheat oven to 375°. Brush a 12x8-inch baking dish with oil. In a pie plate, mix honey and lemon juice. On a sheet of waxed paper, mix sesame seeds, flour, paprika, and mustard. Dip both sides of each breast in the honey mixture; coat one side of each breast in the sesame mixture. Place, sesame side down, in prepared baking dish. Bake for 20 minutes. Turn, and bake for 20 minutes, or until fork-tender.

SERVES 4

2 tablespoons honey
2 tablespoons lemon juice
2 tablespoons sesame seeds
2 tablespoons flour
1/2 teaspoon paprika
1/4 teaspoon dry mustard
2 boneless, skinless chicken breasts, halved

California: Buehler Vineyards, White Zinfandel
France: Labouré-Roi, '93 Vouvray, Loire Valley

TURKEY BREAST

Roslyn Goldstine
Beverly Hills, CA

Someone in my butcher's shop shared this recipe with me one day when I was lamenting over what new, yummy entrée I could make other than "the same old thing."

1 cup chopped fresh parsley
5 cloves garlic, minced
1½ cups lemon juice
1 cup olive or canola oil
4 tablespoons chopped fresh rosemary, or 4 teaspoons dried and crumbled
1 teaspoon salt
1 (4- to 5-pound) turkey breast
2 tablespoons margarine
¼ cup drained capers

Combine parsley, garlic, lemon juice, oil, rosemary, and salt in a marinade dish. Add turkey and chill overnight.

Preheat oven to 400°. Pour a third of the marinade in a baking pan with turkey, reserving remaining marinade for the sauce. Bake for 30 minutes, basting occasionally.

Reduce oven temperature to 350°. Bake, basting frequently, for 1 hour, or until turkey is 165°. In a saucepan over medium-high heat, bring remaining marinade to a boil. Whisk in margarine. Add capers.

To serve, slice turkey and spoon sauce over the top.

SERVES 6 TO 8

 California: Signorello Vineyards, '91 Pinot Noir, Proprietor's Reserve

 Italy: Hofstätter, '90 Pinot Nero, Alto Adige, Villa S. Urbano

ROAST TURKEY WITH DRESSING

Ed McMahon
Beverly Hills, CA

Ed "roasts" a great Roast Turkey with Dressing.

Preheat oven to 325°. In a large pot, lightly brown sausage. Add celery and onions; cook for 5 minutes, or until translucent. Stir in nuts, mushrooms, and sage. Remove the pot from the heat. Add herb-seasoned and cornbread stuffing mixes, applesauce, pineapple, marmalade, and brandy. Stir in just enough water to moisten stuffing mixture. Remove neck and giblets from turkey, reserving for gravy if desired. Rinse and dry turkey. Stuff neck and body cavities. Truss. Place, breast side up, in roasting pan. Brush with oil. Roast, uncovered, for 2 hours, basting occasionally. Cover with a tent of aluminum foil, and roast for 2 hours, basting frequently. Check turkey for doneness. When done, transfer to a large platter; let stand for 15 minutes.

To serve, carve turkey, spoon stuffing into a serving dish, and garnish platter with celery leaves.

SERVES 12

 California: Robert Sinskey Vineyards,
      '92 Pinot Noir

 Italy: Monte Antico, '93 Rosso, Tuscany

1 (12-ounce) roll country pork sausage
2 to 3 stalks celery, diced
2 medium onions, chopped
1 cup chopped pecans or walnuts
1 cup chopped mushrooms
1 tablespoon ground sage
1 (8-ounce) package herb-seasoned cubed stuffing mix
1 (8-ounce) package cornbread stuffing mix
1 cup applesauce
8 ounces crushed pineapple
1/2 cup orange marmalade
1/2 cup brandy
1 (12- to 14-pound) turkey
2 tablespoons vegetable oil

RANCH QUAIL

Crystal L. Lyons
Waxahachie, TX

This is the Texas-style quail dish that I created and have served to out-of-state guests and the family for the past eight years. It looks as if the tradition is here to stay.

24 quail
2 cups buttermilk
1/4 cup (1/2 stick) unsalted
    butter
1 cup sherry
1 cup chicken stock
4 ounces mushrooms, chopped
1/2 cup finely chopped pecans
1 cup flour
1 teaspoon salt
1 teaspoon pepper
Vegetable oil for frying
3 cups cooked brown rice
    (from 1 cup uncooked)

Rinse quail and pat dry. Marinate in buttermilk in a large glass mixing bowl for 30 minutes. Meanwhile, melt butter in saucepan over medium heat. Stir in sherry, stock, mushrooms, and pecans. Remove from the heat and set aside. Combine flour, salt, and pepper in a pie plate or other shallow pan.

When ready to cook, preheat oven to 350°. Heat oil in a skillet over medium-high heat until lightly smoking.

Remove quail from marinade, dredge in flour mixture, and sear on all sides in the skillet. Transfer to a baking dish, pour sherry-stock mixture over, cover with aluminum foil, and bake for 1 hour and 30 minutes.

Remove quail from the oven, reserving the drippings in the pan. Place quail around the outer edge of a large serving platter, and cover loosely with aluminum foil. Mix cooked rice with the pan drippings.

To serve, place rice on the serving platter in the center of quail.

SERVES 12

 California: Louis Foppiano Wine Co.,
        '93 Petit Sirah, Reserve
 France: Vidal-Fleury, '93 Côtes de Rhône

GRILLED QUAIL WITH FOURTH OF JULY SALSA

Sharon Loeff
Scottsdale, AZ

When I met my husband, I quickly learned that one of his greatest loves was bird hunting. Eating fine food was also on his "top 10 list." He gave me a 12-gauge shotgun before an engagement ring and took me afield to see what I was made of. There is something special about serving a meal that you have had to work very hard to bring to the table.

DIRECTIONS FOR GRILLED QUAIL:

Combine wine, oil, lime juice, garlic, and cumin in a marinade dish. Add quail, and chill for 6 to 8 hours.

Prepare grill. Remove quail from marinade, wrap a bacon strip around each, and grill for 3 to 5 minutes per side until cooked to desired doneness.

DIRECTIONS FOR FOURTH OF JULY SALSA:

Core, seed, and dice peppers. Core and dice tomatoes. Dice onion. Seed and mince jalapeño. Combine all salsa ingredients.

Serve salsa adjacent to quail. Accompany with black beans and rice. Garnish with cilantro, a tomatillo, and a dab of sour cream.

Note: Salsa is best prepared and eaten the same day.

(PHOTO, PAGE 155)

SERVES 4

 California: Raymond Vineyard & Cellar,
          '90 Cabernet Sauvignon

France: Domaine Dujac, '93, Morey-St.-Denis

QUAIL:

- 1 cup white wine
- 1/2 cup olive oil
- 1/4 cup lime juice
- 2 cloves garlic, minced
- 1 teaspoon cumin
- 8 quail
- 8 bacon strips
  Cilantro, tomatillos, and sour cream for garnish

SALSA:

- 2 red bell peppers
- 1 yellow bell pepper
- 4 tomatoes
- 1 red onion
- 1 jalapeño pepper, or more to taste
- 1/4 cup lime juice
- 1 cup chopped fresh cilantro (about 1 bunch)
- 1/2 teaspoon crushed cumin

PAELLA

E.G. Chamberlin
Corona del Mar, CA

As my Spanish friend, Paco, left the U.S. to return to Spain, he gave me his authentic paella pan and this wonderful recipe. I've served it to delighted guests for more than 20 years, exactly as he did, with crusty bread followed by a simple salad of greens and garlic vinaigrette.

3 pounds chicken, cut in pieces
2 tablespoons olive oil, plus more for brushing on chicken
1 onion, chopped
1 teaspoon paprika
1 (15-ounce) can chopped Roma tomatoes, undrained
6 cups chicken broth
Salt and pepper to taste
1 vial saffron threads, or pinch powdered
3 cups long-grain rice (uncooked)
1 green bell pepper
1 red bell pepper
1/2 to 1 pound medium shrimp
1/2 to 1 pound bay clams or mussels
1 (14.5-ounce) can garbanzo beans
8 ounces pepperoni, thinly sliced
8 ounces frozen peas

Preheat broiler. Brush chicken with oil, and broil for 10 minutes on each side; set aside. In a paella pan or large casserole dish or skillet over medium heat, sauté onion in 2 tablespoons olive oil until translucent. Add paprika, stirring to prevent blackening. Add tomatoes with their juice. Cook until the juice evaporates and sauce thickens. Add chicken broth. Season with salt, pepper, and saffron. Raise heat to high and bring to a boil. Add rice; boil for 5 minutes. Add chicken, pushing down into rice; boil for 10 minutes.

Meanwhile, core, seed, and julienne bell peppers; shell shrimp; and scrub clams. When chicken has boiled for 10 minutes, add peppers, shrimp, clams, garbanzos, and pepperoni, pushing them into the broth. Distribute ingredients in a decorative pattern over the surface. Sprinkle peas over the top. Boil for 10 minutes, or until clams open and shrimp have coral striations.

Remove from the heat, loosely cover with aluminum foil, and let stand for 10 minutes.

SERVES 8

 Spain: CVNE, '88 Rioja, Reserva
 Spain: Bodegas Torres/Sangre de Toro, '91 Rioja

Duck a l'Orange

Joan Fanaberia Bloom
Montreal, Quebec, Canada

During a dinner party to which my children were not invited and had been asked to remain upstairs, a note floated downstairs. It said, "Please send up some duck for us. Sincerely, Stephen and Heidi." Now, 25 years later, I still have that note, and whenever I serve the duck to guests, I show it to them and we all have a good laugh.

DIRECTIONS FOR DUCK WITH BASTING SAUCE:

Heat oven to 425°. Stuff duck with orange quarters, garlic, salt, and pepper. Truss. Place in a shallow pan, breast up, and brush with butter. Pour wine over duck. Roast, uncovered, for 30 minutes. Whisk together all basting sauce ingredients. Reduce temperature to 375°. Roast for 40 minutes, basting twice with the basting sauce. Turn duck; roast for 20 minutes. Meanwhile, prepare Orange Sauce (see erecipe). Turn duck; roast for 30 minutes, basting twice. Spread marmalade thickly on duck; roast for 10 minutes. Remove trussing; quarter duck.

DIRECTIONS FOR ORANGE SAUCE:

Melt 2 tablespoons butter in a skillet over medium heat. Add liver and sauté until brown. In a separate saucepan, heat brandy, light with a long match, wait until the flame subsides, and pour brandy over liver. Add remaining butter, orange peel, and garlic. Simmer for 2 minutes.

Remove the pan from the heat, remove liver, and set the pan aside. Mince liver; set aside. Stir flour, pepper, and ketchup into the skillet. Add orange juice, broth, wine, and marmalade. Return liver to the pan. Bring to a boil, reduce heat, and simmer for 5 minutes.

To serve, pour orange sauce over duck.

(PHOTO, PAGE 158)

SERVES 4

California: Geyser Peak Winery, '93 Shiraz

France: Château Lynch-Bages, '90 Pauillac

DUCK:
- 1 (4- to 5-pound) duck
- 2 unpeeled oranges, quartered
- 1 clove garlic, chopped
- 1 teaspoon salt
- 3 black peppercorns
- 1/2 cup (1 stick) butter, melted
- 1/4 cup Burgundy
- 1/2 cup orange marmalade

BASTING SAUCE:
- 12 ounces apricot nectar
- 1 tablespoon soy sauce
- 1 teaspoon onion powder
- 1 tablespoon honey

ORANGE SAUCE:
- 3 tablespoons butter, divided into 2 tablespoons and remainder
- Duck liver
- 3 tablespoons brandy
- 2 tablespoons grated orange peel
- 1/2 teaspoon minced garlic
- 3 tablespoons flour
- 1/8 teaspoon pepper
- 1/2 teaspoon ketchup
- 1/2 cup orange juice
- 1 cup clear broth
- 1/4 cup Burgundy
- 1/4 cup orange marmalade

SOUPS AND STEWS

SOUPS ARE HOT NOW

Or they're very cold. Witness the Chilled Mango that makes a
marvelous first course in the summer. The hot ones range from a
very tasty Low-Fat Winter Soup to ones that are so hearty they
make a meal once you add some crusty bread, wine, and your
imagination. Recipes like Texas Corn-Sausage Soup fill the bill
and hungry appetites. We're finally learning what most Europeans
have known for ages: that the heartier soups get, the more they
help us to be satisfied with lighter meals. Go figure. Then, go find
a big pot and start making soup for supper tonight.

Beer Beef Stew

Mrs. Jack K. Grissom
Garland, TX

This is a hearty dish that I like to serve when I entertain my bridge club friends at our place near Holly Lake in East Texas. I've had the recipe for 15 or 20 years and forget where it came from. But, I always share it with the many people who have asked for it.

2 pounds lean beef, cut in
   2-inch cubes
½ cup flour
2 to 3 tablespoons oil for
   browning
1 large onion, cut in
   ¼-inch-thick slices
8 to 12 ounces mushrooms,
   quartered
2 garlic cloves, crushed
1½ tablespoons firmly packed
   light brown sugar
¼ cup chopped fresh parsley
1 bay leaf
¾ teaspoon dried thyme
2 teaspoons salt
¼ teaspoon pepper
1 (14.5-ounce) can beef broth
1 can beer
2 tablespoons red wine vinegar

Preheat oven to 325°. Dredge beef with flour, and brown in oil in a skillet. Transfer to a casserole dish, reserving the pan drippings. Add onion and mushrooms to the casserole dish, and set aside. In the pan drippings, brown garlic. Add sugar, parsley, bay leaf, thyme, salt, pepper, broth, and beer. Pour into the casserole dish, covering beef, onions, and mushrooms. Cover, and bake for 2 hours and 30 minutes, or until tender. Uncover, add vinegar, and return to the oven until hot and bubbly. Serve over noodles.

SERVES 4 TO 6

CREAM OF BROCCOLI SOUP WITHOUT THE CREAM

———— Dr. Eugene L. Gottlieb
Sedona, AZ

When I retired from my orthodontics practice, I became the chief cook at our house except for desserts, which are my wife's specialty. This soup is just as good made with asparagus, and can be served cold in the summertime.

Cut broccoli florets from stems, reserving broth and setting aside 2 or 3 florets for garnish. Cut each broccoli stalk into 5 or 6 pieces. In a deep skillet over low heat, melt butter. Add broccoli florets, onion, leek, celery, and potato. Cover, and simmer for 30 minutes, or until vegetables are tender.

Meanwhile, in a large saucepan over medium-high heat, bring stock, bouillon, and broccoli stalks to a boil. Reduce heat to medium-low, and simmer for 30 minutes. Strain stock, discarding stalks, and set aside.

In a blender, purée softened vegetables. Add to stock. Add lemon juice. Season with salt, pepper, and paprika.

To serve, ladle into soup bowls. Cut reserved broccoli florets into small pieces and sprinkle on the soup. Serve hot or cold.

SERVES 4

1 1/2 pounds broccoli
1/4 cup (1/2 stick) unsalted butter
1/2 cup chopped onion
1 cup chopped leek (white part only)
1 stalk celery, chopped
1 baking potato, peeled and diced
3 1/2 cups chicken stock
1 teaspoon powdered chicken bouillon
1 teaspoon lemon juice
Salt, pepper, and paprika to taste

SOUPS AND STEWS 187

CREAMY CARROT SOUP

Arnold M. Palmer
Los Angeles, CA

This is an absolutely delicious soup, served either hot or cold. When I am in a hurry, I use two cans of Swanson (or any brand) chicken broth instead of "homemade."

5 to 6 carrots, peeled
   and sliced
1½ cups chicken broth
1 medium onion, chopped
2 tablespoons white rice
   (uncooked)
Pinch grated fresh nutmeg
Salt and pepper to taste
Grated lemon peel for garnish
Chopped fresh parsley for
   garnish

Place carrots, broth, onion, rice, nutmeg, salt, and pepper in a medium saucepan. Bring to a boil, cover, reduce heat to medium-low, and simmer for 25 to 30 minutes until rice and carrots are tender. Let cool, and purée.

To serve, garnish with lemon peel and parsley.

SERVES 2

CASUALLY ELEGANT TOMATO SOUP

Shelley Mosley Stanzel
Dallas, TX

As a newlywed, I panicked the first time we invited business associates to dinner. They were all European artists and designers with sophisticated tastes. I barely knew how to cook! By chance, I caught a television cooking show and learned the basic recipe for simple tomato soup. I began to experiment and soon developed a foolproof, easy recipe that always prompts guests to ask for seconds.

6 tomatoes
½ cup (1 stick) butter
½ cup minced onions
   Chopped garlic to taste
3 cups chicken stock
½ cup milk or cream

Cut a skin-deep X in the top of each tomato. Drop into boiling water and blanch for 15 seconds. Remove from the pan and immediately plunge into ice water. Slip off the skins, dice, and set aside.

In a saucepan over medium heat, melt butter and sauté onions and garlic until onions are translucent. Add tomatoes. Cook until tomatoes fall apart. Add chicken stock, and simmer for 20 minutes. Stir with a wire whisk until smooth. Add milk, and stir to combine. Strain, discarding the solids.

SERVES 6

TEXAS CORN-SAUSAGE SOUP

Margaret Henry Amaya
Dallas, TX

My daughter in Atlanta gave me this recipe, but it originated in Texas. It makes a meal that is completely satisfying. My husband and I once lived in Germany and learned to love good German cooking. He likes to smoke meats, and I find this recipe comes closest to the dishes we enjoyed in Berlin.

In a stockpot over medium-high heat, sauté onion in oil until translucent. Cut links into small pieces, add to pot, and brown. Peel and chop potatoes, add to stockpot, add water, cover, and cook for 10 minutes, or until tender. Mash or chop up if desired. Add remaining ingredients; simmer for 15 minutes on low heat.

SERVES 4 TO 6

1 large Texas 1015 yellow onion
Vegetable oil for browning
2 pounds smoked sausage links
2 large Irish potatoes
2 cups water
1 stalk celery, diced
½ green bell pepper, seeded and diced
½ cup green onion
2 (14.5-ounce) cans creamed corn
2 tablespoons crushed red pepper
2 tablespoons minced garlic
2 tablespoons pepper
2 tablespoons chopped fresh parsley
2 tablespoons oregano
2 tablespoons bay leaves
2 to 4 tablespoons chopped jalapeños to taste
2 cups water
2 cups buttermilk

BOSTON FISH CHOWDER

Elle R. Rice
Newport Beach, CA

I was born and raised in Boston with a true pride of my heritage. In 1964, I moved to Arizona and then finally to California in 1969, bringing this taste of Boston to the West Coast, where it's been enjoyed many times.

FISH STOCK:

- 1/4 cup (1/2 stick) sweetened butter
- 3/4 cup peeled and chopped carrots
- 3 to 4 medium onions, minced
- 2 stalks celery, chopped
- 1 cup chopped mushrooms
- 2 cups dry white wine
  Pinch salt (optional)
- 12 white peppercorns
- 6 parsley sprigs
- 1 bay leaf
- 1 teaspoon dried thyme
  Bones and heads of 6 or 7 white-fleshed, non-oily fish, viscera and gills removed

FISH CHOWDER:

- 1/2 cup (1 stick) butter
- 1 cup carrots, peeled and sliced into thin pieces
- 2 stalks celery, diced
- 3 large baking potatoes
- 1 cup corn, cut from the cob (2 ears) or frozen
- 2 to 2 1/2 pounds boneless, skinless lean fish, cut into 2-inch chunks
  Sour cream for serving
  Chopped fresh parsley for garnish

To make fish stock, in a 4-quart stockpot over medium heat, melt butter. Add carrots and cook, stirring constantly, for 1 minute. Add onions, celery, and mushrooms. Cook covered, over low heat for 25 to 30 minutes, stirring occasionally until vegetables are tender and lightly colored. Add remaining ingredients, cover with water, raise heat to medium-high, and bring to a boil. Reduce heat to medium-low, and simmer with lid askew for 30 minutes. Remove from the heat, let cool, and pour through a cheesecloth-lined strainer, discarding the solids. Taste the stock. If it lacks intensity, return it to the pot and boil for 15 to 20 minutes. Cover, chill, and remove any solid fat that rises to the surface.

To make fish chowder, in a large stockpot over medium heat, melt butter. Add carrots, and cook, stirring constantly, for 1 minute. Add celery, potatoes, corn, fish chunks, and fish stock. Stir to combine, and cook until heated through.

To serve, put a dollop of sour cream in each bowl. Pour in chowder. Sprinkle with parsley.

Note: Flounder, sole, or other mild fish is recommended for the stock. For the chowder, cod, hake, haddock, monkfish, halibut, ocean pollack, sea bass, or catfish is recommended.

MAKES 2 TO 3 QUARTS

California: Monterey Vineyards, '94 Johannisberg Riesling

Portugal: Taylor, Fladgate & Yeatman, Dry Sherry

CURRIED CHICKEN AND LENTIL SOUP

Joyce Goldstein
San Francisco, CA

This is quite a hearty soup. If you increase the amount of chicken, you will have a meal in a bowl. Serve it with a leafy salad tossed with slices of melon, papaya, or mango, in a lemon or lime based vinaigrette.

Put lentils in a small saucepan. Add enough water to come 2 inches above lentils. Bring to a boil. Reduce heat to medium-low, and simmer for 25 minutes, or until tender. Set aside.

In a sauté pan, bring stock to a boil. Reduce the heat to medium-low, and poach chicken breasts for 6 to 8 minutes until tender when pierced. Remove chicken from stock, reserving stock. Let chicken cool enough to handle, cut into bite-sized pieces, and set aside.

In a saucepan over medium heat, melt butter, and sauté onions for 10 minutes, or until translucent. Add curry, ginger, and garlic, and cook for 2 minutes. Add reserved chicken stock and coconut cream, and simmer for 10 minutes. Add tomatoes. Drain lentils, add to the saucepan, raise the heat to medium-high, and bring to a boil. Reduce the heat to medium-low. Add lemon juice, salt, pepper, and chicken, and cook until heated through.

To serve, ladle into bowls and top with mint.

SERVES 6

3/4	cup brown lentils
4	cups chicken stock
2	boneless, skinless chicken breasts, halved
3	tablespoons butter
2	onions, diced
2	teaspoons curry powder
1/2	teaspoon ginger
1	teaspoon minced garlic
1/4	cup coconut cream
1	(14.5-ounce) can plum tomatoes, diced
1	teaspoon lemon juice
1	teaspoon salt
1/2	teaspoon pepper
3	tablespoons chopped fresh mint

Spain: Paul Cheneau, Blanc de Blanc

France: F.E. Trimbach, '94 Pinot Blanc, Alsace

CHILLED MANGO SOUP

Nancy Martinez
Dallas, TX

When mango season is at its peak and we are at our house in Mexico, hardly a day goes by without some of this glorious fruit on our table. My mother added this recipe to our mango repertoire. I serve it in individual glass icers, so it looks as good as it tastes and makes a refreshing and colorful beginning to a meal.

2 large mangoes
1½ cups chicken broth, chilled
1 cup plain yogurt
1 teaspoon sugar (optional)
1 tablespoon dry sherry
Salt and white pepper to taste

Peel, pit, and chop mangoes. Purée in a food processor with remaining ingredients, and chill for at least 2 hours. Garnish with mint.

Note: Mango varieties with less fiber, such as Staulfo, are best. To peel, pit, and dice mangoes, cut lengthwise through the skin on both sides, peel skin back, and cut the flesh off the pit in long vertical slices. Mangoes are messy and juicy, mango juice stains, and many people are allergic to the skin, so you may want to use gloves.

SERVES 4

CHILLED YELLOW PEPPER SOUP WITH SCALLOP CEVICHE VERDE

Stephan Pyles
Dallas, TX

DIRECTIONS FOR CHILLED YELLOW PEPPER SOUP:

Spear bell peppers with a fork and hold over low heat, turning until skin darkens and splits. Place in a paper bag, and let stand for 10 minutes. Meanwhile, soak saffron in water for 10 minutes. Peel peppers, and put in a medium saucepan with saffron and water. Add onion, carrot, garlic, chili, and stock. Bring to a boil, reduce the heat to low, and simmer for 5 minutes. Transfer to a blender, and blend for 1 minute. Scrape down the sides, and blend for 1 minute, or until smooth. Strain into a mixing bowl, and chill. Blend in cream, milk, and salt.

DIRECTIONS FOR SCALLOP CEVICHE VERDE:

Marinate scallops in lime juice for 1 hour in the refrigerator. Meanwhile, husk and mince tomatillos, and place in a mixing bowl. Seed and dice tomato; add to bowl. Seed and mince chilies; add to bowl. Peel, pit, and dice avocado; add to bowl. When scallops are done marinating, drain, reserving 1 tablespoon lime juice. Add to bowl with reserved lime juice and remaining ingredients. Chill for 30 minutes.

To serve, ladle the Chilled Yellow Pepper Soup into chilled bowls. Garnish each bowl with a generous portion of the Scallop Ceviche Verde and a tablespoon of sour cream.

(PHOTO, PAGE 157)

SERVES 4

California: Benziger of Glen Ellen, '93 Sémillon

Oregon: Henry Estate, '94 Riesling, Umpqua Valley

SOUP:

- 3 medium yellow bell peppers
- 1/4 teaspoon saffron threads
- 1 tablespoon warm water
- 1/2 cup chopped onion
- 1/4 cup chopped carrot
- 1 clove garlic, minced
- 1/2 serrano or jalapeño chili, seeded
- 1 1/2 cups chicken stock
- 1/2 cup heavy cream
- 1/2 cup milk
  Salt to taste
- 4 tablespoons sour cream for garnish

CEVICHE:

- 8 ounces sea scallops, thinly sliced
- 1/4 cup lime juice
- 3 medium tomatillos
- 1/2 small tomato
- 3 serrano chilies
- 1 small avocado
- 1 clove garlic, minced
- 4 tablespoons diced scallions
- 1 tablespoon olive oil
- 1 teaspoon minced fresh basil
  Salt to taste

Lentil and Vegetable Soup

Katy Massoud
Dallas, TX

After I married into a Lebanese family, I decided to try to make my own version of lentil soup. I really like vegetables, so I concocted this recipe, which has both. It may not be pure Lebanese, but it's delicious.

1 cup lentils
1 to 2 ham hocks
8 to 12 cups water
1 bay leaf
2 carrots
2 turnips
1 large potato
2 stalks celery
2 small tomatoes
6 ounces string beans
1 large onion
1 tablespoon olive oil
Salt and pepper to taste
1/2 cup chopped fresh Swiss chard

Soak lentils in water overnight. Rinse and drain lentils. Place with ham hocks, water, and bay leaf in a large stockpot over medium heat. Cover, and cook for 15 to 20 minutes until lentils are tender.

Meanwhile, peel and chop carrots, turnips, and potato; add to stockpot. Chop celery, tomatoes, and string beans; add to pot. Cook for 10 minutes.

Meanwhile, chop onion, and sauté in oil in a separate pan until translucent. Add to stockpot. Add salt and pepper and Swiss chard. Cook for 10 minutes, or until all vegetables are tender.

Serve with lemon wedges and parsley.

SERVES 6 TO 8

 California: Château St. Jean, Vin Blanc
 California: Martin Brothers Winery, Aleatico

SWEET POTATO SOUP WITH CILANTRO PESTO

Mrs. vanAlen Hollomon
Dallas, TX

This soup is my own version of one that I enjoyed recently at Popolos restaurant in Dallas. It combines some of the best tastes to be enjoyed in Southwestern cooking.

DIRECTIONS FOR SWEET POTATO SOUP:

In a stockpot over medium heat, melt butter, and sauté onion until tender. Add remaining ingredients, and cook for 20 minutes, or until potatoes are fork-tender. Transfer the soup to a blender, and purée. If necessary, thin with additional chicken stock.

DIRECTIONS FOR CILANTRO PESTO:

Blend all pesto ingredients in a food processor to form a smooth paste.

To serve, ladle soup into bowls. Float a spoonful of pesto (at room temperature) on top. Accompany with grilled chicken or salmon topped with pesto.

SERVES 4

SOUP:
- 2 tablespoons butter
- 1 onion, chopped
- 2 or 3 medium sweet potatoes, peeled and sliced
- 1 quart chicken stock
- 1/8 teaspoon cayenne, or to taste

PESTO:
- 1/4 cup pine nuts
- 3 garlic cloves
- 1 bunch cilantro, stems removed
- 1/2 jalapeño, seeded and chopped
- 1/4 cup olive oil
- 3 tablespoons lime juice
- Salt to taste

LOW-FAT WINTER SOUP

Doris B. Suttin
North Miami Beach, FL

I spend about 10 days out of every month in Dallas, and it's there that I do most of my cooking for my boyfriend. He will not eat any fat at all. So I created this soup one cold, rainy day, and he loved it. For me, it was a good way to chase away the winter blues.

1 tablespoon vegetable oil
4 carrots, peeled and sliced
4 celery stalks, sliced
1 small onion, diced
1/2 yellow bell pepper, seeded and sliced
1/2 red bell pepper, seeded and sliced
1/2 orange bell pepper, seeded and sliced
8 cups water
1 (14.5-ounce) can whole tomatoes
1 teaspoon parsley
1/4 teaspoon thyme
1/2 teaspoon sour salt
1/2 teaspoon kosher salt
1/4 teaspoon pepper

In a large saucepan over medium-high heat, warm oil, and sauté carrots, celery, onion, and bell peppers until tender. Add remaining ingredients. Bring to a slow rolling boil for 1 minute. Reduce heat to medium-low, and simmer for 1 hour. Adjust seasonings to taste.

Serve with rice or noodles and hot crusty bread.

MAKES 6 SERVINGS

CREAMY TOMATO BISQUE WITH LUMP CRABMEAT AND A CHIFFONADE OF FRESH BASIL

Susan Parsell
Charleston, SC

I'm a transplanted Texan who now enjoys the foods of my new home in South Carolina so much that, when I had the opportunity, I bought into a restaurant. My chef, Donald Barickman, makes this wonderful soup with tomatoes from his grandparents' garden.

Drain crabmeat, pick out any shells, and set aside. In a heavy-bottomed stockpot over medium heat, warm oil, and sauté onion and garlic for 2 minutes, stirring constantly, until onion is translucent. Reduce the heat to low, and make a roux by adding flour and stirring until combined. Cook for 5 minutes, stirring constantly. Raise the heat to medium, and add half of broth, stirring vigorously. Cook, stirring constantly, until broth begins to thicken and becomes smooth. Gradually add remaining broth and bouillon. Cook, stirring constantly, until broth thickens. Raise the heat and bring to a boil. Reduce to medium-low, and simmer for 5 minutes. Drain juice from canned tomatoes into the stockpot. Cut tomatoes in half, remove seeds, dice, and add to stockpot. Add ½ cup basil, tomato sauce, and tomato juice. Simmer for 10 minutes. Skim off and discard any skin that forms. Add cream. Bring to a simmer, skim again if necessary, and add salt and pepper.

Ladle the soup into bowls. Garnish with crabmeat and remaining basil.

MAKES 8 SERVINGS

- 8 ounces lump crabmeat for garnish
- ¼ cup plus 1 teaspoon extra-virgin olive oil
- ½ cup chopped onion
- 1 teaspoon minced garlic
- ½ cup flour
- 3 cups chicken broth, divided in half
- 1 chicken bouillon cube
- 1 (14.5-ounce) can whole Italian-style tomatoes, undrained
- ¾ cup chopped fresh basil, divided into ½ cup and remainder
- 2 (14.5-ounce) cans tomato sauce
- 2 cups tomato juice
- 1 cup heavy cream
- ½ teaspoon salt (optional) Dash white pepper (optional)

Cajun Shrimp Jambalaya

Mrs. K.R. Tharp
Dallas, TX

This authentic Cajun recipe is over 100 years old and was given to my grandmother by a dear friend. Over four generations of our family have enjoyed it to this day.

1 cup white rice (uncooked)
3 slices bacon, cut up
1 onion, chopped
1½ large green bell peppers, seeded and chopped
3 cloves garlic, crushed
1 (6-ounce) can tomato paste
Dash paprika
3 tablespoons chopped fresh thyme, or 1 tablespoon dried
½ teaspoon salt
¼ teaspoon red pepper
2 (14.5-ounce) cans crushed tomatoes
½ pound cooked ham, diced
1½ pounds shrimp, cleaned and cooked
¼ cup chopped fresh parsley, or 2 tablespoons dried

Cook rice according to the package directions, and set aside. In a large skillet over medium heat, cook bacon until light brown. Add onion, green peppers, and garlic, and sauté until tender. Blend in tomato paste, paprika, thyme, salt, and red pepper. Stir in rice, tomatoes, ham, shrimp, and parsley. Cook until heated through.

SERVES 8

 Spain: Emilio Lustau, Deluxe Cream Sherry, Solera
 Portugal: Blandís, Madeira, Rainwater

WHITE GAZPACHO SOUP

Carole G. Markoff
Beverly Hills, CA

I really can't recall where I first obtained this recipe. At any rate, I know that it is a favorite with all my guests. I do so much volunteer work that my entertaining is usually limited to holiday dinners which I like to build around a theme.

Peel cucumbers; mince in food processor. Add garlic, sour cream, 1/2 cup yogurt, salt, and pepper; blend. Adjust consistency by adding stock if too thick or more yogurt if too thin. Add Tabasco®, and adjust seasoning to taste.

Place in a covered container and chill overnight.

To serve, garnish with tomatoes, scallions, parsley, and almonds. (PHOTO, PAGE 156)

SERVES 6

California: Callaway Vineyard, Pinot Gris, Temecula
Portugal: Blandís Reserve (5 years), Verdelho

2 medium cucumbers
2 cloves garlic, crushed
1 pint sour cream
1/2 to 3/4 cup plain yogurt
   as needed
Salt and pepper to taste
1/4 to 1/2 cup chicken stock
   (if needed)
3 dashes Tabasco®
Chopped tomatoes, scallions,
   and parsley for garnish
Slivered almonds
   for garnish

Sauces and Dressings

Sauces and dressings are often what makes the difference between a ho-hum meal and an interesting one. Before cooking, they're called marinades. At the table, they're the secret of a successful salad. And what would pasta be without a zesty sauce? Nothing else on the menu offers such opportunities for originality and experimentation with flavors. We found our chef panelists all to be enthusiastic supporters of the new art of *infusion*. To us amateurs, that means flavoring oils with just the right herbs and spices, and that opens up a whole new world of good-tasting food!

APPLE CHUTNEY

Suzanne G. Keith
Houston, TX

My mother married in Calcutta in 1920. After living on rubber plantations in India, Africa, and South America, she developed into a very imaginative cook and hostess. I grew up loving curry, and thinking chutney was a staple to be whipped up with any fresh fruit, like other mothers made Jell-O™.

4 medium tart, firm apples
1 onion, chopped
2 teaspoons mustard seed
1 cup raisins
1 cup firmly packed light
    brown sugar
1½ tablespoons chili peppers,
    finely chopped
2 tablespoons minced garlic
4 (2-inch) pieces fresh
    gingerroot, minced
  Zest and juice of 1 lemon
½ cup apple juice

Peel, core, and chop apples.

Combine all ingredients in a medium saucepan, and bring to a boil over medium-high heat. Reduce heat to medium-low, and simmer for 5 minutes, or until apples are cooked but retain their shape. Chill until ready to serve.

Serve with chorizo pork.

MAKES 3 CUPS

202 SAUCES AND DRESSINGS

Béarnaise Sauce

Ebe Frasse
San Jose, CA

I am a fifth-generation Californian who loves to cook and entertain guests on my terrace, which overlooks orchards and the city of San Jose. I usually grill steaks for eight or 10 friends and always offer this Béarnaise Sauce which they all love with their steaks.

In a small saucepan over medium heat, simmer wine, vinegar, tarragon, and onion until the liquid is reduced to 2 tablespoons. Strain, discarding tarragon and onion. Put egg yolks in a double boiler, and slowly beat in the liquid with a wire whisk. Heat over hot, but not boiling, water, beating constantly with a wire whisk, until slightly thickened. Beat in cold butter in small portions. Add melted butter by drops, and stir to combine.

Serve with tournedos of beef, French-style.

SERVES 6

- 1/4 cup dry white wine
- 2 tablespoons tarragon wine vinegar
- 1/2 teaspoon dried tarragon
- 1 tablespoon minced green onion
- 3 egg yolks, lightly beaten
- 2 tablespoons cold butter
- 1/2 cup (1 stick) butter, melted

Chocoholics' Hot Fudge Sauce

Bonnie Aaron Levin
Los Angeles, CA

This recipe was given to me years ago by my late aunt. It is simple to make and has thrilled chocoholics from Chicago to Los Angeles.

Melt all ingredients in a double boiler over low heat, stirring constantly, until smooth.

Note: Sauce may be refrigerated in a microwave-safe glass jar. When ready to serve, remove lid, and warm in a pan of hot water or microwave. If the sauce has hardened, thin it with sour cream.

MAKES 2 1/2 CUPS

- 4 ounces semisweet chocolate
- 2 ounces unsweetened chocolate
- 40 marshmallows
- 3/4 cup sour cream
- 2 teaspoons vanilla extract
  Few drops almond extract

QUICK HOLLANDAISE

Joan Sheppard
Godfrey, IL

As a Christmas morning tradition at our house, my husband always fixes Eggs Benedict, which everyone loves. This is his tried and true recipe, which he is allowing me to share with all of you.

½ cup (1 stick) butter
4 egg yolks
2 to 3 tablespoons lemon juice to taste
¼ teaspoon salt
Dash pepper

Melt butter. Meanwhile, place yolks, lemon juice, salt, and pepper in a blender. With the blender running at high speed, slowly add hot butter in a thin, steady stream.

Serve on shrimp, vegetables, fish, or Eggs Benedict.

MAKES 1 CUP

BARBECUE SAUCE

Cindy Kypreos
Fort Worth, TX

In 1955, while my father was stationed in Iceland, he made friends with a tribe of Eskimos. They gave him this Barbecue Sauce recipe, but made him promise never to give it to anyone else. It was his most prized possession for years, but on my wedding day, he gave it to me. I think enough time has passed for me to share it with you.

1 small red onion, chopped
1 tablespoon mustard
2 tablespoons Worcestershire sauce
2 cloves garlic, peeled and sliced
1 tablespoon sugar
1 tablespoon hickory smoke salt
¼ cup lemon juice
½ cup vegetable oil
1 teaspoon Tabasco® sauce
2 teaspoons hickory sauce
1 cup ketchup
1 cup water
1 tablespoon seasoned salt

Mix all ingredients together and chill for 24 hours.

MAKES 4 CUPS

DILL SAUCE

Evy Rappaport
Beverly Hills, CA

This is my favorite all-purpose sauce. I use it whenever I serve gravlax and assorted other fish entrées and vegetables. I even find it works as a base to many homemade soups.

In a small bowl, combine dark mustard, Chinese hot mustard, Bavarian grainy mustard, and dry mustard. Add sugar and vinegar; mixture will be like paste. Stir with a wire whisk until blended. Add oil; blend. Stir in dill. Transfer to an airtight jar and chill until ready to use.

Note: Dill Sauce will keep for several weeks. For less bite, substitute rice wine vinegar for the white vinegar.

MAKES ²/₃ CUP

- 2 tablespoons dark mustard, highly seasoned
- 1 tablespoon Chinese hot mustard
- 1 tablespoon Bavarian grainy mustard
- 1 tablespoon dry mustard
- 3 tablespoons sugar
- 2 tablespoons white vinegar
- ⅓ cup vegetable oil
- 3 tablespoons snipped fresh dill

GREEN GODDESS DRESSING

Sue Zelickson
Minneapolis, MN

This is a wonderful dressing my mother made for family gatherings, holidays and special dinners. Everyone loved it, and we used the leftover dressing whenever there was any, as a dip.

Blend all ingredients in a blender or food processor. Chill for at least 2 hours.

To serve, toss with torn-up romaine lettuce, sliced cucumbers, and diced green bell peppers. Or serve as a dip for raw vegetables or as a topping for crab mold.

MAKES 3 CUPS

- 1 (2-ounce) can chopped anchovies, or 2 squirts paste
- 3 tablespoons snipped fresh chives, or 1 tablespoon dried
- 1 tablespoon lemon juice
- 3 tablespoons vinegar
- 1 cup sour cream
- 1 cup mayonnaise
- ½ cup chopped fresh parsley
  Salt and pepper to taste

MANGO SAUCE

Patricia A. Parkinson
Humble, TX

My husband and I enjoy cooking together and creating our own recipes out of whatever we find that looks tempting in the market. Mangoes, limes, and bananas are plentiful in ethnically diverse Houston, so we have a ready supply for lots of experimenting. We use this sauce on toasted bagels or stirred into steamed summer squash and onions. It's a great marinade, too!

2 mangoes
1 banana (optional)
⅔ cup sugar, or to taste
Juice of 2 large limes, or to taste
1 tablespoon brandy (optional)

To peel, pit, and dice mangoes, cut lengthwise through the skin on both sides, peel skin back, and cut flesh off the pit in long vertical slices. Peel and chop banana. In a saucepan over low heat, simmer mangoes and banana with sugar and lime juice, stirring frequently, for 25 minutes. Add brandy and simmer for 5 minutes, or until sugar is absorbed and mangoes appear glazed.

Serve over chicken or pork cutlets, and accompany with wild rice. Or serve over ice cream or waffles.

Note: For a thicker sauce, dissolve 2 teaspoons cornstarch in ¼ cup white wine and add during last 5 minutes of cooking.

MAKES 2 CUPS

GRILLED FRUIT RELISH

Catherine A. Byles
Dallas, TX

I never make anything the same way twice, but this is the basic recipe for the fruit relish we like to use on meats grilled outside in the summertime. It's a little like the salsa at Blue Mesa restaurant, and a little like chutney, and delicious with pork or chicken.

2 peaches
2 plums
¼ cup diced red onion
1 tablespoon sugar
1 tablespoon minced fresh sage leaves
1 tablespoon balsamic vinegar
1 tablespoon butter, melted

Grill or broil peaches and plums until fruit is soft and skin blackens. Plunge into cold water, and slip off and discard skins. Pit and dice the fruit. Add remaining ingredients, and stir to combine.

Serve with grilled pork or chicken.

MAKES 1 CUP

Mango-Pineapple Salsa

Dallas Shea
San Francisco, CA

My husband and I celebrated our second wedding anniversary at Poipu Beach in Kauai. Every evening at the Hyatt Regency Club, we feasted on a sumptuous appetizer buffet, highlighted by this delicious salsa. Here is my version, which we now enjoy at home with fond memories. We are already planning our next year's celebration at this great resort.

1 cup pitted, peeled, and diced mango
1 cup diced pineapple
1 cup seeded and diced tomato
½ cup diced red onion
¼ cup diced green onion (white part only)
¼ cup snipped fresh chives
½ cup diced red bell pepper
3 tablespoons chopped fresh cilantro
1 serrano chili, seeded and minced
2 tablespoons lime juice
2 tablespoons extra-virgin olive oil
Salt and pepper to taste

Combine all ingredients in a small bowl. Cover, and chill for 1 to 2 hours to allow seasonings to blend.

Serve with crunchy coconut shrimp, shrimp cocktail, grilled shrimp, or grilled chicken or fish.

Note: Mangoes are messy and juicy, mango juice stains, and many people are allergic to the skin, so you may want to use gloves.

MAKES 5 CUPS

Spicy Mayonnaise

Mollie H. Grober
Fort Smith, AR

This is my friends' favorite birthday or Christmas gift. It's wonderfully tart, and sometimes I change it a little by substituting tomato paste and basil for the onion and Worcestershire sauce when we use it on smoked turkey. However, my family likes it on just about anything.

1 yolk of a large egg at room temperature
1 cup vegetable oil, divided into ¼ cup and remainder
3 tablespoons lemon juice, strained
½ teaspoon salt
½ teaspoon sugar
½ teaspoon dry mustard
⅛ teaspoon paprika
Dash cayenne, or to taste
1 teaspoon grated onion
1 teaspoon Worcestershire sauce

Blend egg yolk and ¼ cup oil in a blender for a couple of seconds. Add lemon juice, salt, sugar, mustard, paprika, cayenne, onion, and Worchestershire, and blend for 10 seconds. With blender running, slowly pour in remaining oil. Blend until thick.

(PHOTO, PAGE 154)

MAKES 1 CUP

Sour Cream Horseradish Sauce for Prime Rib

Mr. and Mrs. Eric Lieber
Beverly Hills, CA

For prime rib, yes. But my television producer husband loves it so much that he puts it on everything but his breakfast cereal. I always include it on the menu of my two big parties each year–at Christmas and at Oscar time.

Combine all ingredients and stir until smooth. Chill until ready to serve.

SERVES 4 TO 6

4 tablespoons sour cream
2 tablespoons ground fresh horseradish
1/2 teaspoon Worcestershire sauce
1/2 teaspoon dry mustard
4 drops Tabasco® sauce
1/2 teaspoon salt
Pinch white pepper

Mint Pesto Sauce

Christine M. Strohm
Sierra Madre, CA

I love lamb and find this sauce so much better than any mint jelly. It can be spread on the meat just before the final roasting or grilling is done. I think the goat cheese and nuts really make a difference.

In a food processor, mince garlic. Pull mint leaves from the stems, and add to garlic. Add cheese and nuts, and process until combined. With the food processor running, slowly add oil and blend until smooth.
Note: The pesto may be stored in an airtight container in the refrigerator for up to 5 days.

MAKES 1 CUP

2 large cloves garlic, peeled
1 (2-ounce) bunch mint
4 ounces goat cheese
2/3 cup walnuts or pine nuts, toasted (about 3 ounces)
1/4 cup extra-virgin olive oil

Shiitake Mushroom and Shallot Sauce

Suzanne M. Goodman
Santa Ana, CA

I've prepared this sauce for many special occasions, but always being sure to use only the best meat. The butcher I bought meat from for years no longer has a retail shop, but continues to deliver his high-quality meats to his ever-faithful clientele, which includes me. One more thing: This sauce is richly flavored, with no salt and almost no fat.

1 pound shiitake mushrooms
5 cups (40 ounces) salt-free beef stock, divided into 1 cup and remainder
1 pound shallots
  Cooking spray to coat enameled pot
1 cup merlot
1 bay leaf

Clean mushrooms; remove and reserve the stems; cut the caps into 1/3-inch-thick slices, and set aside.

In a small saucepan over medium-low heat, simmer the stems in 1 cup stock for 25 minutes, or until stock is reduced to 1/2 cup. Strain, reserving stock in a container with a pour spout and discarding the stems. Peel shallots. Coat a heavy 3-quart enameled pot with cooking spray, and sauté shallots, stirring constantly, over medium heat for 10 minutes, or until lightly browned. Remove from the pot, and set aside. Spray the pot again, and sauté mushroom slices over high heat for 5 minutes, or until liquid is released. Remove mushrooms from the pot, reserving the liquid in the pot. Cover mushrooms, and set aside. Add the mushroom liquid to the reduced beef stock; cover and set aside. Return shallots to the pot. Add merlot, bring to a rolling boil, and boil until wine is reduced to 1 tablespoon. Add remaining beef stock and bay leaf; bring to a boil. Reduce heat to medium-low, and simmer until liquid is reduced to 2 cups. Discard bay leaf. Return mushrooms to the pot. Add reserved mushroom-stock mixture, raise the temperature to medium-high, and bring to a boil. Reduce heat to medium-low, and simmer for 5 minutes.

Serve with roasted veal loin.

Note: Sauce may be prepared a day before serving, covered, and chilled.

MAKES 6 1/2 TO 7 CUPS

BASIC RED SAUCE

Catherine Handelsman
Glencoe, IL

My husband and I are near vegetarian and dedicated gardeners, so we needed a pasta sauce we could enjoy three or four times a week and vary with whatever's current in our garden. Sometimes we spice it up (alla arrabiata) with dried chilies, extra garlic, and a pat of butter, or we add shrimp or scallops. This sauce freezes well. Mangia, mangia!

Peel onion, carrots, and garlic. Shred with celery in a food processor. Transfer to a large stockpot. Add oil, and cook over medium-low heat for 10 minutes. Add tomatoes, oregano, sugar, salt, pepper, and chilies, and stir to combine. Simmer for 1½ to 2 hours.

To serve, pour over pasta.

Note: Two medium zucchinis may be substituted for carrots. Ten fresh medium tomatoes or 14 Italian plum tomatoes, peeled and diced, may be substituted for the canned.

MAKES 6 TO 8 CUPS

1 large onion
3 large carrots
4 cloves garlic
3 large stalks celery
¼ cup extra-virgin olive oil
3 (14.5-ounce) cans crushed tomatoes
1½ cups chopped fresh oregano, or ½ cup dried
½ cup sugar
1 teaspoon salt
2 teaspoons pepper, or to taste
2 to 3 dried chili peppers to taste

FRESH HERB VINAIGRETTE

Ardis Bartle
Houston, TX

This is so good that at Christmastime I bottle it and decorate the bottles with festive gold and red ribbons. It's always a hit.

In a bowl, combine vinegar, basil, dill, thyme, garlic, and shallot. Slowly whisk in olive oil. Season to taste. Whisk again before using.

MAKES 1 CUP

¼ cup red wine vinegar
1 tablespoon fresh chopped basil
½ teaspoon fresh snipped dill
½ teaspoon minced thyme
1 tablespoon minced garlic
1 teaspoon minced shallot
¾ cup olive oil
Salt and pepper to taste

VEGETABLES

We had more vegetable recipes submitted than any other single category. On many menus, they've moved up from a supporting role to a starring one. There are so many ways to combine vegetables, and new ways to cook them besides boiling, steaming, and baking. Grilling is the newest fashion in vegetable cookery. Almost every day, we discover a new vegetable, a new variety of a favorite one, or even a new way vegetables can contribute to our health. All this talk makes you want to go out and spade up the garden, doesn't it?

Marinated Asparagus

— Amanda Shams
Atlanta, GA

This is the only green vegetable my 10- and 12-year-old daughters will eat. In fact, Samantha, who is the "elegant" one, always wants it served on a silver platter with tongs. Grown-ups love it, too, as I can testify, having served it to my Gourmet Club many times.

1½ pounds asparagus
4 tablespoons red wine vinegar
1 tablespoon Dijon mustard
1 teaspoon salt
¼ teaspoon pepper
½ teaspoon paprika
1 to 2½ teaspoons sugar to taste
1 shallot, minced
½ cup olive oil
2 eggs, hard-boiled
1 tablespoon diced red bell pepper

Steam asparagus until tender; set aside in a shallow serving dish, uncovered, to let cool. Chill, uncovered, for at least 10 minutes. Meanwhile, in a small mixing bowl, whisk together vinegar, mustard, salt, pepper, paprika, sugar, and shallot. Slowly add oil, stirring to combine. Cover, and chill for at least 10 minutes.

Separate egg whites from yolks. Grate whites over asparagus. Grate yolks over whites. Sprinkle red pepper on top. Drizzle the dressing over asparagus. (PHOTO, PAGE 154)

SERVES 4

BODACIOUS BEANS

Jo Dunn
Sugar Land, TX

As a native Texan, I was practically raised on ham and beans. But realizing how important it is to lower fat intake, I was thrilled when a friend suggested using turkey instead. I combined both our recipes to come up with this one, and it's just as smoky and delicious as the old way.

Pick through beans, discarding any rubble, and soak overnight in a pot of water.

Drain and rinse beans. Transfer to a stockpot, cover with water, and bring to a boil over medium-high heat. Skim off foam. Add remaining ingredients, stir to combine, cover, reduce heat to medium-low, and simmer for 1 hour and 30 minutes. Uncover, and simmer for 1 hour, stirring frequently to prevent sticking.

Remove turkey legs, debone, and remove skin. Return turkey meat to the stockpot. Cook until thick.
Serve with Jalapeño Cornbread Muffins (Page 54).

SERVES 8 TO 10

1 pound beans or black-eyed peas (uncooked)
1 (14.5-ounce) can chopped tomatoes with chilies
1 green bell pepper, seeded and chopped
1 head garlic, chopped
1 (8-ounce) can tomato sauce
5 stalks celery, chopped
4 green onion tops, snipped
1 Texas 1015 onion, chopped
1/2 cup chopped fresh parsley, or 1/4 cup dried
1 teaspoon chili powder
1 tablespoon sugar (omit when using black-eyed peas)
Creole seasoning to taste
Chopped fresh okra to taste (optional)
2 smoked turkey legs

Cuban Black Beans

Jeri Greenberg
Washington, D.C.

A friend, who is a Cuban expatriate, shared her husband's family recipe with me. In Cuba, it's just not a meal without a dish of spicy black beans. In addition to being delicious, they are low in fat.

1 pound black beans
  (uncooked)
1 large onion, chopped
1 green bell pepper, chopped
1 tablespoon oregano
1 tablespoon cumin
2 large cloves garlic, minced
2 tablespoons vinegar
1/4 teaspoon pepper
2 teaspoons salt

In a stockpot over medium-low heat, mix together beans, onion, green pepper, oregano, cumin, garlic, vinegar, and pepper. Cover with water, and simmer for 6 hours. Stir in salt.

To serve, spoon over rice.

SERVES 8

Top-Secret Green Beans

Marjorie H. Watkins
Glencoe, IL

For years, I refused to tell what I added to my green beans to give them a unique flavor and texture. One daughter who loves the beans, but hates anchovies, wishes the secret ingredient had remained a mystery to her.

2 pounds green beans
1 rounded tablespoon
  anchovy paste
2 tablespoons olive oil
3 tablespoons unsalted butter
2 teaspoons minced garlic
1/2 cup chopped fresh Italian
  flat-leaf parsley

Trim green beans; cut diagonally into bite-sized pieces. Steam until crisp-tender. Remove, and cover with aluminum foil to keep warm, reserving cooking water. Whip anchovy paste into olive oil. Melt butter in a skillet over medium-high heat; sauté garlic until golden. Stir in anchovy paste-oil mixture, beans, and 1 tablespoon or more as desired reserved steaming liquid. Cook, stirring occasionally, until heated through.

To serve, toss with parsley.

SERVES 6 TO 8

Tuscan-Style White Beans

Elaine Y. Tucker
St. Louis, MO

Years ago, when I was a buyer for Neiman Marcus, I lunched with the Pratesi family at a small restaurant in Pistoria, near Florence. It was January, we sat by the fireside and I tasted this dish for the first time. I have made it many times since.

Pick through beans, discarding any rubble, and soak overnight in a pot of water.

Drain and rinse beans. Preheat oven to 300°. In a large saucepan over medium-high heat, bring 4 cups water to a boil. Add beans, prosciutto, sage, leek, and oil, and bring to a boil. Transfer to a casserole dish, cover, and bake for 2 hours. Add tomatoes, cover, and bake for 30 minutes.

To serve, stir in vinegar, salt, and pepper.

SERVES 8

- 2 cups (12 ounces) Great Northern white beans (uncooked)
- 4 cups water
- 1/4 pound prosciutto, chopped
- 2 teaspoons dried sage
- 1 leek, white part only, chopped
- 2 tablespoons olive oil
- 1 (28-ounce) can plum tomatoes, drained and chopped
- 1 tablespoon balsamic vinegar
- 1/2 teaspoon salt
- 1/2 teaspoon pepper

BROCCOLI-STUFFED ONIONS

Elizabeth M. Wood
Dallas, TX

For more than 25 years, this dish has been changing the minds of people who thought they didn't like onions or broccoli or both. It's a wonderful side dish for special dinners. At Christmastime, I sprinkle it with paprika for a festive look.

3 medium Spanish onions,
   peeled and cut in half
1 (10-ounce) package frozen
   chopped broccoli
1/2 cup grated Parmesan cheese
1/3 cup mayonnaise
2 teaspoons lemon juice
2 tablespoons butter or
   margarine
2 tablespoons flour
1/4 teaspoon salt
2/3 cup milk
1 (3-ounce) package cream
   cheese, cubed

Preheat oven to 375°. Parboil onions in salted water for 10 to 12 minutes. Meanwhile, cook broccoli according to package directions. Drain onions and broccoli. Remove centers of onions, leaving 3/4-inch edges. Place onion shells in a baking dish. Chop onion centers; combine with broccoli, Parmesan, mayonnaise, and lemon juice. Spoon into onion shells. In a saucepan over medium heat, melt butter. Blend in flour, salt, and milk. Cook until thick, stirring constantly. Remove from heat; blend in cream cheese. Spoon over stuffed onions. Bake, uncovered, for 20 minutes.

SERVES 6

Broccoli and Olives with Garlic and Hot Pepper Vinaigrette

Joyce Goldstein
San Francisco, CA

This spicy vinaigrette would be good on cauliflower or zucchini as well. Serve hot or at room temperature.

Heat oil in a small saucepan. Add pepper flakes, and steep until oil is red. Let cool, strain, add vinegar and garlic, and season with salt and pepper. Cut florets from broccoli stems, reserving both. Peel stems. Bring a large pot of salted water to a boil. Add broccoli florets and stems, and cook until crisp-tender. Drain.

To serve warm: Warm vinaigrette and olives in a small saucepan, and spoon over broccoli. Serve immediately.

To serve as a salad: Plunge broccoli into ice water to retain color. Drain, and wipe dry. Chill until needed. Remove from refrigerator, and let stand until room temperature. Place on a salad platter or on individual salad plates. Drizzle with vinaigrette. Sprinkle with olives. (PHOTO, PAGE 145)

SERVES 4 TO 6

½ cup olive oil
2 teaspoons hot pepper flakes
2 tablespoons red wine vinegar
2 cloves garlic, minced
    Salt and pepper to taste
1 large or 2 small heads
    broccoli
1 cup pitted and sliced black
    olives

CARROT LOAF

Sara M. Dunham
Baton Rouge, LA

This is a favorite for all our family gatherings, whether they are in Baton Rouge or at our Barrel Springs Ranch in Texas. We serve it with almost any entrée because it looks elegant and tastes so good.

2 pounds carrots, peeled and cut into ¼-inch pieces
½ cup (1 stick) unsalted butter, divided into ¼ cup, 2 tablespoons, and 2 tablespoons
4 ounces mushrooms, sliced
8 ounces spinach, stems removed
5 eggs
4 ounces grated Swiss cheese
1 teaspoon salt
1 teaspoon pepper

Line an 8½x4½x2½-inch loaf pan with aluminum foil, and grease the foil. In a sauté pan over medium heat, melt ¼ cup butter, and sauté carrots until tender. Remove from the pan, dice, and set aside in a large mixing bowl. Preheat oven to 400°. In the same sauté pan over high heat, melt 2 tablespoons butter, and sauté mushrooms for 2 minutes. Remove from the pan, dice, and add to carrots. In the same pan, melt 2 tablespoons butter, and sauté spinach until wilted. Chop, and set aside separately.

In a medium mixing bowl, beat together eggs and cheese; add to carrot mixture, and stir to combine. Season with salt and pepper. Spread half of the carrot mixture in the prepared loaf pan, cover with spinach, and add remaining carrot mixture. Place in a shallow pan of warm water, and bake for 1 hour and 15 minutes, or until a knife inserted in the center comes out clean.

To serve, invert onto a serving platter and remove the foil.

(PHOTO, PAGE 145)

SERVES 6

EAST INDIAN CAULIFLOWER

Mrs. Robert W. Stuart III
Dallas, TX

We stepped from the Orient Express into the most delightful village and a cottage which was to be our home for several months. Our housekeeper from India had the most wonderful variations for curry, from which we adapted this recipe.

Steam cauliflower for 5 minutes, or until tender to the touch; set aside. In a small bowl, whisk together yogurt, sour cream, and lemon juice; set aside. Warm oil in a large non-stick frying pan over medium heat; sauté onion and bell pepper for 5 minutes, or until tender. Add ginger, ground coriander, cumin, turmeric, and ground red pepper. Cook, stirring constantly, for 1 minute. Add cauliflower; cook, stirring constantly, for 2 minutes. Reduce heat to low. Stir in yogurt mixture, and cook for 2 minutes, stirring constantly.

To serve, sprinkle with cilantro.

(PHOTO, PAGE 151)

SERVES 4

- 1 head cauliflower, separated into florets
- 1/2 cup yogurt
- 1/2 cup sour cream
- 2 tablespoons lemon juice
- 1 teaspoon olive oil
- 1 large onion, cut into thin slices
- 1 red bell pepper, cut into thin strips
- 1 tablespoon minced fresh gingerroot
- 2 teaspoons ground coriander
- 3/4 teaspoon cumin
- 3/4 teaspoon turmeric
- 1/4 teaspoon ground red pepper
- 1/4 cup minced fresh cilantro

Corn Pudding

Mrs. Robert J. Epperson
Satin, TX

Last Christmas, I was inspired to publish a book of family recipes for all my relatives. This easy-to-prepare corn pudding recipe always makes a hit, especially with the men in my family.

3 eggs, beaten lightly
1 pint milk
1 tablespoon plus 1 teaspoon sugar
1 teaspoon salt
1 tablespoon plus 1 teaspoon butter or margarine, melted
3/4 cup corn, cut from the cob (1 1/2 ears), or canned or frozen
Chopped green chili to taste (optional)
Chopped onion to taste (optional)
Grated cheese to taste (optional)
Paprika to taste (optional)

Preheat oven to 450°. Grease a glass baking dish. Combine eggs, milk, sugar, salt, butter, and corn in the prepared dish. Place in a shallow pan of warm water. Bake for 45 minutes.

To serve, sprinkle with chili, onion, cheese, and paprika.

SERVES 4

SHRIMP-STUFFED EGGPLANT CREOLE

Jackie Cox
Houston, TX

This is a New Orleans recipe used by both my mother and my aunt at Thanksgiving, Christmas, and other times during the year. We especially enjoy it at Christmas, when a large group of relatives and friends who love good food, recipes, and people gather together.

Grease a cookie sheet. Parboil eggplant for 15 minutes, or until almost tender. Cut in half lengthwise, leaving stems intact to hold the shape. Scoop out and chop the flesh; set aside. Place shells on the prepared cookie sheet; set aside.

Preheat oven to 400°. Pour 1 cup water over bread, press out excess moisture, and set aside. In a sauté pan over medium-high heat, warm oil. Add onions, and sauté until tender. Add garlic and celery; cook for 2 minutes. Add chopped eggplant, bread, butter, salt, pepper, and cayenne. Cook, stirring constantly, until bread blends in. Remove from heat. Gradually stir in eggs, and blend. Add shrimp and parsley, and stir to combine. Spoon a portion of the mixture on each eggplant shell. Sprinkle with cheese. Bake for 20 minutes.

SERVES 4

- 2 eggplants
- 1 cup water
- 6 slices dried bread, crusts removed
- 1/4 cup cooking oil
- 2 medium onions, chopped
- 2 garlic cloves, minced
- 1/4 cup minced celery
- 2 tablespoons butter or margarine
- 2 teaspoons salt
- 1/8 teaspoon pepper
- 1/8 teaspoon cayenne
- 2 eggs, slightly beaten
- 9 ounces small shrimp
- 1/4 cup minced fresh parsley
- 1/4 cup grated Parmesan cheese

GRILLED PORTOBELLO MUSHROOMS

Debi Davis
Dallas, TX

I've been a vegetarian for 10 years. Recently, a friend introduced me to the "meaty" mushrooms known as portobellos. They are excellent grilled, and now I have them as often as possible.

1 to 2 pounds portobello
    mushrooms
1/2 cup olive or canola oil
1/4 cup red wine vinegar
3 tablespoons balsamic vinegar
2 cloves garlic, minced
1 teaspoon firmly packed
    light brown sugar
1 teaspoon celery seeds
1/2 teaspoon dry mustard
1/2 teaspoon salt
    Ground pepper to taste
10 cracked peppercorns
1 to 2 tablespoons chopped
    fresh parsley, or 1 to 2
    teaspoons dried
1 tablespoon Worcestershire
    sauce

Remove and discard mushroom stems. In a gallon-size freezer bag, blend mushroom caps with remaining ingredients. Seal, and massage gently to mix. Chill for 2 hours.

Prepare and light a charcoal grill. Drain mushrooms, reserving marinade. Place mushrooms on metal skewers or in a vegetable grill basket. Grill, hollow side up, over medium-hot coals for 6 minutes, basting every minute with the marinade; do not turn.

SERVES 4

 California: Carmenet Vineyard,
        '93 Dynamite Cabernet
 Oregon: Domaine Drouhin, '91 Pinot Noir

MUSHROOM BARLEY CASSEROLE

Mrs. Ronald Goldstein
Atlanta, GA

When we have had enough pasta and potatoes, this quick and easy casserole is the perfect solution. It's equally good with beef, chicken or fish, and everyone loves the change of pace.

If using morel mushrooms, soak morel mushrooms in warm water for 30 minutes. Drain. Chop into pieces.

Preheat oven to 400°. Combine morels with mushrooms, barley, bouillon, butter, rosemary, and water in a 1½-quart casserole dish. Cover, and bake for 1 hour, or until barley is tender and all liquid is absorbed.

SERVES 4

 California: Santa Barbara Winery, '91 Pinot Noir

Italy: Fonterutoli, '90 Ser Lapo, Riserva

½ ounce dried morel
mushrooms (optional)
8 ounces mushrooms, sliced
¾ cup barley (uncooked)
3 beef or chicken bouillon
cubes
1 tablespoon butter
½ teaspoon dried rosemary,
crumbled
2 cups boiling water

Heavenly Baked Onions

Olivia Dee Franklin
Dallas, TX

Baked onions have always been a favorite at our house, but once I tasted them flavored with balsamic vinegar in a restaurant, I was determined to work on my own homemade version. It's the broiling that really intensifies the flavors as it browns the onions and thickens the sauce.

2 large sweet yellow onions,
    unpeeled, halved
2 tablespoons butter
1 1/2 tablespoons lemon juice
1 tablespoon spicy brown
    mustard
1/2 cup to 1 cup chicken broth
    as needed
    Balsamic vinegar to taste

Preheat oven to 375°. Place onions on end in a small cast-iron skillet or baking dish; do not cut off root, as the root and outer peel hold the onions' shape. Melt butter with lemon juice in a small saucepan. Add mustard, and stir to combine. Spread half the mixture over the cut surface of onions. Pour enough chicken broth in the pan to come halfway up the side of onions. Bake for 30 minutes. Drizzle balsamic vinegar over onions. Add more broth if necessary to come halfway up the side of onions. Bake for 30 minutes, or until fork-tender.

Preheat broiler. Spread remaining mustard mixture over onions, leaving onions in broth-filled baking dish. Broil on the center rack of the oven until onions are browned and broth thickens.

To serve, spoon broth over onions.

SERVES 2

Fabulous Kale with Tomatoes and Onions

Elizabeth E. Solender and Gary L. Scott
Dallas, TX

Knowing how important it is for women to eat foods high in calcium, we experimented on our friends and came up with this recipe. The kale is lightly cooked, so it stays a bright green. It's a far cry from the old Southern way of cooking vegetables with lots of pork fat until they are limp and soggy. It is extremely easy to prepare, and it is great alone or served on rice. It's guaranteed to become a favorite.

Peel and chop onion and garlic. Separate kale leaves from stems, discarding stems and any tough leaves. Tear kale leaves into pieces. In a heavy skillet over medium-high heat, sauté onion in oil for 2 minutes. Add garlic, and sauté for 2 minutes. Add tomatoes with their juice, breaking up tomatoes with a spoon. Add salt and pepper. Cook, stirring constantly, until the mixture simmers. Simmer for 3 to 4 minutes until liquids are reduced. Place kale on top, cover, and cook for 2 minutes. Lightly press kale into the mixture with a large spoon, cover, and cook for 2 minutes, or until kale is dark green and slightly crisp.

To serve, ladle over rice.

SERVES 4

1 medium onion
3 to 4 cloves garlic
1 bunch kale
2 tablespoons olive oil
1 (14.5-ounce) can whole tomatoes, undrained
Salt and pepper to taste

Potato Puffs

Anita Reiter
Roswell, GA

This recipe is an old favorite of mine. When I entertain, my husband Joe, my children, my grandchildren, and our guests all love them. They make any main course look so much more elegant–and the taste is unbelievable!

10 potatoes
2 large onions, minced
½ cup vegetable oil
   Salt and pepper to taste
1 (1 pound, 1.25-ounce) box
   frozen puff pastry sheets,
   defrosted

Peel and chop potatoes. Place in a large pot of water. Bring to a boil, and boil until tender. Drain, and mash in a large mixing bowl until firm and smooth. In a skillet over medium-high heat, sauté onions in oil until tender. Add onions with some of the oil from the pan to potatoes. Season with salt and pepper.

Preheat oven to 400°. Roll out a pastry sheet to ⅛-inch thick. Lay a strip of the potato mixture along one long edge of the pastry sheet. Roll the long edge of the dough over the potatoes to the middle. Fold the other side of the dough over the rolled dough so that the flat dough edge overlaps the rolled dough. Cut into 1-inch pieces.

Create a nest for the potato filling in each puff by folding the loose end of dough over one end of the roll. Push down slightly on the puff, reshaping as necessary to form a sphere.

Bake on ungreased cookie sheets for 10 to 12 minutes until golden.

MAKES 80 PUFFS

Sweet Potato Soufflé

Elizabeth Winkler
Anderson, SC

I have a friend who calls me long-distance every Thanksgiving to get this recipe. She doesn't keep it; she says it gives her a good excuse to call me just before the holiday.

Peel and chop sweet potatoes. Place in a large pot of water. Bring to a boil, and boil until tender. Meanwhile, grease a 1½-quart baking dish. When potatoes are cooked, drain and mash.

Preheat oven to 350°. In a large mixing bowl, combine potatoes with sugar, salt, melted butter, eggs, milk, and vanilla. Transfer to the prepared baking dish. In a small mixing bowl, combine brown sugar, flour, and nuts; cut in butter. Sprinkle over soufflé. Bake for 25 minutes.

SERVES 8 TO 10

1½ pounds sweet potatoes
½ cup sugar
½ teaspoon salt
⅓ stick butter or margarine, melted
2 eggs
½ cup milk
1 teaspoon vanilla extract
½ cup firmly packed light brown sugar
¼ cup flour
½ cup nuts
2 tablespoons butter or margarine

Mashed Potatoes with Garlic Purée

Marilyn J. Tenser
Beverly Hills, CA

I have my cousin, who is a gourmet cook, to thank for this recipe. Even when I serve it on my plain white china (where it almost disappears on the plate), it's a great dish – light, fluffy, and irresistible to my guests.

1 head garlic
1 tablespoon olive oil
1 pound potatoes
3/4 cup half-and-half, divided into 1/4 cup and 1/2 cup
1/4 cup (1/2 stick) butter
2 teaspoons thyme

Preheat oven to 275°. Cut a half inch off the top of garlic; remove some of the skin from the outside, keeping the head intact. Place in a small baking dish. Drizzle olive oil over garlic. Cover, and bake for 1 hour. Meanwhile, peel and chop potatoes. Place in a large pot of water. Bring to a boil, and boil until tender. Drain, and set aside in a large mixing bowl. When garlic is baked, remove from oven, uncover, squeeze garlic cloves out of the skins, and place in a blender or food processor. Add 1/4 cup half-and-half, blend to combine, and add to potatoes. Add remaining half-and-half, butter, and thyme, and whip with an electric mixer until smooth and creamy.

SERVES 6

Secret Potatoes

Caryn Kay
Glencoe, IL

These potatoes were served at a dinner I attended, but it was up to me to figure out a way to duplicate the taste. When I serve them, someone always tries to guess the secret ingredient. I always tell, but not until after dinner.

1/2 cup olive oil, divided into 6 tablespoons and 2 tablespoons
2 pounds red potatoes, cut into small wedges
1 large Vidalia onion, cut into chunks
1 red bell pepper, seeded and cut into 1-inch pieces
1/4 cup white wine
1 teaspoon oregano
1 envelope onion soup mix
1/4 cup grated Parmesan cheese

Preheat oven to 350°. Combine 6 tablespoons oil, potatoes, onion, red pepper, wine, oregano, and onion soup mix in a baking dish. Bake for 1 hour, or until potatoes are golden brown and crisp. Sprinkle with remaining oil and Parmesan cheese. Bake for 10 minutes.

SERVES 6

BROILED STUFFED RADICCHIO

Joyce Goldstein
San Francisco, CA

The radicchio may be blanched and stuffed ahead of time, then put under the broiler or placed in a hot oven. If you use this method, baste it with a little virgin olive oil mixed with balsamic vinegar.

Bring a large pot of salted water to a boil. Add radicchio, and cook for 2 minutes, constantly pushing radicchio under the water. Drain, lightly pressing to release excess moisture. Carefully open radicchio heads; tuck a piece of mozzarella in each head. Overlap the leaves to cover cheese. Whisk together oil and vinegar in a small cup. Preheat broiler. Place radicchio packets on a broiler pan; sprinkle with salt and pepper. Brush with oil-vinegar mixture, reserving leftover mixture. Broil for 3 minutes, turn, brush with oil-vinegar mixture, and broil for 3 minutes.

Note: If radicchio heads are large, cut in half.

As an alternative method, place stuffed radicchio in an oiled baking pan, spoon on oil-vinegar mixture, and bake at 400° for 20 minutes, or until tender, and browned, and cheese melts.

SERVES 4

4 small heads radicchio
1/3 pound fresh mozzarella, cut into 4 finger-shaped pieces
1/4 cup extra-virgin olive oil
2 tablespoons balsamic vinegar
Salt and pepper to taste

RATATOUILLE

John E. Crosby Jr.
Midland, TX

I love eggplant prepared almost any way. A friend recommended this recipe as the best way to use it. I serve it hot as a vegetarian main course or cold as a salad.

1 eggplant
1 teaspoon salt
3 small zucchini
8 ounces mushrooms
1 green bell pepper
3 stalks celery
1 medium onion
3 tomatoes
2 cloves garlic
3 tablespoons olive oil
1 teaspoon dried basil
1 teaspoon dried oregano
1 teaspoon dried parsley
1 teaspoon dried thyme
1 teaspoon dried marjoram
1 teaspoon lemon pepper
3 tablespoons Worcestershire
   sauce

Peel eggplant, cut into 1/2-inch cubes, and place in a colander. Sprinkle with salt, mix, and let stand to drain. Meanwhile, chop zucchini, mushrooms, green pepper, celery, onion, and tomatoes into bite-sized pieces. Mince garlic. In a 4-quart Dutch oven over medium-high heat, warm oil. Add zucchini, green pepper, celery, onion, and tomatoes. Stir in garlic, basil, oregano, parsley, thyme, marjoram, and lemon pepper. Sauté for 5 minutes. Add mushrooms and eggplant, and stir to combine. Add Worcestershire. Reduce heat to medium, cover, and cook, stirring occasionally, for 30 minutes, or until vegetables are crisp-tender.

SERVES 6 TO 8

Brown Rice Pilaf with Nuts and Raisins

Sharon Popham
Dallas, TX

I first enjoyed this dish at a friend's house. I have now prepared it so many times for my own dinner parties that I have to keep a record of those who have had it. It's particularly wonderful to serve in the fall, when the aroma fills the house, creating a cozy, comfortable feeling as guests arrive.

In a medium saucepan over medium-high heat, melt butter, and sauté onion until translucent. Add rice, reduce heat to low, and cook for 3 minutes, or until grains are coated with butter and brown slightly. Add stock, stir to combine, and season with salt and pepper. Bring to a boil. Cover, reduce heat to medium-low, and simmer for 45 minutes, or until all the liquid is absorbed.

Meanwhile, plump raisins in wine for 30 minutes; drain. Remove rice from heat. Stir in raisins and remaining ingredients.

To serve, transfer to a serving bowl and garnish with mint. Serve as an accompaniment to carrot or mint soup, tenderloin, or carrots sautéed with mint.

SERVES 4

1/4 cup (1/2 stick) unsalted butter
1/4 cup chopped onion
1 cup brown rice (uncooked)
2 1/2 cups chicken stock
1 teaspoon salt
1/4 teaspoon pepper
1/2 cup golden raisins
1/2 cup dry white wine
2 tablespoons unsalted butter, melted
3/4 cup almonds, toasted
1/2 cup chopped fresh mint

CRANBERRY WILD RICE

Dawn Washer
Corona del Mar, CA

Every Thanksgiving, we drive north to San Luis Obispo, where my son and his wife live, and the San Francisco family contingent meets us there. We have a grand time over the weekend, which culminates in a big outdoor feast in a favorite park. This is the dish I am always asked to bring.

9 cups chicken broth,
    divided in half
1 cup wild rice (uncooked),
    rinsed and drained
2 cups brown rice (uncooked)
2 tablespoons butter or
    margarine
2 medium onions, diced
2 celery stalks, diced
1 cup dried cranberries
1 teaspoon cinnamon
    Grated zest of 1 orange
2 teaspoons dried thyme
2 teaspoons dried marjoram
1 teaspoon dried sage
    Salt and pepper to taste
1 cup chopped pecans

In a heavy saucepan over medium-high heat, bring 4½ cups broth to a boil. Reduce heat to medium-low, add wild rice, and cook for 45 minutes, or until tender. Meanwhile, in a separate heavy saucepan over medium-high heat, bring remaining broth to a boil, stir in brown rice, reduce heat to low, and simmer for 25 minutes. Fluff brown rice, and add to wild rice.

Preheat oven to 350°. In a sauté pan over medium-high heat, melt butter. Add onions, celery, and cranberries. Sprinkle with cinnamon. Cook for 5 minutes, or until the vegetables wilt. Add remaining ingredients. Toss with rice. Cover, and bake for 20 minutes.

(PHOTO, PAGE 158)

SERVES 8 TO 10

Shallot Compote

Charlie Trotter
Chicago, IL

Simple grilled or broiled meat and fish can be made exciting with this simple compote of shallots, jalapeños, and apple. Great food does not need to be complicated, but it must be delicious and interesting. Don't be afraid to dress up a simple family dinner with a little excitement.

In a sauté pan over medium heat, melt butter. Add onions and jalapeños, cover, and sweat until tender. Add apple, and stew for 1 minute. Add vinegar, wine, orange juice, honey, and brown sugar. Bring to a boil, reduce heat to medium-low, and simmer for 2 minutes. Strain liquid into a heavy saucepan. Cover the vegetable-apple mixture to keep warm. Cook the liquid over medium-high heat until reduced to 6 tablespoons with a syrupy consistency. Season with salt and pepper, and fold into the vegetable-apple mixture.

Serve as an accompaniment to beef, lamb, venison, or red wine-salmon dishes.

(PHOTO, PAGE 161)

SERVES 4 TO 6

- 3 tablespoons butter
- 1 pound Walla Walla or other shallots, peeled and cut in 1/8-inch slices
- 3 tablespoons seeded and chopped jalapeños
- 1 Gala apple, cored, peeled, and chopped
- 1/4 cup rice wine vinegar
- 1 1/2 cups pinot noir
- 1 1/2 cups orange juice
- 2 tablespoons lavender or other honey
- 1 tablespoon firmly packed light brown sugar
- Salt and pepper to taste

TERRINE OF GRILLED SALSIFY AND TINY LEEKS WITH

Salsify is a root vegetable admired by the nobility of Europe for its subtle taste and texture. I like using it in combination with the tiny leeks to create a flavor/texture combination that is elegant, yet exciting. The Black Truffle Vinaigrette adds another dimension of sophistication and taste complexity.

TERRINE OF GRILLED SALSIFY AND TINY LEEKS:

2 pounds salsify (oyster plant), peeled
1 quart milk
1 quart water
1 tablespoon plus 1 teaspoon salt, divided
Butter for browning
1/2 carrot, chopped
1/2 onion, chopped
1/2 celery stalk, chopped
6 bunches baby leeks, cleaned and trimmed to show 3 inches of green
1 1/2 cups vegetable stock or water
10 sheets (leaves) gelatin
Vegetable oil for brushing mold
1 pound spinach, stems removed

TERRINE OF GRILLED SALSIFY AND TINY LEEKS:

In a large pot over medium heat, simmer salsify with milk, water and 1 tablespoon salt for 10 to 15 minutes until tender. Remove salsify from the liquid, and let cool. Grill salsify, or brown with butter in a heavy saucepan. Set aside to cool, cutting any thick pieces in half. In the same saucepan, melt butter. Add carrot, onion, and celery; brown, stirring occasionally to prevent burning. Add leeks, vegetable stock, and remaining salt. Steam until tender. Remove from the heat, and let cool. Strain into a large bowl, and set the vegetable mixture aside. Add gelatin to liquid, and stir to dissolve. Brush a 24x2x2-inch terrine mold with oil. Line with plastic wrap, leaving a border of plastic wrap large enough to encase the terrine. Dip salsify in gelatin, wipe off excess, and place a layer in the bottom of the mold. Dip some of the vegetable mixture in gelatin, wipe off excess, and add a layer on top of the salsify. Alternate gelatin-dipped layers of salsify and vegetable mixture until the mold is almost full, ending with salsify and reserving leftover gelatin. Press slightly on the mold, seal the plastic wrap, and weigh down the terrine with a small board. Chill for at least 2 hours.

BLACK TRUFFLE VINAIGRETTE

Charlie Trotter
Chicago, IL

BLACK TRUFFLE VINAIGRETTE:
1 canned black truffle the size
   of a large marble
1 teaspoon rice vinegar
1 tablespoon white truffle oil
¼ tablespoon hazelnut oil
   Salt and pepper to taste

Meanwhile, drop spinach into boiling water and blanch. Remove from pan, and immediately plunge into ice water. Remove from water, and blot dry. In a saucepan over low heat, warm reserved gelatin. Lay out enough plastic wrap to encase the terrine. Cover the plastic wrap with a layer of spinach leaves. Brush with gelatin. When the terrine is chilled, invert to unmold, remove the plastic wrap, and place terrine on spinach. Encase the terrine with spinach, pressing slightly to help spinach adhere. Wrap in plastic, and chill for at least 10 minutes.

BLACK TRUFFLE VINAIGRETTE:

Drain truffle, reserving 2 teaspoons juice. Chop truffle, place in a mixing bowl with reserved juice and remaining ingredients, and combine.

To serve, without removing plastic wrap, cut the terrine in ½-inch slices. Place a slice in the center of each individual plate. Remove plastic wrap from each slice. Drizzle 1 teaspoon of Black Truffle Vinaigrette over each slice.

Note: The plastic wrap helps the terrine hold its shape while it is being sliced.

MAKES 1 TERRINE

Spinach Artichoke Casserole

Gail Greene
Garland, TX

In my work as a food stylist on television commercials, I know how important it is to make an attractive presentation of any food. This is one of my favorites to layer in a glass dish or quiche dish and decorate with red pepper rings, a tomato rose bouquet, or asparagus.

3 (10-ounce) boxes chopped spinach
2 strips bacon, diced
1 large onion, minced
2 tablespoons butter or margarine, melted
2 (14-ounce) cans quartered artichokes, drained, cut in half
1 1/4 cups shredded Parmesan cheese, divided into 3/4 cup and remainder
1 pint sour cream
1 (2-ounce) jar diced pimiento, drained (optional)
1/2 teaspoon grated fresh nutmeg
Salt and pepper to taste

Preheat oven to 350°. Grease a 9x13x2-inch casserole dish. Cook spinach according to package directions; drain, squeeze lightly in a towel to remove additional moisture, and set aside to cool.

In a skillet over medium heat, cook bacon until crisp; remove from the skillet and drain on paper towels, reserving the drippings in the skillet. Sauté onion in bacon drippings until translucent. Remove onion from the skillet, and transfer to a large mixing bowl. Add spinach, bacon, melted butter, artichokes, 3/4 cup Parmesan, sour cream, pimiento, nutmeg, salt, and pepper. Pour into the prepared casserole dish. Sprinkle remaining Parmesan over the top. Bake for 35 to 40 minutes until top is golden; if top does not brown, broil for several minutes to brown.

SERVES 8

 California: Kendall-Jackson Winery, '94 Sauvignon Blanc
 California: Etude Wines, '92 Pinot Noir

SPINACH SOUFFLÉ

Mrs. Lyndon B. Johnson
Stonewall, TX

Lady Bird's continued contribution is greatly appreciated.

Preheat oven to 350°. Grease a casserole dish. In a skillet over medium-high heat, melt butter, and sauté onion until translucent. Add flour to form a roux. Add milk, salt, and pepper; stir until smooth. Beat yolks until slightly thickened and pale yellow. Stir into the skillet. Add spinach and cheese.

Beat egg whites until they stand in soft peaks, and fold into the mixture. Transfer to the prepared casserole dish. Place in a shallow pan of warm water. Bake for 50 minutes.

SERVES 2

1 tablespoon butter
1/4 cup chopped onion
2 tablespoons flour
1 cup milk or light cream
1/2 teaspoon salt
1/8 teaspoon pepper
3 eggs, separated
1 cup chopped cooked spinach
1/2 cup grated cheese

DESSERTS

Doesn't everyone love a happy ending? This chapter is full of them. Something interesting for every sweet tooth. Sophisticated palates will love Tiramisù. Traditionalists will find comfort in recipes like Streusel-Topped Peach Pie. Some of these have been handed down from generation to generation by family members who could cook up a storm in New England or the deep South. We all know that a knockout dessert can be the main attraction of any dinner, so just imagine the impact of a party with any six of these 36 masterpiece desserts.

AMARETTO COCONUT CREAM CAKE

Howard S. Ehrlich
Parkland, FL

While vacationing in the Caribbean, we sampled this delectable dessert and decided we couldn't leave the island without it. We settled for the recipe, which was much easier to pack!

3 eggs
1/3 cup plus 2 tablespoons sugar, divided
1/8 cup warm water
1 1/2 tablespoons gelatin
1 cup amaretto
1 tablespoon almond extract
3 pints heavy cream
4 ounces shredded coconut, toasted, or more to taste
2 1/2 cups graham cracker crumbs
1/4 cup (1/2 stick) butter, melted

With an electric mixer, beat eggs and 1/3 cup sugar in a large mixing bowl at high speed until fluffy (approximately 5 minutes). In a small bowl, mix water and gelatin, and heat to dissolve; add amaretto and extract and let cool. Slowly add to the egg mixture. Whip cream until stiff; fold into the mixture. Add coconut, reserving approximately 2 tablespoons for garnish.

In a separate bowl, mix together graham crackers with remaining sugar; stir in melted butter and mix. Spread the cracker mixture over the bottom, and approximately 1 inch up the sides, of an 8x3-inch springform pan. Pour in the cake mixture; garnish with toasted coconut. Chill for 3 to 4 hours.

To serve, run a knife around the sides of the springform pan to release the cake.

SERVES 12 TO 16

 California: Schramsberg, Crémant
 Italy: Ferrari, Sparkling Wine, Brut

APPLE CAKE

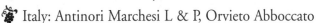

Linda Goldberg
Natick, MA

When I became engaged, I asked my grandmother, Bubbie, for the recipe for her apple cake. She gave it to me in handfuls and glassfuls. I knew from the smile on her face that it pleased her that I had asked. After experimenting, I finally was able to duplicate her cake, and now it has become a family favorite for three generations.

Preheat oven to 325°. Grease a 2-quart or 8x12-inch glass pan. Peel, core, and slice apples; set aside. Mix sugar and butter by hand; add eggs. Add flour, baking powder, vanilla, and salt.

Line prepared pan with a thin layer of dough. Cover with a layer of apples. Sprinkle cinnamon and lemon juice on top; the amount will depend on the tartness of the apples. Spread remaining dough on top. Cover with remaining apples. Sprinkle brown sugar over apples. Bake for 1 hour, or until a toothpick inserted in the center comes out clean.

MAKES 16 SERVINGS

 California: Fetzer Vineyards, '94 Gewürztraminer

Italy: Antinori Marchesi L & P, Orvieto Abboccato

- 3 pounds apples
- 2 cups sugar
- 1/2 cup (1 stick) butter or margarine
- 4 eggs
- 2 cups sifted flour
- 2 teaspoons baking powder
- 2 teaspoons vanilla extract
  Pinch salt
  Cinnamon and lemon juice to taste
- 3 tablespoons light brown, firmly packed sugar or jam

APPLESAUCE CAKE

Joyce Pate Capper
Fort Worth, TX

If you're tired of giving (or getting) recycled fruit cakes, this is the answer. I make it just as soon as the weather turns cool and the aroma makes everyone feel as if the holidays are already here.

1½ teaspoons baking soda
½ cup brandy, wine, or hot water
½ cup (1 stick) butter or shortening
2 cups sugar
1 cup raisins
1 cup chopped walnuts
2½ cups flour
1 teaspoon allspice
1 teaspoon cinnamon
1 teaspoon cloves
1 teaspoon nutmeg
2 tablespoons cocoa
2 cups (16 ounces) applesauce
¼ teaspoon salt

Preheat oven to 350°. Generously grease a bundt pan. Dissolve baking soda in brandy and set aside. In a large mixing bowl, cream butter and sugar with electric mixer. Dust raisins and nuts with flour, and add to butter. Add remaining ingredients and dissolved baking soda; mix. Put in bundt pan, and bake for 1 hour and 15 minutes.

MAKES 16 SLICES

 California: Robert Pecota Winery,
Moscato di Andrea

Italy: Ronchi di Cialla, '91 Verduzzo

FANCY FRESH APPLE CAKE

Vicki Midyett
Richardson, TX

As a home economist, I am always on the lookout for outstanding recipes and try several new ones every week. I found this moist, delicious cake over 20 years ago while flipping through vintage magazines. It makes a very pretty presentation on a glass pedestal cake stand.

DIRECTIONS FOR CAKE:

Preheat oven to 350°. Generously grease and flour 3 (9-inch-diameter) cake pans. Sift flour again with baking soda and salt to combine. In a small bowl, combine apples, walnuts, and lemon peel. In a large mixing bowl, combine sugar, oil, and eggs; beat with a wooden spoon. Add the dry ingredients and stir until smooth. Add the apple mixture; stir until combined. Spread evenly into pans. Bake 30 to 40 minutes until top of cake springs back when lightly touched. Cool in pans for 10 minutes. Remove from pans and cool on wire racks.

DIRECTIONS FOR FROSTING:

In a medium bowl, beat cream cheese, butter, egg yolk, and vanilla with an electric mixer on medium speed until light and creamy. Add confectioners' sugar and beat until desired spreading consistency. Frost between each layer as well as the sides and top. Press walnut pieces into frosting on the sides of the cake. Chill until ready to serve.

SERVES 10 TO 12

 Neiman Marcus Cuvée, CJTK '90

Italy: Contratto, Moscato d'Asti, Tenuta Tre Pini

CAKE:

- 3 cups flour, sifted
- 1 1/2 teaspoons baking soda
- 1 1/2 teaspoons salt
- 3 cups peeled, cored, chopped tart cooking apples (about 4 medium apples)
- 1/2 cup walnuts, coarsely chopped
- 1 teaspoon grated lemon peel
- 2 cups sugar
- 1 1/2 cups vegetable oil
- 2 large eggs

FROSTING:

- 8 ounces cream cheese, softened
- 1 tablespoon butter, softened
- 1 yolk of a large egg
- 1 teaspoon vanilla extract
- 16 ounces confectioners' sugar
- 1 cup chopped walnuts for garnish

APRICOT CAKE

Irene Kuzyk
Kew Gardens, NY

I was born in the Ukraine, where this recipe goes back four generations in my family. Children love it and it keeps forever–but at our house it disappears very quickly.

1 cup (2 sticks) unsalted butter, semi-frozen
2¼ cups flour
1 teaspoon baking powder
2 tablespoons sour cream
¼ cup sugar
4 eggs, separated
Dash vanilla extract
1 (16-ounce) jar apricot preserves
Confectioners' sugar for dusting

Cut butter into small pieces and work into flour until mixture is crumbly. Add baking powder. Mix in sour cream, sugar, egg yolks, and vanilla. Work the mixture by hand until a smooth ball can be formed, taking care not to overmix. Form a third of the dough into a ball; wrap in plastic wrap, aluminum foil, or waxed paper. Freeze for at least 2 hours. Spread the remainder of the dough by hand into an ungreased 9x13x2-inch baking pan, bringing the dough up an inch on the sides. Cover with foil or plastic wrap and chill for at least 2 hours.

When ready to bake, preheat oven to 350°. Over chilled dough in baking pan, spread apricot preserves evenly. Beat egg whites until they stand in soft peaks, and spread over preserves. Coarsely grate the frozen dough ball over egg whites, covering them completely. Bake for 35 to 45 minutes until the sides come away from the pan. Remove from the oven, and let cool on a wire rack.

To serve, dust with confectioners' sugar and cut into squares.

Note: Multiple batches of dough can be prepared at one time. Dough can be spread into aluminum cake pans, stacked with each layer separated by foil, and frozen. Dough balls can be frozen in freezer bags.

(PHOTO, PAGE 148)

MAKES 16 TO 18 SERVINGS

 California: Freemark Abbey Winery, '92 Late Harvest Edelwein

 Italy: Maculan, '93 Torcolato

BAILEY'S® IRISH CREAM CHEESECAKE

Susan (Mrs. Bill) Roberds
Dallas, TX

Even though we're both adults, my sister and I have not outgrown our sibling rivalry of who can make the best cheesecake in the family. Our "rivalry" reaches its peak each year during the Christmas season, when cheesecake is the traditional dessert served at our family's Christmas Eve dinner. Usually, my sister's cheesecake is the family favorite, but not last year, when I made this recipe.

DIRECTIONS FOR CHEESECAKE:

Preheat oven to 325°. Grease the bottom and sides of a 10-inch springform pan. Using a fork, combine cracker crumbs, brown sugar, cinnamon, and melted butter in a medium mixing bowl until blended. Press evenly onto the bottom and 1 inch up the sides of prepared pan. Chill for 30 minutes.

Wipe the mixing bowl clean, and beat cream cheese in it until smooth. Add sugar, and beat until smooth, scraping the sides of bowl as needed. Add eggs, one at a time, scraping the sides after each addition.

Beat 10 minutes, or until smooth. Beat in vanilla and liqueur until mixed. Pour into springform pan and bake for 1 hour and 15 minutes, or until the center is the consistency of set gelatin. Let cool on a wire rack away from drafts.

DIRECTIONS FOR GLAZE:

Scald cream, stir in chocolate and vanilla, and chill for 10 minutes. Drizzle glaze on top of cooled cheesecake and chill overnight. When ready to serve, remove sides of pan.

To serve, garnish with whipped cream and shaved chocolate.

SERVES 8 TO 10

CHEESECAKE:

- 2 cups graham cracker crumbs
- 1/2 cup firmly packed light brown sugar
- 1 teaspoon cinnamon
- 1/2 cup (1 stick) unsalted butter, melted
- 2 1/4 pounds cream cheese, softened
- 1 1/2 cups sugar
- 5 large eggs at room temperature
- 1 teaspoon vanilla extract
- 1 cup Bailey's® Irish Cream

GLAZE:

- 1 cup whipping cream
- 8 ounces semisweet chocolate, chopped
- 1 teaspoon vanilla extract

 California: Ferrari-Carano, Eldorado Gold

Italy: Alois Lageder, Moscato Rosa

Warm Chocolate Custard Cake

This is another of our trademark dishes at Star Canyon, one that has been on the menu since we opened. The chocolate cake was inspired by a recipe of Julia Child's that I first made for her when I was working as a chef's assistant for the Great Chef's Program at the Mondavi Winery in Napa in 1981. This version is a little more sinful! It's a good dessert to serve at the end of a meal if you're trying to impress-- it's really rich, and a chocoholic's delight. It should be served at room temperature.

CAKE:

- 1 cup heavy cream
- 10½ ounces semisweet baking chocolate, chopped
- 2 ounces unsweetened chocolate, chopped
- 5 eggs
- ⅓ cup sugar
- 1 teaspoon vanilla extract

DIRECTIONS FOR WARM CHOCOLATE CUSTARD CAKE:

Place a round of parchment or waxed paper in the bottom of a 9-inch-diameter cake pan. Butter and flour the pan and paper. Preheat oven to 350°. In a medium saucepan, bring cream to a boil; remove from heat. Add both chopped chocolates; stir to blend. Cover and cook over low heat 5 minutes, or until chocolate melts. Stir to blend; set aside.

Place eggs, sugar, and vanilla in a metal bowl and set over simmering water. Whip until warm to the touch (about 1 minute); remove from heat. Beat with an electric mixer at high speed for 7 to 10 minutes until tripled in volume. Gently whisk a fourth of the egg mixture into the chocolate. Gently fold in remaining egg mixture, taking care to deflate the egg mixture as little as possible.
Pour into the cake pan and place inside a slightly larger pan. Pour boiling water into the larger pan until it comes halfway up the side of the smaller pan. Bake for 50 minutes, or until an inserted toothpick or skewer comes out clean. Remove from the oven and let stand in the water for 30 minutes, or until cool. Invert on a platter and remove the parchment paper.

Note: To slice the cake, dip a knife in hot water, as this cake can be crumbly.

WITH CANDIED LEMON SAUCE

— Stephan Pyles
Dallas, TX

CANDIED LEMON SAUCE:
- 1/2 cup sugar
- 1 cup heavy cream
- 1/2 cup (1 stick) unsalted butter, cut into bits
- Pinch salt
- 1 tablespoon Grand Marnier
- 1 tablespoon lemon juice
- 6 to 8 lemons (1 1/2 pounds)
- 1 1/3 cups sugar

DIRECTIONS FOR CANDIED LEMON SAUCE:
In a saucepan, cook sugar, cream, butter, and salt over moderate heat, stirring until butter is melted and the mixture is smooth. Remove from the heat; stir in Grand Marnier and lemon juice, and let cool. Transfer to a small bowl, cover, and chill until thick. Meanwhile, cut an inch from the top and bottom of lemons. Using a sharp knife, remove peel in 1/2-inch strips, leaving a third of the pulp attached. Place peel in a large pot, cover with cold water, and slowly bring to a boil, uncovered. Boil rapidly for 3 minutes; drain. Return peel to the large pot and repeat the procedure 3 more times, beginning with cold water each time. When finished, return the peel to the pot and do not add water. Mix in sugar and cook, uncovered, over very low heat, turning frequently with a wooden spoon, for 1 to 1 1/2 hours until glazed. Drain on wire racks over waxed paper.

Note: Blanching the peel 4 times removes all but a pleasing trace of bitterness. The peel and sugar must be cooked very slowly; if the liquid evaporates too quickly, the peel will be insufficiently cooked.

To serve, top the cake with Candied Lemon Sauce.

SERVES 8 TO 10

California: Heitz Wine Cellars, '89 Grignolino, Port

Portugal: Graham, '91 Port, Oporto

CHOCOLATE MELTING CAKES

Melinda Jayson
Dallas, TX

With a busy law practice, I don't do a lot of cooking on a regular basis, but I love to spend a day cooking for the fun of it with my sister. She's an ardent collector of cookbooks, and we enjoy doing impressive things for special occasions. These cakes are a favorite, primarily because the warm ganache centers add extra richness.

14 ounces bittersweet chocolate, divided into 2 ounces and 12 ounces
6 tablespoons heavy cream
6 tablespoons unsalted butter
5 large eggs, separated
10 tablespoons sugar, divided into 6 tablespoons and 4 tablespoons
1/2 teaspoon vanilla extract
3/4 cup ground almonds
Confectioners' sugar for dusting
Strawberries or raspberries for garnish

Chop 2 ounces chocolate into small pieces. Heat cream in a small saucepan until bubbles appear around the edge. Drop chocolate pieces into cream, let stand several minutes, and stir until smooth. Pour ganache into 6 squares of a plastic ice cube tray. Freeze until solid.

Grease an extra large, 6-cup muffin pan. Melt butter and remaining chocolate in a double boiler. Stir until smooth, and let cool slightly. In a medium bowl, combine egg yolks, 6 tablespoons sugar, and vanilla. Beat with an electric mixer until slightly thickened and pale yellow (5 to 8 minutes). Add chocolate-butter mixture and combine. Fold in almonds. In a separate bowl, beat remaining sugar with egg whites until stiff; fold into the egg yolk-chocolate mixture. Spoon 3 tablespoons of the batter into each cup of the muffin pan. Place a frozen ganache cube in the center of each. Spoon remaining batter over tops, making sure ganache cubes remain centered and are completely covered. Freeze until solid, at least 1 hour.

When ready to bake, preheat oven to 375°. Bake for 20 to 25 minutes. Let cool 5 to 10 minutes. Carefully invert the muffin pan over a clean towel and remove cakes with a spatula. To serve, dust with confectioners' sugar. Garnish with berries. Note: If frozen ganache cubes are difficult to remove from the ice cube tray, dip the bottom of the tray in hot water.

MAKES 6 INDIVIDUAL CAKES

California: Martin Brothers Winery, '93 Moscato Allegro

Italy: Rallo, Diego & Figli, Marsala

CRANBERRY POUND CAKE

Gerry Granacki
Fort Worth, TX

I like to serve this cake in the winter because fresh cranberries are readily available. Somehow, the flavors in the cake seem to warm your insides. It freezes well and always makes a big impression on my guests.

DIRECTIONS FOR CRANBERRY POUND CAKE:

Preheat oven to 325°. Grease and flour a 10-inch tube pan and place a round of baking parchment in the bottom. Toss berries with ¼ cup flour; set aside. Sift remaining flour with baking powder and salt; set aside. In a large bowl, cream butter and sugar. Add eggs, one at a time, beating well after each addition. Add vanilla and beat until fluffy. Add zest. Fold in the dry ingredients. Beat until well-blended and a stiff batter forms. Gently stir in berries. Spoon the batter into prepared pan. Bake for 1 hour and 15 minutes, or until a wooden pick inserted in the middle comes out clean.

DIRECTIONS FOR GLAZE:

Beat juice and confectioners' sugar until smooth. Cool the cake for 10 minutes in the pan on a rack. Run a knife around the edges of the pan and center tube. Invert over a serving plate. Peel off baking parchment. Glaze with the juice mixture.

To serve, let glaze harden and cut into wedges.

Note: When cranberries are out of season, use fresh blueberries instead, substituting lemon zest for orange zest and lemon juice for orange juice in glaze.

SERVES 10 TO 12

CAKE:
- 12 ounces cranberries, washed and drained
- 3 cups flour, divided into ¼ cup and remainder
- 1 teaspoon baking powder
- ½ teaspoon salt
- 1 cup (2 sticks) butter, softened
- 2 cups sugar
- 4 large eggs at room temperature
- 1½ teaspoons vanilla extract
- Grated zest of 1 orange (optional)

GLAZE:
- ¼ cup orange juice
- 2 cups confectioners' sugar

California: Firestone Vineyard,
'94 Johannisberg Riesling, Select Harvest

Italy: Cinzano, Asti Spumante

Golden Cointreau® Cake

Mary Kleckner
Dallas, TX

I make this cake several times a year. The nicest thing about the recipe is that you can make it two or three weeks ahead of time and freeze it, so you don't have to worry about having dessert handy.

CAKE:

8 large eggs
1 1/2 cups sugar
1/3 cup freshly squeezed orange juice, strained
1 cup flour
1 1/2 teaspoons Cointreau®
1/2 teaspoon vanilla extract
1/4 teaspoon salt
1/2 teaspoon cream of tartar

FROSTING:

1/2 cup (1 stick) unsalted butter
2 3/4 cups confectioners' sugar
1/2 teaspoon salt
6 tablespoons Cointreau® or more as needed to thin to desired spreading consistency

SERVES 10 TO 12

DIRECTIONS FOR GOLDEN COINTREAU® CAKE:
Preheat oven to 325°. Separate eggs, putting yolks in one large mixing bowl and whites in another. Beat yolks with an electric mixer on medium speed until thick and smooth. Slowly beat in sugar; continue beating until smooth and pale yellow. Add orange juice, and blend thoroughly. Sift flour twice and sprinkle over yolk mixture; gently fold in flour with a whisk. Fold in Cointreau® and vanilla.

Add salt to bowl with egg whites, and beat until white and foamy. Add cream of tartar and beat for 4 minutes, or until the egg whites hold a stiff peak. Fold a third of the egg whites into the batter to lighten it. Fold in remaining egg whites. Spoon into an ungreased 10-inch angel food cake pan. Bake for 1 hour and 15 minutes, or until a toothpick inserted in the middle comes out clean. Cover cake and let stand in the pan overnight. Run a knife around the edges of the pan and invert the cake onto a serving plate.

DIRECTIONS FOR COINTREAU® FROSTING:
Cut butter into pieces and place in a large mixing bowl. Sift confectioners' sugar into the bowl. Add salt, and beat with an electric mixer on medium speed until blended. Slowly add 6 tablespoons Cointreau®. Beat until smooth. Add additional Cointreau® as needed for desired spreading consistency.

Note: As an alternative to the frosting, soak 1 pint sliced strawberries in 3 tablespoons Cointreau® until soft, sweeten with superfine sugar to taste, spoon over cake, and add a dollop of crème fraîche. (PHOTO, PAGE 148)

Calif: Andrew Quady, Orange Muscat
Italy: Antinori Marchesi L & P, Vin Santo

ABSOLUTELY DIVINE DEVIL'S FOOD CAKE

Cindy Brooks
St. Louis, MO

One of my coworkers shared this recipe with the group. Now we all blow our diets for this cake! Don't be put off by the beets; they help to make it very rich and delicious.

DIRECTIONS FOR DEVIL'S FOOD CAKE:

Preheat oven to 350°. Grease the bottom and sides of 2 (9-inch-diameter) cake pans and dust with flour or cocoa. Melt chocolate in double boiler; set aside to cool slightly. Drain beet juice into a small bowl. Chop beets into small, thin pieces, and add to juice; set aside. In a large bowl, beat butter, sugar, eggs, and vanilla with an electric mixer until fluffy. Reduce speed to low; beat in melted chocolate. In a medium mixing bowl, stir together flour, baking soda, and salt. Alternately beat flour (in fourths) and buttermilk (in thirds) into the chocolate mixture. Mix until blended. Add beets and juice; mix until blended. Pour into prepared pans, and bake for 30 to 35 minutes. Cool in pans for 10 minutes; remove from pans and cool to room temperature on wire racks.

DIRECTIONS FOR FROSTING:

Heat cream in a saucepan over medium heat until just boiling. Reduce heat to low; add chocolate and vanilla, and stir until smooth. Chill in a glass bowl, stirring every 10 minutes, until the consistency of set pudding. Continue to chill, stirring every 5 minutes, until the consistency of fudge. Let stand at room temperature until the desired spreading consistency is achieved.

Frost cake; let it stand at room temperature until frosting is set. (PHOTO, PAGE 158)

SERVES 8 TO 10

CAKE:

- 3 ounces unsweetened chocolate
- 1 (8¼-ounce) can beets
- ½ cup (1 stick) butter at room temperature
- 2½ cups firmly packed dark brown sugar
- 3 large eggs at room temperature
- 2 teaspoons vanilla extract
- 2 cups flour
- 2 teaspoons baking soda
- ½ teaspoon salt
- ½ cup buttermilk

FROSTING:

- 2 cups whipping cream
- 24 ounces (3 cups) semisweet chocolate chips
- 2 teaspoons vanilla extract

 Germany: Egon Müller Scharzhof, Scharzhofberger, Riesling BA

 Italy : Agricola Masi, '94 Recioto della Valpolicella

GRAHAM CRACKER CAKE

Mary K. Petsche
Arlington, TX

My aunt Lilla, who was a live-in cook for a wealthy family in Cleveland, gave me this recipe back in the '50s. She began cooking at age 13 and knew how to make anything taste good. This was one of her favorites.

CAKE:

- 1 cup (2 sticks) butter or shortening
- 2 cups sugar
- 4 large eggs, separated
- 1 teaspoon baking powder
- 3¼ cups graham cracker crumbs (from about 44 crackers)
- 1 teaspoon vanilla extract
- 1½ cups milk
- 1 cup chopped walnuts

FROSTING:

- 1 cup milk
- 1 large egg
- ½ cup sugar
- ¼ cup (½ stick) sweetened butter
- 8 ounces confectioners' sugar

DIRECTIONS FOR GRAHAM CRACKER CAKE:

Preheat oven to 350°. Grease and flour an 8x8x2-inch baking pan, and line with parchment paper. In a large mixing bowl, cream butter with sugar; add egg yolks one at a time, beating after each addition. Stir baking powder into crumbs, and add to the batter. Mix vanilla with milk; add to the batter. Stir in walnuts. Beat egg whites until they stand in soft peaks; fold into the batter. Pour into prepared pan. Bake for 35 minutes, or until a toothpick inserted in the center of the cake comes out clean. Let cool to room temperature.

DIRECTIONS FOR FROSTING:

In a heavy saucepan, cook milk, egg, and sugar over low heat until thick and custard-like. Let cool. Cream butter with confectioners' sugar. Slowly beat milk mixture into butter until light and creamy.

To serve, frost cake.

SERVES 8 TO 10

California: Robert Mondavi Winery, '93 Sauvignon Blanc, Late Harvest

Spain: Hidalgo Vinicola, Oloroso Sherry

BOILED RAISIN CAKE

Virginia Crawford
Jackson, MO

This is a very old recipe that I remember my mother making when I was a child. I always loved the spicy aroma in the kitchen as it cooked, and eagerly awaited eating a piece while it was still warm.

DIRECTIONS FOR BOILED RAISIN CAKE:

Preheat oven to 350°. Grease and flour a 1½-quart loaf pan. Place raisins and water in a medium saucepan, and cook over medium heat until 1 cup of liquid remains. Cream sugar and shortening; add raisins with cooking liquid.

In a separate bowl, sift together flour, baking soda, cinnamon, nutmeg, and salt; add to shortening mixture. Mix in vanilla and pecans. Pour into loaf pan. Bake for 40 to 50 minutes until a wooden toothpick inserted in the center comes out clean.

DIRECTIONS FOR GLAZE:

In a medium bowl, sift sugar. Add water and beat until smooth. If too thick, add more water and beat. Drizzle over the top of the warm cake. Let glaze harden before serving.

Serve with a cup of Mango Ceylon tea.

SERVES 10 TO 12

California: Mirassou Vineyards, '94 Pinot Blanc, Late Harvest

Italy: Antinori Marchesi L & P, '92 Muffato della Sala

CAKE:

1 cup raisins
2 cups cold water
1 cup sugar
2 tablespoons shortening or butter
2 cups flour
1 teaspoon baking soda
1 teaspoon cinnamon
1 teaspoon nutmeg
½ teaspoon salt
1 teaspoon vanilla extract
½ cup chopped pecans

GLAZE:

1½ cups confectioners' sugar
3 to 4 tablespoons hot water as needed

PINEAPPLE CAKE

Marilyn Firnett
Chatsworth, CA

I grew up in Iowa on a farm without electricity or gas. I can remember my grandmother making this cake on a wood stove. One Christmas, she made a special gift for me–a blue composition book containing all the recipes she had invented, including this one. I treasure it to this day.

CAKE:

- 2 tablespoons butter, softened
- 1 cup sugar
- 1 large egg
- 1 cup milk
- 1 teaspoon pineapple extract
- 2 cups flour
- 4 teaspoons baking powder
- 1/8 teaspoon salt

FILLING:

- 1 cup milk, divided into 3/4 cup and 1/4 cup
- 1/2 cup sugar
- 4 tablespoons flour
- 1/8 teaspoon salt
- 1 yolk of a large egg
- 1 teaspoon butter
- 1/2 teaspoon pineapple extract
- 4 ounces crushed pineapple, drained

DIRECTIONS FOR PINEAPPLE CAKE:

Preheat oven to 350°. Grease and flour 2 (8-inch-diameter) cake pans, and line with parchment paper. In a large bowl, cream butter and sugar with an electric mixer. In a small bowl, whisk together egg, milk, and extract; add to the butter mixture. Combine remaining cake ingredients with a fork; add to the batter. Beat for 3 minutes. Pour into prepared pans. Bake for 20 minutes, or until a toothpick inserted in the middle comes out clean. Let cool in the pans for 5 minutes. Invert onto wire racks, and peel off parchment paper.

DIRECTIONS FOR FILLING:

Pour 3/4 cup milk into a double boiler over medium heat. In a mixing bowl, whisk together sugar, flour, salt, egg yolk, and remaining milk. When milk in double boiler is hot, add the flour mixture. Cook, stirring constantly, until very thick. Stir in butter. Let cool. Stir in extract and crushed pineapple.

To serve, spread filling between the cake layers and frost with a plain white icing.

SERVES 6 TO 8

Fresh Lemon Ice Cream

Kathee Kraker
Cupertino, CA

Our family and friends particularly enjoy this refreshing dessert after a dinner of fresh salmon, grilled on our patio by the pool.

Cut approximately ⅓ off the end of each lemon. Carefully ream out juice and reserve ⅓ cup strained juice to use in ice cream. Scrape shells clean with a spoon. Freeze until ready to use. In a large mixing bowl, combine cream and sugar, stirring until sugar dissolves. Blend in lemon peel and reserved juice. Pour into a shallow pan. Freeze for 4 hours, or until firm. Spoon into frozen lemon shells.

To serve, garnish with fresh mint leaves, strawberries, and a few strands of lemon zest.

As an alternative to serving in lemon shells, the ice cream can be served in champagne flutes. Alternate scoops of ice cream with bittersweet chocolate sauce and top with a whipped cream rosette and a candied violet.

Note: This recipe can be adapted to other citrus fruits such as grapefruit and oranges.

(PHOTO, PAGE 164)

MAKES 8 SERVINGS

8 large lemons
2 cups whipping cream
1 cup sugar
1 tablespoon grated lemon peel
Mint leaves, strawberries, and lemon zest for garnish

Banana Cream Pie

Charlotte A. Elwert
Bloomfield Hills, MI

My family has long been engaged in the wholesale food business, and I have always had great interest in cooking as an art. I own the Cordon Bleu video and devour each and every issue of *Cook's Illustrated*. I even attended the New Orleans Cooking School and French cooking classes across the river in Windsor, Ontario.

PASTRY CREAM:

- 4 cups whole milk
- 8 yolks of large eggs
- 1⅓ cups sugar
- ⅔ cup flour
- ½ teaspoon salt
- 3 tablespoons unsalted butter
- 4 teaspoons vanilla extract, divided in half
- 7 ripe bananas
- 2 cups chilled whipping cream
- 3 tablespoons confectioners' sugar
- Lemon juice to toss on banana garnish

NO-ROLL PIE CRUST:

- ¾ cups (1½ sticks) unsalted butter
- ¼ cup sugar
- 1 tablespoon confectioners' sugar
- 2 cups flour
- Cooking spray to coat tart dish

SERVES 8

DIRECTIONS FOR PASTRY CREAM:

In a small heavy saucepan, scald milk. Remove from heat. In a medium bowl, whisk yolks until pale and thick. In a medium heavy saucepan, mix sugar, flour, and salt; gradually whisk in milk. Whisk some of the milk mixture into yolks. Return yolks to the milk mixture in the saucepan. Cook over medium heat, whisking constantly for 5 minutes, or until the mixture boils and thickens. Add butter and 2 teaspoons vanilla; whisk for 2 minutes. Pour into a bowl. Press plastic wrap onto the surface of pastry cream to prevent skin from forming. Cover; chill until set.

DIRECTIONS FOR NO-ROLL PIE CRUST:

Preheat oven to 300°. Melt butter in a medium heavy saucepan. Remove from heat. Add sugar and confectioners' sugar; stir to combine. Stir in flour. Cool for 15 minutes (dough will still be warm). Use dough immediately. Coat a 10-inch-diameter fluted ceramic tart dish with 2-inch-high sides or a glass pie dish with cooking spray. Press dough to ¼-inch thickness into the bottom and up the sides of prepared dish. Trim edges and crimp. Chill for at least 30 minutes. Bake for 40 minutes, or until golden brown. Let cool on a wire rack; cover.

Peel bananas and cut into ¼-inch slices. Using an electric mixer, whip cream, confectioners' sugar, and remaining vanilla in large bowl until soft peaks form. Arrange half of sliced bananas on pie crust, overlapping slightly. Spoon pastry cream over banana layer. Top with remaining bananas, reserving 8 slices for garnish. Toss lemon juice on garnish slices to prevent discoloration. Top pie with whipped cream. Chill for 1 to 4 hours.

Garnish with remaining banana slices and serve chilled.

Note: Pastry cream and crust can be prepared one day ahead.

BRANDY ALEXANDER PIE

Madlyn Daniel
Chicago, IL

The first time I made this pie, I thought it was only so-so. But when we tasted it the next day, it was wonderful! Since then, I always make it a day ahead of time.

Sprinkle gelatin over cold water in a saucepan. Add 1/3 cup sugar, salt, and egg yolks; whisk to blend. Cook over low heat, stirring constantly, until gelatin dissolves and the mixture foams and thickens slightly; do not boil. Remove from heat and stir in cognac and crème de cacao. Chill until the mixture thickens slightly. Beat egg whites until they stand in soft peaks; gradually beat in remaining sugar, and fold into chilled mixture. Whip cream until it holds medium peaks and fold in. Pour into crust. Chill for several hours or overnight.

To serve, whip remaining cream, lightly sweeten with sugar, and garnish. If you are handy with a pastry tube and decorator's tip, this is the time to show off. Finish with chocolate curls.

SERVES 6 TO 8

- 1 (1/4-ounce) envelope unflavored gelatin
- 1/2 cup cold water
- 2/3 cup sugar, divided in half
- 1/8 teaspoon salt
- 3 large eggs, separated
- 1/4 cup cognac
- 1/4 cup crème de cacao
- 2 cups heavy cream, divided into 2 equal portions
- 1 (9-inch-diameter) graham cracker crust
- Chocolate curls for garnish

California: Joseph Phelps Vineyards,
          '93 Scheurebe, Late Harvest
Italy: Pellegrino, '93 Passito di Pantelleria

SOUR CREAM APPLE PIE

Linda R. Dunn
Swampscott, MA

I am an avid reader of cookbooks and read cookbooks for pleasure. It seems to me we are going back to comfort foods, and that certainly is the character of this pie. I make it with McIntosh or Gala apples and serve it hot or cold. It's an especially good finish to a roast beef dinner.

PIE:

1 large egg
½ cup sugar
2 tablespoons flour
¼ teaspoon salt
2 tablespoons lemon juice
1 cup sour cream
4 cups peeled, thinly sliced, cooked apples (4 or 5 medium apples)
1 (9-inch-diameter) pie crust, unbaked

TOPPING:

½ cup firmly packed light brown sugar
¼ cup flour
1 teaspoon cinnamon
¼ cup (½ stick) butter, chilled

DIRECTIONS FOR SOUR CREAM APPLE PIE:

Preheat oven to 400°. In a small bowl, mix egg, sugar, flour, salt, and lemon juice with a whisk. Beat in sour cream. Place apples in pie crust. Pour mixture over top. Bake for 15 minutes.

DIRECTIONS FOR TOPPING:

Process topping ingredients in order listed in a food processor until crumbly. Sprinkle over pie. Reduce oven temperature to 350°. Bake for 30 to 40 minutes until apples are tender when pierced with the tip of a knife.

Serve with coffee.

SERVES 6 TO 8

 California: Far Niente Winery, '93 Dolce
 Italy: Carlo Hauner, '93 Malvasia delle Lipari

STREUSEL-TOPPED PEACH PIE

Connie Caldwell
McKinney, TX

My mother found this recipe inside a flour sack years ago. Frankly, we call it "the best peach pie you will ever eat." It's so easy and always wins raves.

DIRECTIONS FOR PIE SHELL CRUST:

Preheat oven to 375°. Using a fork, combine crust ingredients in order given to form a soft dough. Shape dough into a ball by hand and press into a 9-inch pie pan. Flute the edges.

DIRECTIONS FOR FILLING:

Combine peaches, confectioners' sugar, and flour. Toss lightly until peaches are evenly coated with sugar and flour. Spoon into unbaked pie shell crust.

DIRECTIONS FOR CRUMB MIXTURE:

Combine crumb mixture ingredients to form a crumbly mixture. Distribute evenly over peaches. Bake for 40 to 50 minutes until top is golden.

Serve with vanilla ice cream.

SERVES 6 TO 8

California: Andrew Quady, Essencia
France: Château Moncontour, '94 Vouvray

PIE SHELL CRUST:
1½ cups flour
2 teaspoons sugar
½ teaspoon salt
½ cup cold, mild-flavored cooking oil
2 tablespoons milk

FILLING:
5 cups peeled, pitted and sliced peaches
½ cup confectioners' sugar
⅓ cup flour

CRUMB MIXTURE:
¾ cup flour
½ cup firmly packed light brown sugar
½ teaspoon cinnamon
⅓ cup butter or margarine

AUSTRALIA TORTE

Barbara Williams
Dallas, TX

This recipe took me to Paris! It all began when my niece entered a chocolate recipe contest and her Australian torte won her the grand prize–a trip for two to Paris–and she invited me to go with her. The secret of its smooth texture is that half the mixture is baked and half is chilled.

1¼ cups (2½ sticks) plus 1 tablespoon butter, softened
1½ cups sugar
9 eggs, separated
Zest of 1 large orange
10½ ounces bittersweet or semisweet chocolate, melted
3 tablespoons shortbread cookie crumbs

Preheat oven to 375°. Lightly grease a 9-inch-diameter springform pan. Cream butter and sugar until light and smooth. Add egg yolks, one at a time, blending well after each addition. Add orange zest and chocolate.

In a separate bowl, beat egg whites until they stand in soft peaks; gently fold into the chocolate mixture. Set aside half of this mixture. Fold shortbread crumbs into remaining half.

Pour crumb batter into springform pan and bake for 30 to 35 minutes until the center is firm to the touch. Let cool at room temperature without removing the outside ring of the pan. When the base has cooled completely, spread reserved chocolate mixture over the baked base to form the top layer. Chill for several hours or overnight. Remove the outside ring of the pan.

To serve, garnish with whipped cream, grated chocolate, and orange peel.

Note: For a more finished top layer, pipe the second layer onto the baked layer to create large decorative swirls.

SERVES 10 TO 12

CHOCOLATE MOUSSE

Bonnie (Mrs. Irving) Schiffman
Dallas, TX

Decadence for the chocoholic! This was a favorite in the era of "BCC" (Before Cholesterol Consideration). It is easily prepared in advance and can be served in individual portions or in a large crystal bowl for buffets.

Chill a medium metal or ceramic bowl in the freezer. In a double boiler, melt semisweet and unsweetened chocolate, butter, and coffee. Stir until smooth and creamy. Stir in extract. Remove from heat, transfer to a large bowl, and let cool at room temperature.

In a metal mixing bowl, beat egg yolks and ¼ cup sugar with an electric mixer until thick and pale yellow. Beat in amaretto. Place over simmering water, and beat for 4 to 5 minutes until hot and foamy. Remove from heat, and place over a bowl filled with ice cubes. Beat for 4 to 5 minutes until cooled, thickened, and creamy in texture; set aside.

In the chilled bowl, beat egg whites, gradually adding ¼ cup sugar until stiff. Stir a cup of egg whites into the chocolate mixture. Fold in remaining egg whites and cooled egg yolk mixture. Whip cream with remaining sugar and vanilla until stiff. Fold into chocolate mixture until smooth. Spoon mousse into stemmed glasses or into a large bowl and chill before serving.

To serve, top with whipped cream.

SERVES 12 TO 15

12 ounces semisweet chocolate
2 ounces unsweetened chocolate
6 tablespoons unsalted butter
6 tablespoons strongly brewed coffee
1 teaspoon almond extract
6 eggs, separated
¾ cup superfine sugar, divided in thirds
¼ cup amaretto
1 pint heavy cream
½ teaspoon vanilla extract

GRANDMA'S CHOCOLATE HEAVEN

Elise Perelman
Katonah, NY

This very rich chocolate cake is one of Grandma's secret recipes that she saved for special occasions. Everyone at the table looked forward to it from the time they sat down. Pure heaven!

CAKE:
- 2²/₃ cups semisweet chocolate chips
- 2 cups (4 sticks) butter
- 1¹/₄ cups sugar
- 1 cup light cream
- 1 tablespoon vanilla extract
- ¹/₂ teaspoon salt
- 8 large eggs

GLAZE:
- 1 cup semisweet chocolate chips
- 2 tablespoons butter
- 2 tablespoons half-and-half
- 1 tablespoon vanilla-flavored coffee creamer
- 2 tablespoons light corn syrup

CHOCOLATE HEAVEN CAKE:

Preheat oven to 350°. Grease a 10x3-inch springform pan. In a 3-quart saucepan, melt chocolate chips, butter, sugar, cream, vanilla, and salt over low heat. Stir until smooth. Set aside. In a large mixing bowl, slightly whisk eggs. Slowly add warm chocolate mixture, beating until blended. Pour into prepared pan and bake for 45 minutes, or until a toothpick inserted 2 inches into the cake comes out clean. Let cool, wrap in plastic, and chill for 2 to 3 hours until cake is sturdy.

GLAZE:

Melt chocolate chips and butter over low heat until smooth. Remove from heat. Beat in half-and-half, coffee creamer, and corn syrup.

Unwrap cake and loosen the edges with a knife until it slides off easily. Line cake plate with waxed paper and place cake in the center. Glaze. Chill until glaze is hard.

Serve with whipped cream.

Note: An extra tablespoon of half-and-half can be substituted for coffee creamer in the glaze.

SERVES 10 TO 12

 Portugal: Blandís Reserve (5 years), Verdelho
 Italy: Frescobaldi, Vin Santo

MILLION-DOLLAR BROWNIES

Mrs. Marvin B. Ganek
Highland Park, IL

The recipe for these brownies was given to me years ago by a friend of my daughter. They are expensive to make and certainly not low-calorie, but definitely the ultimate indulgence and well worth the dollars and the calories.

Preheat oven to 350°. Grease and flour a 13x9x2-inch baking pan. In a double boiler over low heat, combine caramels and evaporated milk. Cover and simmer until caramels melt, stirring occasionally; keep warm with lid askew and water barely simmering.

In a 2-quart saucepan over low heat, combine chocolate and butter, stirring occasionally, until melted. Remove from heat; let cool to room temperature.

In a large bowl, beat eggs with an electric mixer at high speed until foamy. Gradually add sugar, continuing to beat until slightly thickened and pale yellow.

In a separate bowl, sift together flour, baking powder, and salt; gradually add to the egg mixture. Mix. Blend in the cooled chocolate mixture and vanilla. Spread half of the chocolate batter into prepared pan. Bake for 6 minutes, or until set. Remove from oven.

Spread caramel mixture over baked chocolate batter. Sprinkle chocolate chips on top. Add half of pecans into remaining chocolate batter. Spoon over caramel layer. Sprinkle remaining pecans over top. Bake for 30 minutes, or until the top layer of the batter is set. Let cool in baking dish. Chill for 2 hours in the baking dish.

Note: If brownies are not chilled, they will be difficult to cut.

MAKES 35 BROWNIES

- 1 (14-ounce) package individually wrapped caramel candies
- 1/3 cup evaporated milk
- 8 ounces German's sweet chocolate
- 6 tablespoons butter
- 4 large eggs
- 1 cup sugar
- 1 cup flour, sifted
- 1 teaspoon baking powder
- 1/2 teaspoon salt
- 2 teaspoons vanilla extract
- 6 ounces chocolate chips
- 1 cup chopped pecans, divided in half

BUTTER TOFFEE

Jayne (Mrs. Jerry) Gross
The Woodlands, TX

This is candy for adults! And friends can't wait to receive it as gifts. I begin making it around Thanksgiving time and have shipped it everywhere–Chicago, Amarillo, and to a son in college.

1 cup (2 sticks) butter at refrigerator temperature
1¼ cups sugar
⅛ teaspoon cream of tartar
1 cup chopped pecans
3½ ounces milk chocolate
3½ ounces semisweet chocolate
¾ to 1 cup pecans, grated, to taste

Lightly oil an 11x17-inch cookie tray with edges. In an aluminum pan, mix butter and sugar. Cook over high heat, stirring constantly with a wooden spoon. As butter melts and the mixture simmers around the edges, add cream of tartar. Stir vigorously. When mixture comes to a rolling boil, add chopped pecans. Cook, stirring constantly until mixture turns a medium tan color and is slightly thinned. Pour immediately into prepared cookie tray, spreading evenly over sheet.

Break up chocolates. Immediately strew on toffee, let melt, and spread. Sprinkle grated pecans on top of chocolate while still hot.

Let stand to harden. Break in pieces to serve.

MAKES 3 DOZEN PIECES

Big Dipper Biscotti

Joyce M. Konigsberg
Ross, CA

I devised this recipe in honor of our 15th wedding anniversary. It's a hybrid, combining the best features of mondelbrot and biscotti, just as our marriage combines the best features of Jewish and Italian cultures.

Preheat oven to 350°. Soak cherries and apricots in liqueur for 30 minutes. Lightly grease 2 cookie sheets. Strain cherries and apricots and set aside, reserving 2 teaspoons liqueur. In a large bowl, cream butter, sugar, and eggs. Add zest, reserved liqueur, and extract; stir and set aside. Sift flour again with baking powder, salt, and cinnamon. Combine the dry ingredients with the egg mixture. Add almonds and rehydrated fruits. Mix together with a fork; shape the dough into a ball by hand. Lightly flour a board. Knead dough on floured board for a few minutes. Split dough in half. Form each half by hand into a 1-inch-thick rope-like roll. Flatten each roll until it is 3 inches wide. Place on cookie sheet 2 inches apart and bake for 40 to 45 minutes until lightly browned. Remove to a breadboard, and cut diagonally while warm into 1/2-inch-wide slices.

Place slices, cut side up, on second cookie sheet. Bake on the top shelf of the oven until toasted, turn, and toast the other side. While the cookies are cooling, lay out aluminum foil or waxed paper. Melt the chocolate. Dip one side of the Biscotti into the chocolate and set, plain side down, on foil until chocolate hardens.

Serve with sherry.

Note: Cherry or peach liqueur can be substituted for almond.

(PHOTO, PAGE 152)

MAKES ABOUT 2 DOZEN

1/4 cup finely chopped dried cherries
1/4 cup finely chopped dried apricots
1/4 cup almond liqueur
1/4 cup (1/2 stick) sweet butter, softened
3/4 cup sugar
2 large eggs
Grated zest of 1 small orange
1/4 teaspoon almond extract
2 1/4 cups flour, sifted
1 1/2 teaspoons baking powder
1/4 teaspoon salt
1 1/2 teaspoons cinnamon
1/2 cup coarsely chopped almonds
6 ounces bittersweet chocolate

Pistachio-White Chocolate Chip Cookies

Suzanne Mitchell
Southfield, MI

My bachelor neighbor loves these cookies so much that he brings me the white chocolate whenever he comes over for dinner, just so I'll make a batch for him.

1¼ cups (2½ sticks) butter
2 cups firmly packed light brown sugar
2 large eggs
2 teaspoons vanilla extract
2½ cups flour
1 teaspoon baking soda
1 teaspoon baking powder
½ cup old-fashioned rolled oats
12 ounces white chocolate chips
1⅓ cups pistachios, coarsely chopped

Preheat oven to 350°. With an electric mixer at medium speed, cream butter with sugar in a large bowl. Beat in eggs and vanilla. In a medium bowl, combine flour, baking soda, baking powder, and oats. Gradually add the flour mixture to the butter mixture and combine. Stir in chocolate chips and pistachios.

Drop batter by heaping teaspoons about 2 inches apart onto ungreased cookie sheets. Bake for 8 to 10 minutes until light golden brown. Let cool slightly on cookie sheets; remove to wire racks to cool completely.

Serve with pistachio ice cream.

(PHOTO, PAGE 159)

MAKES 4 DOZEN

SESAME-SEEDED COOKIES

Lucia Giangrasso
Jamaica Plain, MA

This is an old Italian recipe that I remember my grandmother making for holidays such as Easter and Christmas. They are not too sweet, are very crisp, and keep well in a tightly covered container. Make a big batch; they go very fast!

Preheat oven to 400°. Grease a cookie sheet or use a non-stick sheet. Cream shortening. Add eggs, one at a time, mixing well. Add vanilla, anise, sugar, baking powder, and flour. Knead with floured hands. Shape into oval balls. Dip each dough ball in milk and roll in sesame seeds. Place on prepared cookie sheet. Bake for 15 to 20 minutes until golden brown.

MAKES 4 DOZEN

1¾ cups shortening
2 eggs
1 teaspoon vanilla extract
¼ teaspoon anise flavoring
1 cup sugar
1 teaspoon baking powder
4 cups flour
½ cup milk
1 pound sesame seeds

Banana Macadamia Nut Phyllo Tart

Mark Militello
Miami, FL

CRUST:

- ½ cup (1 stick) unsalted butter
- 8 sheets phyllo dough or strudel dough
- 3 to 4 tablespoons confectioners' sugar as needed

FILLING:

- ½ cup (1 stick) unsalted butter
- 4 large eggs
- 1 cup light corn syrup
- 1 cup firmly packed light brown sugar
- 2 teaspoons vanilla extract
- ½ teaspoon salt
- 4 ounces (½ cup) unsalted macadamia nuts
- 1 medium ripe banana
- 2 to 3 tablespoons confectioners' sugar for dusting
- 1 cup heavy cream for garnish

DIRECTIONS FOR CRUST:

Lightly grease a 10-inch-diameter springform pan. Melt butter, and let cool. Line prepared pan with a sheet of phyllo dough, gently easing the dough into the bottom and sides of the pan without tearing it. Sprinkle confectioners' sugar on the dough and brush with melted butter. Placing each layer perpendicular to the previous one, layer remaining sheets of phyllo dough in the pan, brushing with melted butter and dusting with confectioners' sugar. Reserve leftover butter.

DIRECTIONS FOR FILLING:

Preheat oven to 325°. In a small saucepan, melt butter, and let cool to room temperature. In a large bowl, combine eggs, corn syrup, brown sugar, vanilla, and salt; whisk until mixed. Whisk in butter. Arrange nuts over the bottom of the crust. Peel the banana, cut into ¼-inch slices, and arrange on top of nuts. Pour the egg mixture on top. Gently fold the phyllo dough over the filling. Brush the top with butter remaining from the crust assembly; sprinkle with confectioners' sugar. Bake for 1 hour, or until filling is set, but still soft. Let cool to room temperature, and remove the sides of the pan. Lightly dust with confectioners' sugar. Beat the cream to soft peaks.

To serve, cut the tart into wedges. Serve each with a ruff of whipped cream.

Note: Crust must be prepared before filling.

SERVES 8

 Germany: Egon Müller Scharzhof, '93 Auslesen Riesling, Forst Kirchenstücl

 France: Louis Roederer, Carte Blanche

CARAMELIZED PUMPKIN FLAN

Joyce Goldstein
San Francisco, CA

Creme caramel is comfort food at its best. This variation on the classic dessert is perfect for the holidays. It's easy to prepare and best made the day before so there's no last-minute anxiety when entertaining.

Preheat oven to 325°. Melt 1 cup sugar and water in a small saucepan, stirring until sugar is dissolved. Cook over high heat until sugar caramelizes to a rich, warm brown; do not stir. Pour carefully into the bottom of 8 custard cups or oven-proof ramekins.

In a bowl, combine pumpkin, zest, cinnamon, nutmeg, ginger, and salt. In a medium saucepan, heat cream with remaining sugar until bubbles form around the edge of the pan; remove from the heat. In a large metal or ceramic bowl, beat eggs lightly with a fork; add the pumpkin mixture. Gradually add hot cream and vanilla. Mix until smooth. Pour over the caramelized sugar in the custard cups. Place the cups in a baking pan. Add enough hot water to the pan to come halfway up the sides of the cups. Cover the pan with aluminum foil. Bake for 45 minutes, or until custard is set and a knife inserted in the custard comes out clean. Remove the cups from the water and let stand on a rack or baking pan at room temperature for 30 minutes. Cover and chill for at least 2 hours or overnight.

To serve, run a knife around the inside edge of each cup and turn the custards out onto plates or shallow dessert bowls.

Note: Cooked mashed sweet potatoes or yams could be used instead of pumpkin.

| 1 1/2 cups sugar, divided into 1 cup and remainder |
| 3 tablespoons water |
| 1 cup canned pumpkin (half of a 16-ounce can) |
| Grated zest of 1 orange |
| 1 teaspoon cinnamon |
| 1/4 teaspoon nutmeg |
| 1/2 teaspoon ginger |
| 1/4 teaspoon salt |
| 1 1/2 cups light cream |
| 3 eggs |
| 1 teaspoon vanilla extract |

SERVES 8

California: Santa Barbara Winery, '93 Sauvignon Blanc, Late Harvest

California: Gan Eden, '93 Black Muscat, San Joaquin Valley

Kahlúa® Crème Brûlée

Veronica Dalton
Scottsdale, AZ

Once the guests have arrived, I like to spend my time with them, not in the kitchen. So I do this recipe ahead of time, and without fail, the guests rave about the coffee and Kahlúa® richness of this elegant dessert. In fact, there is never any left!

7 yolks of large eggs
1/4 cup sugar
4 cups whipping cream
1 tablespoon freeze-dried instant coffee granules
1/2 cup Kahlúa®
1 tablespoon vanilla extract
2/3 cup firmly packed light brown sugar

Preheat oven to 325°. In a medium metal or ceramic bowl, whisk together egg yolks and sugar until slightly thickened and pale yellow. In a medium saucepan, stir together cream and coffee. Bring to a boil over medium heat, stirring to dissolve coffee granules. Slowly whisk hot cream into egg yolks. Whisk in Kahlúa® and vanilla. Ladle into 8 round broilerproof 1/2-cup ramekins. Set in a shallow baking pan; add enough boiling water to the pan to come halfway up the sides of the ramekins. Bake for 30 minutes, or until the tops are set. The custards will remain jiggly until completely chilled. Remove from the water bath, and let cool to room temperature. Cover and chill overnight.

Preheat broiler. Press brown sugar through a sieve over the custards in an even, fluffy layer. Wipe excess sugar from the edges of the dishes. Broil 5 to 6 inches from the heat source until sugar liquefies and begins to caramelize, being careful not to burn sugar. Chill for 1 to 5 hours.

To serve, garnish with mint leaves and raspberries or chocolate-covered coffee beans.

SERVES 8

 California: Andrew Quady, Orange Muscat
 Italy: Rivetti, '94 Moscato d'Asti

French Fresh Fruit Flan

Linda Underdown
Birmingham, MI

Every year, a group of my high school friends meet for a reunion in Naples, Florida. It was there that I learned the recipe for this delicious and colorful dessert. It's always the pièce de résistance at any meal. Now, even my daughter, Amy, has made it for her high school French class.

DIRECTIONS FOR ALMOND CRUST:

Preheat oven to 375°. In a food processor, combine almonds, butter, sugar, and flour. Add egg yolk and extracts. Blend until dough holds together. Press onto bottom and sides of an 11-inch tart pan with a removable bottom. Bake for 15 minutes, or until golden brown. Let cool.

DIRECTIONS FOR FILLING:

Mix all filling ingredients with electric mixer until smooth. Spread evenly on cooled tart crust. Chill for 30 minutes, or until firm.

DIRECTIONS FOR GLAZE:

Mix glaze ingredients in a small saucepan, and cook on low heat until hot. Strain through a fine sieve, and let cool.

DIRECTIONS FOR TOPPING:

Arrange fruit in concentric circles or another attractive pattern on top of filling. Brush with glaze. Let stand for 1 to 2 hours for glaze to harden.

Serve slightly chilled or at room temperature.

Note: Almond Crust can be made one day ahead.

(PHOTO, PAGE 160)

SERVES 10 TO 12

California: Andrew Quady, Elysium Black Muscat

France: Barton and Guestier (B&G), '88 Sauternes

ALMOND CRUST:
- 1/2 cup ground almonds
- 1/2 cup (1 stick) butter, softened
- 1/2 cup sugar
- 1 1/2 cups flour
- 1 yolk of a large egg
- 1 teaspoon vanilla extract
- 1/2 teaspoon almond extract

FILLING:
- 8 ounces cream cheese, softened
- 3 tablespoons sugar
- 2 tablespoons amaretto
- 1 teaspoon vanilla extract
- 1/2 teaspoon almond extract

GLAZE:
- 1/2 cup apricot preserves or orange marmalade
- 1 tablespoon lemon juice
- 2 tablespoons amaretto

TOPPING:
- 3 to 4 cups fresh fruit, such as:
  - Strawberries, halved with stems intact
  - Kiwis, peeled and sliced in rounds
  - Peaches, peeled, sliced, and dipped in lemon juice to preserve color
  - Raspberries
  - Blueberries

CRANBERRY APPLE CRISP

Laura Wertheimer
Washington, D.C.

Every Thanksgiving, I struggle to find the perfect dessert for that special meal. Pumpkin pie, pumpkin cheesecake, pumpkin ginger soufflé, pumpkin chiffon pie—I tried them all. Then I started anew. This recipe is the result and has been a family favorite ever since its debut.

FILLING:

16 tart baking apples
12 ounces fresh or frozen cranberries (if frozen, do not defrost)
⅓ pound dried, pitted sour cherries
2 teaspoons cinnamon
1 cup sugar
Juice and rind of 2 lemons

TOPPING:

1 cup old-fashioned rolled oatmeal
1 cup flour
1 cup firmly packed light brown sugar
¾ cup (1½ sticks) unsalted butter

DIRECTIONS FOR FILLING:

Preheat oven to 350°.

Grease a 10- to 12-inch-deep Dutch oven or high-sided glass baking dish. Peel, core, and slice apples. Add remaining filling ingredients and mix to combine.

DIRECTIONS FOR TOPPING:

In a food processor, combine topping ingredients and pulse until coarse crumbs form.

Sprinkle topping over the filling. Bake for 60 to 70 minutes.

SERVES 12 TO 14

 California: Iron Horse Vineyards, Blanc de Pinot Noir

 California: De Loach Vineyards, '94 Gewürztraminer, Late Harvest

CRANBERRY TORTE

Marianne P. Hinrichs
Corona del Mar, CA

In our family, it just would not have been Thanksgiving or Christmas without this festive delight. It's as pretty to serve as it is delicious.

DIRECTIONS FOR CRANBERRY TORTE:

Preheat oven to 375°. Grease a jelly roll pan or 2 (9-inch-diameter) baking pans. In a large bowl, beat egg yolks and sugar until light. Add water. In a separate bowl, mix flour, baking powder, nuts, dates, salt, and lemon rind; combine with yolks. Beat egg whites until they stand in soft peaks; fold into mixture. Spread in prepared jelly roll pan or baking pans. Bake for 25 to 30 minutes until the center is firm to the touch. Meanwhile, prepare filling (see filling recipe). When torte is done, remove from oven and let cool on a wire rack. If baked in one long sheet, cut in half to form 2 layers.

DIRECTIONS FOR CRANBERRY FILLING:

Bring sugar and water to a boil over medium heat in a saucepan; boil for 5 minutes. Add cranberries and orange rind. Cook for 1 minute, or until all the berries pop. Mix cornstarch with cold water and add to berries. Cook for 2 minutes. Chill until ready to serve.

To serve, spread filling on one torte layer; top with second torte layer. Top with whipped cream.

SERVES 10 TO 12

🍷 California: Ficklin Vineyards, Ruby Port
🍇 Italy: Pellegrino, Sweet Marsala

TORTE:

- 4 eggs, separated
- 1 cup sugar
- 1/2 cup water
- 1 cup flour
- 2 teaspoons baking powder
- 1 cup chopped walnuts
- 1 cup sliced dates
- 1/4 teaspoon salt
- Grated rind of 1/2 lemon

FILLING:

- 3/4 cup sugar
- 1 cup water
- 2 cups cranberries
- Grated rind of 1 orange
- 1 tablespoon cornstarch
- 1 tablespoon cold water

Strawberry Jelly Roll

Pam Morse
Houston, TX

Many years ago, my aunt told me that if I really wanted to impress my guests, all I had to do was serve her strawberry jelly roll. It is well worth the effort and is delicious.

JELLY ROLL:

- 4 large eggs, separated
- 3/4 cup sugar, divided into 1/4 cup and 1/2 cup
- 1 teaspoon vanilla extract
- 2/3 cup flour
- 1 teaspoon baking powder
- 1/8 teaspoon salt
- Confectioners' sugar for dusting

FILLING:

- 1 pint whipping cream
- Sugar to taste
- 1 pint strawberries, sliced

DIRECTIONS FOR STRAWBERRY JELLY ROLL:

Preheat oven to 375°. Grease and lightly flour a cookie tray with sides. In a large bowl, beat yolks until slightly thick and pale yellow. Gradually beat in 1/4 cup sugar; add vanilla. In a medium bowl, beat egg whites until soft peaks form. Gradually add 1/2 cup sugar and beat until stiff peaks form. Fold egg whites into yolks. Wipe out the medium bowl and sift together flour, baking powder, and salt in it; fold into the egg mixture. Spread batter evenly in cookie tray. Bake for 10 minutes, or until cake springs back when lightly touched. Meanwhile, sprinkle sifted confectioners' sugar lightly on a towel. When the cake is done, immediately loosen sides and turn onto towel, using a spatula if necessary to loosen the bottom. Starting at the narrow end, roll up cake and towel together into a log to shape cake. Let cool on a rack. When cake is room temperature, unroll.

DIRECTIONS FOR FILLING:

Whip cream to medium peak stage and sweeten with sugar to taste. Sweeten strawberries with sugar to taste.

Combine cream and berries and spread on the cake. Gently roll up into a log shape. Slice with a serrated knife. Let stand for 10 to 15 minutes.

Serve with additional sliced strawberries and whipped cream.

SERVES 6 TO 8

Strawberries Diable

Virginia Kopacz Valley
Corona del Mar, CA

On our honeymoon in Europe, my husband and I dined in a charming Austrian restaurant in Innsbruck named Kapelles, where no one but the chef spoke any English. The food was magnificent, especially the dessert, which the chef made specially for us because we were on our honeymoon. The whole restaurant joined in the celebration, making it quite an evening.

Remove strawberry stems, and cut strawberries into thick slices. In a heavy saucepan over medium heat, melt sugar until light brown and caramelized. Remove from heat; let cool slightly. Stir in orange and lemon juice (combined juices should measure 1 cup). Raise heat to medium-high, and stir until all particles are dissolved. Add strawberries, and bring to a boil. Reduce heat to medium-low. Simmer for 15 minutes, or until liquid is reduced by half, sprinkling pepper over berries while simmering; do not stir. Let cool at room temperature. Chill for 1 hour and 30 minutes to 2 hours.

To serve, spoon ¼ cup sauce on a flat plate. Place a scoop of ice cream on top slightly to one side of the center of the plate and a dollop of whipped cream slightly to the other side. Sift confectioners' sugar over plate to dust.

Note: The sauce may be frozen. For a more exotic flavor, use ½ cup orange juice and ¼ cup orange-flavored liqueur.

SERVES 4

2 pints strawberries
4 tablespoons sugar
¾ cup orange juice
Juice of 1 lemon
5 black peppercorns, crushed
Vanilla ice cream
Whipped cream, sweetened with sugar to taste
Confectioners' sugar for garnish

TIRAMISÙ

Christine Fluor
Newport Beach, CA

My two young daughters, Daria and Kira, have become tiramisù critics and love to order it in restaurants so they can compare it to Mom's. So far, though, my recipe wins. Maybe it's because they get to help make it and lick the beaters afterward.

1 tablespoon instant espresso powder
½ cup hot water
4 tablespoons brandy, divided in half
1 cup whipping cream
½ cup sugar
8 ounces mascarpone cheese
1 yolk of a large egg
1 (7-ounce) package crisp, dry lady fingers
1 tablespoon cocoa powder

Set a medium mixing bowl in the freezer to chill. Dissolve espresso powder in hot water in a quiche or pie pan. Stir in 2 tablespoons brandy, and set aside. In the chilled bowl, whip cream with an electric mixer on high speed until thick. Add sugar, mascarpone, egg yolk, and remaining brandy. Beat at medium speed until combined. Beat on high speed until thick and fluffy with the consistency of whipped cream.

Divide mascarpone mixture, lady fingers, and cocoa powder into thirds. Dip each lady finger into the dissolved espresso, coating both sides without letting them get soggy. Place lady fingers side by side in the bottom of a glass bowl. Spread a third of the mascarpone mixture on top. Sift a third of the cocoa powder on top. Repeat this process two more times. Chill until ready to serve.

To serve, spoon onto chilled dessert plates or into shallow dessert bowls.

SERVES 4

 California: Heitz Wine Cellars, Tawny Port
 Italy: G. Bologna Moscato d'Asti

Cooking Terms

Al dente - (Italian, "to the tooth") A description of pasta cooked only to the point of doneness - with slight resistance when chewed, not overcooked.

Blanch - To cook in boiling water briefly, usually to loosen skin for easy removal, enhance color and decrease bitterness, prolong storage life, or extract excess salt. Foods should be plunged into cold water immediately afterwards to prevent further cooking.

Chiffonade - (French, "made of rags") Thin ribbons or shreds of herbs, leafy greens, or other vegetables, often used to garnish soups.

Clarified, or drawn, butter - Unsalted butter with milk solids extracted. Its higher smoke point enables cooking at higher temperatures. To clarify butter, melt over low heat, skim off froth, and pour the clear yellow liquid into a container, discarding the milky residue.

Deglaze - To form a sauce to accompany a dish by adding water stock, wine, or liquor to a pan in which food has been cooked after the cooked food and excess fat have been removed. The liquid is cooked over high heat and stirred to release browned bits and remaining drippings from the bottom of the pan.

Nap - To completely cover food with an ultra-thin, even layer of sauce.

Parboil - To cook in boiling water until almost halfway cooked. Often used as a time-saving technique so that dense foods such as carrots will cook in the same amount of time in stir-fries and sautés as do the other ingredients.

Ramekin - An individual 3- to 4-inch diameter porcelain or earthenware baking dish akin to a miniature soufflé dish.

Roux - Equal quantities of butter and flour cooked together and used as a base for sauces or as a thickening agent.

Zest - The colored portion of the skin of a citrus fruit. Unlike *rind*, the term *zest* does not include the white pith portion of the skin.

Weights and Measures

1 quart = 4 cups = 64 tablespoons = 32 fluid ounces
1 pint = 2 cups = 32 tablespoons = 16 fluid ounces
1/2 pint = 1 cup = 16 tablespoons = 8 fluid ounces
1 tablespoon = 3 teaspoons = 1/2 fluid ounce
Dash = less than 1/8 teaspoon

Metric liquid measurements:
3.785 liters = 1 gallon
.9463 liters = 1 quart
4732 liters = 1 pint
1/4 liter, approximately = 1 cup

Metric dry measurements:
1.101 liters = 1 quart
.551 liters = 1 pint

Metric weights:
30 grams, approximately = 1 ounce
454 grams, approximately = 1 pound

All temperatures are given in degrees Fahrenheit (°F).
To convert °F to °C, subtract 32°, multiply by 5, and divide by 9.

INDEX

INDEX OF WINES

* Please refer to recipe page for complete wine selection.

Contributors

A

Janys Abate – Eastchester, NY, 141
Nancy Adams – Rancho Santa Fe, CA, 171
Beverly Kabakoff Adilman – Chicago, IL, 45
Emma Afra – Miami, FL, 98
Mary Louise Albritton – Chattanooga, TN, 35
Mary Frances Engle Alford – Henderson, TX, 49
Margaret Henry Amaya – Dallas, TX, 189

B

Bonnie Baker – Playa del Rey, CA, 72
Susan H. (Mrs. William Torry) Barbee – Weslaco, TX, 36
Ardis Bartle – Houston, TX, 211
Joyce Baseman – Alexandria, VA, 42
Pamela Baxter – New York, NY, 87
Cheryl Q. Behan – St. Louis, MO, 108
Edna B. Benna – Reno, NV, 116
Cheryl Bennett – Forest Park, IL, 119
Karen Benning – Dallas, TX, 121
Barbara Bernstein – Los Angeles, CA, 58
Linda G. Bishop – Dallas, TX, 40
Joan Fanaberia Bloom – Montreal, Quebec, Canada, 183
Caroline Bourestom – St. Cloud, MN, 33
Ruth M. Branham – Dallas, TX, 25
A. Bremer – Houston, TX, 144
Cindy Brooks – St. Louis, MO, 253
Barbara Bush – Houston, TX, 167
Catherine A. Byles – Dallas, TX, 206

C

Connie Caldwell – McKinney, TX, 261
Joyce Pate Capper – Fort Worth, TX, 244
Margaret C. Carter – Dallas, TX, 78
E.G. Chamberlin – Corona del Mar, CA, 182
Marilyn Jones Chapman – Seabrook, TX, 83
Joan Chognard – Menlo Park, CA, 169
Barbara E. Church – San Diego, CA, 54
Gail L. Coleman – Farmington Hills, MI, 66
Gary Collins – Beverly Hills, CA, 54
Jackie Cox – Houston, TX, 223
Sandra Crawford – Mineral Wells, TX, 77
Virginia Crawford – Jackson, MO, 255
Freda D. Cronic – Griffin, GA, 173
John E. Crosby Jr. – Midland, TX, 232

D

Veronica Dalton – Scottsdale, AZ, 272
Madlyn Daniel – Chicago, IL, 259
Debi Davis – Dallas, TX, 224
Tomas de la Mata – Dallas, TX, 44
Ann S. Degenhart – Lake Worth, FL, 74
Susan Z. Diamond – Melrose Park, IL, 41
M. Susan Douglas – Topeka, KS, 68
Ginger (Mrs. John E.) Dudley – Comanche, TX, 106
Sara M. Dunham – Baton Rouge, LA, 220
Linda R. Dunn – Swampscott, MA, 260
Jo Dunn – Sugar Land, TX, 215
Patricia J. Dutt – Chicago, IL, 110

E

Howard S. Ehrlich – Parkland, FL, 242
Charlotte A. Elwert – Bloomfield Hills, MI, 258
Mrs. Robert J. Epperson – Satin, TX, 222
Patti Estabrooks – Laguna Beach, CA, 57

F

B. Rhoads Fearn – Santa Maria, CA, 22
James D. Felter – Scottsdale, AZ, 37
Dawn Adels Fine – Miami, FL, 129
Melodie Finks – Salem, IL, 115
Marilyn Firnett – Chatsworth, CA, 256
Mrs. Harold Fishman – St. Louis, MO, 176
Margaret Fletcher – Houston, TX, 24
Carol (Mrs. Luis) Flores – Houston, TX, 118
Christine Fluor – Newport Beach, CA, 278
Olivia Dee Franklin – Dallas, TX, 226
Ebe Frasse – San Jose, CA, 203
Barbara Frederich – San Jose, CA, 120
Rona L. Freedland – Bloomfield Hills, MI, 113
Karen Frommer – Bedford Corners, NY, 28

G

Nancy K. Galdi – Tucson, AZ, 117
Mrs. Marvin B. Ganek – Highland Park, IL, 265
Margane M. Gatto – Miami Lakes, FL, 91
Mona Ghazal – Houston, TX, 130
Lucia Giangrasso – Jamaica Plain, MA, 269
Linda Goldberg – Natick, MA, 243
Esther W. Goldman – New Rochelle, NY, 124

CONTRIBUTORS

G (continued)

Joyce Goldstein – San Francisco, CA, 61, 86, 99, 191, 219, 231, and 271
Mrs. Ronald Goldstein – Atlanta, GA, 225
Roslyn Goldstine – Beverly Hills, CA, 178
Suzanne M. Goodman – Santa Ana, CA, 210
Dr. Eugene L. Gottlieb –Sedona, AZ, 187
Susan Gottlieb – Richboro, PA, 56
Gerry Granacki – Fort Worth, TX, 251
Jeri Greenberg – Washington, D.C., 216
Gail Greene – Garland, TX, 238
Carol Grimm – Coral Springs, FL, 123
Mrs. Jack K.Grissom – Garland, TX, 186
Mollie H. Grober – Fort Smith, AR, 208
Jayne (Mrs. Jerry) Gross –The Woodlands, TX, 266

H

Catherine Handelsman – Glencoe, IL, 211
Jean Hankin – Honolulu, HI, 168
Carol M. Harrison – Fort Lauderdale, FL, 39
Judy Walke Havener – Fort Worth, TX, 35
Rosalind Hertzog – Scarsdale, NY, 133
Marianne P. Hinrichs – Corona del Mar, CA, 275
Mrs. vanAlen Hollomon – Dallas, TX, 195

J

Janina Parrott Jacobs – St. Clair Shores, MI, 143
Louise (Mrs. Robert) Jayson – Dallas, TX, 43
Melinda Jayson – Dallas, TX, 250
Angela Jhin – Tiburon, CA, 132
Jane Jobst – Rochester Hills, MI, 63
Mrs. Lyndon B. Johnson – Stonewall, TX, 239
Mrs. Jimmy J. Jones – Houston, TX, 57
Mrs. Robert E. Jones – Benton, AR, 37

K

Jackie Kanner – St. Petersburg, FL, 95
Ann-Rose Kaplan – Tarzana, CA, 73
Phyllis Katz – New Albany, OH, 24
Caryn Kay – Glencoe, IL, 230
Louise Kazanjian – Pompano Beach, FL, 109
Suzanne G. Keith – Houston, TX, 202
Matthew Kenney – New York, NY, 85, 97, and 174
Barbara (Mrs. Gary) Kent – Las Vegas, NV, 104
Diane Kessler – Newport Beach, CA, 18
Mary Kleckner – Dallas, TX, 252

K (continued)

Lisa Klein – Houston, TX, 76
Paul-Michael Klein – North Miami Beach, FL, 142
Gem Wallis Klinar – Kingsport, TN, 137
Montelle Kline – Miami, FL, 166
Joyce M. Konigsberg – Ross, CA, 267
Kathee Kraker – Cupertino, CA, 257
Irene Kuzyk – Kew Gardens, NY, 246
Cindy Kypreos – Fort Worth, TX, 204

L

Kimberly Lakin – Kansas City, MO, 60
Sylvia C. Landers – Norfolk, NE, 50
Bonnie Aaron Levin – Los Angeles, CA, 203
Christine Horner Lewis – Plano, TX, 138
Mr. and Mrs. Eric Lieber – Beverly Hills, CA, 209
Evilon (Mrs. Eric) Littlejohn – Dallas, TX, 111
Sharon Loeff – Scottsdale, AZ, 181
Crystal L. Lyons –Waxahachie, TX, 180
Dottie Lyons – Santa Maria, CA, 101

M

Sarah Magner – Chicago, IL, 176
Sandy Mallin – Las Vegas, NV, 140
Mrs. John A. Manno Sr. – Shreveport, LA, 48
Carole G. Markoff – Beverly Hills, CA, 199
Nancy Martinez – Dallas, TX, 192
Katy Massoud – Dallas, TX, 194
Ed McMahon – Beverly Hills, CA, 179
Liz Ghiselin Mercier – Houston, TX, 71
Vicki Midyett – Richardson, TX, 245
Mark Militello – Miami, FL, 67, 88, and 270
Ronnie Milsap – Nashville, TN, 139
Elizabeth Morris Minahan – Dallas, TX, 96
Suzanne Mitchell – Southfield, MI, 268
Mrs. Guy Edward Moman – Tuscaloosa, AL, 75
Elaine D. Montgomery – Garland, TX, 122
Joanna Morford – Chandler, AZ, 34
Pam Morse – Houston, TX, 276
Janet Mothershed – Clemmons, NC, 82

N, O

Mrs. Terrell Newberry Jr. – Spring, TX, 172
Julie G. Oelman – Hinsdale, IL, 29

CONTRIBUTORS

P

Arnold M. Palmer – Los Angeles, CA, 188
Brenda J. Pangborn – Bloomfield Hills, MI, 55
Patricia A. Parkinson – Humble, TX, 206
Susan Parsell – Charleston, SC, 197
Elise Perelman – Katonah, NY, 264
Mary K. Petsche – Arlington, TX, 254
Jacqueline K. Pletscher – San Diego, CA, 58
Sharon Popham – Dallas, TX, 233
Mrs. Ronald C. Prati Sr. – Irving, TX, 59
Gayle Price – Pacific Grove, CA, 128
Stephan Pyles – Dallas, TX, 92, 193, and 248

R

Evy Rappaport – Beverly Hills, CA, 205
Sherrie L. Reddick – Wichita Falls, TX, 48
Anita Reiter – Roswell, GA, 228
Elle R. Rice – Newport Beach, CA, 190
Dr. Fay A. Riddle – La Grange, GA, 70
Susan (Mrs. Bill) Roberds – Dallas, TX, 247
Paula Robinson – Houston, TX, 137
Sylvia F. Rollins – Chicago, IL, 27
Elizabeth Romero – Los Mochis, Mexico, 69
Janet Rosenblatt – Boston, MA, 177

S

Mr. and Mrs. V.W. Sanders – Beverly Hills, CA, 125
Mrs. Edgar C. Sayles Sr. – Huntington Beach, CA, 20
Bonnie (Mrs. Irving) Schiffman – Dallas, TX, 263
S.C. Schultz – Marietta, GA, 32
Scott Schwimer – Beverly Hills, CA, 21
Fonda M. Scott – Los Angeles, CA, 23
Amanda Shams – Atlanta, GA, 214
Saundra Reiter Shapiro – Marietta, GA, 100
Dallas Shea – San Francisco, CA, 207
Karen Sheetz – Newport Beach, CA, 26
Janet Shepherd – Atlanta, GA, 136
Joan Sheppard – Godfrey, IL, 204
Ann Siner – Phoenix, AZ, 38
Elizabeth E. Solender and Gary L. Scott – Dallas, TX, 227
Mara Squar – Tarzana, CA, 51
Shelley Mosley Stanzel – Dallas, TX, 188
Christine M. Strohm – Sierra Madre, CA, 209
Mrs. Robert W. Stuart III – Dallas, TX, 221
Annlyn C. Stufflebeam – Plano, TX, 114
Liz Sublewski – Chicago, IL, 131

S (continued)

Doris B. Suttin – North Miami Beach, FL, 196
Eileen H. Swartz – Swampscott, MA, 135
Janet Swedburg – Axtell, NE, 53
Carol Sweet – Houston, TX, 84

T

Laura M. Taylor – Atlanta, GA, 62
Marilyn J. Tenser – Beverly Hills, CA, 230
Mrs. K.R. Tharp – Dallas, TX, 198
Patty (Mrs. Tignor) Thompson – Dallas, TX, 52
Charlie Trotter – Chicago, IL, 235 and 236
Elaine Y. Tucker – St. Louis, MO, 217
Andrea L. Tuggle – Dallas, TX, 32

U, V

Linda Underdown – Birmingham, MI, 273
Virginia Kopacz Valley – Corona del Mar, CA, 277

W

Carole Warburton – Sherman Oaks, CA, 134
Diane A. Ward – Los Angeles, CA, 19
Dawn Washer – Corona del Mar, CA, 234
Marjorie H. Watkins – Glencoe, IL, 216
Laura Wertheimer – Washington, D.C., 274
Janet Wilhelmi – Joliet, IL, 26
Barbara Williams – Dallas, TX, 262
Karol Wilson – Dallas, TX, 105
Patricia A. Wilson – Channelview, TX, 90
Linda K. Wind – Dallas, TX, 44
Elizabeth Winkler – Anderson, SC, 229
Elizabeth M. Wood – Dallas, TX, 218
Bess Worden – Wauwatosa, WI, 112

Y, Z

Selma Young – Scottsdale, AZ, 94
S. Kelly Young-Finkel – Fort Lauderdale, FL, 170
Sue Zelickson – Minneapolis, MN, 205

I would like to order additional copies of Neiman Marcus Cookbooks:

☐ *No Jacket Required* ($25.⁰⁰) | ☐ *Pigtails and Froglegs* ($19.⁹⁵) | ☐ *Pure & Simple* ($19.⁹⁵)
_____ quantity | _____ quantity | _____ quantity
☐ FOR MYSELF ☐ AS A GIFT | ☐ FOR MYSELF ☐ AS A GIFT | ☐ FOR MYSELF ☐ AS A GIFT

MAIL TO: NAME _____

ADDRESS _____

CITY, STATE, ZIP _____

IF GIFT, GIFT CARD SHOULD READ: _____

_____

ENCLOSED IS MY CHECK OR PLEASE CHARGE MY ACCOUNT (PLUS APPLICABLE TAXES AND $5.25 FOR SHIPPING):
☐ NEIMAN MARCUS   ☐ AMERICAN EXPRESS

ACCOUNT# _____ EXP. DATE _____

SIGNATURE _____

Mail to: Neiman Marcus Cookbooks: P.O. Box 3188, Dallas, TX 75221 or call: 1-800-624-7253

I would like to order additional copies of Neiman Marcus Cookbooks:

☐ *No Jacket Required* ($25.⁰⁰) | ☐ *Pigtails and Froglegs* ($19.⁹⁵) | ☐ *Pure & Simple* ($19.⁹⁵)
_____ quantity | _____ quantity | _____ quantity
☐ FOR MYSELF ☐ AS A GIFT | ☐ FOR MYSELF ☐ AS A GIFT | ☐ FOR MYSELF ☐ AS A GIFT

MAIL TO: NAME _____

ADDRESS _____

CITY, STATE, ZIP _____

IF GIFT, GIFT CARD SHOULD READ: _____

_____

ENCLOSED IS MY CHECK OR PLEASE CHARGE MY ACCOUNT (PLUS APPLICABLE TAXES AND $5.25 FOR SHIPPING):
☐ NEIMAN MARCUS   ☐ AMERICAN EXPRESS

ACCOUNT# _____ EXP. DATE _____

SIGNATURE _____

Mail to: Neiman Marcus Cookbooks: P.O. Box 3188, Dallas, TX 75221 or call: 1-800-624-7253

I would like to order additional copies of Neiman Marcus Cookbooks:

☐ *No Jacket Required* ($25.⁰⁰) | ☐ *Pigtails and Froglegs* ($19.⁹⁵) | ☐ *Pure & Simple* ($19.⁹⁵)
_____ quantity | _____ quantity | _____ quantity
☐ FOR MYSELF ☐ AS A GIFT | ☐ FOR MYSELF ☐ AS A GIFT | ☐ FOR MYSELF ☐ AS A GIFT

MAIL TO: NAME _____

ADDRESS _____

CITY, STATE, ZIP _____

IF GIFT, GIFT CARD SHOULD READ: _____

_____

ENCLOSED IS MY CHECK OR PLEASE CHARGE MY ACCOUNT (PLUS APPLICABLE TAXES AND $5.25 FOR SHIPPING):
☐ NEIMAN MARCUS   ☐ AMERICAN EXPRESS

ACCOUNT# _____ EXP. DATE _____

SIGNATURE _____

Mail to: Neiman Marcus Cookbooks: P.O. Box 3188, Dallas, TX 75221 or call: 1-800-624-7253

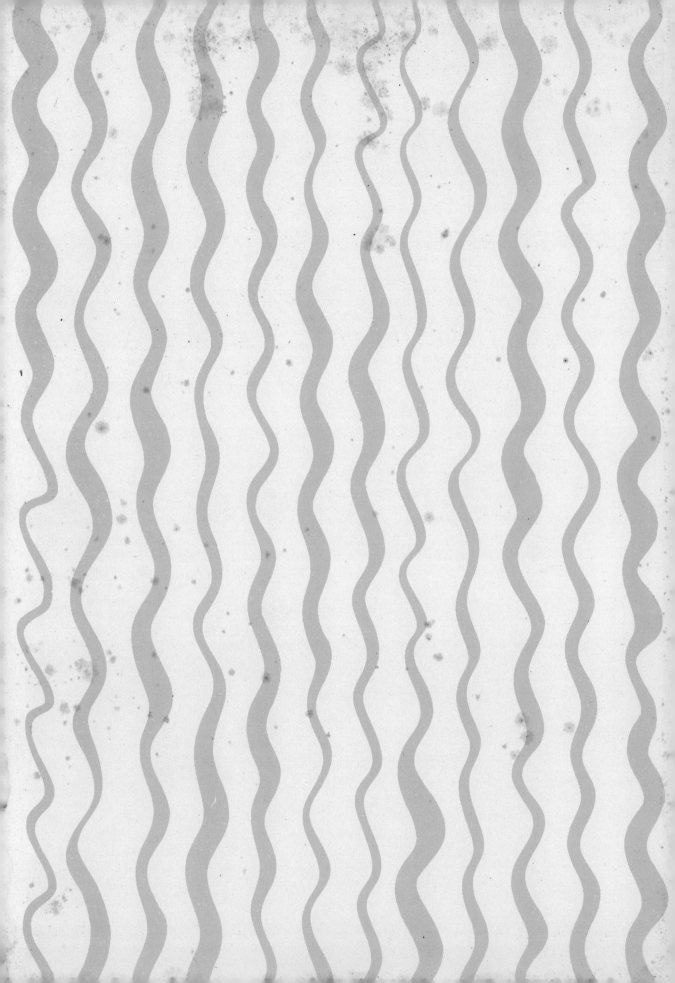